An easily read, hope-filled, engaging, 'how to' book
To endorse this book requires you to know about the author. Alan is a passionate follower of Jesus and walks the talk of being a peacemaker. I have been privileged to journey alongside Alan as co-mediator, conflict coach and co-trainer of peacemaking principles. To be a peacemaker requires courage as God opens our eyes to areas where we are in need of repentance and that courage is evident in Alan's life.

From this place of authenticity, Alan provides an easily read, hope-filled, engaging, 'how to' book on navigating the rough and rocky road of conflict in Christian communities. If 'conflict is to be lived in the context of reconciliation', this book helps leaders navigate conflict to God's honour. It outlines biblical peacemaking principles for leading conflict and then takes them one step further by providing a practical framework with transformative steps for leaders to implement when conflict arises. So, whether you are the leader of a Christian community, or one of the members, this book provides invaluable assistance in the face of conflict.

Wendy Konemann, Clinical Counsellor, Trauma Therapist,
Conflict Coach, Public Speaker, Mediator, Trainer, PeaceWise, Australia

Fresh and enormously helpful – a lifeline
There is no shortage of books on the subject of conflict resolution. So it was with surprise and appreciation that I found Alan Kelshaw's contribution to be both fresh and and enormously helpful. That there is a need for biblical and wise practical advice in this area should be self-evident. Everywhere we look we continue to see conflict in Christian communities. In fact we have long come to understand that conflict is a natural part of the process of being in community. However, to continue allowing conflict to become destructive of community should not be something we are happy to live with.

As a practitioner of community leadership, I need advice which is accessible and practical. Alan's work provides both a framework for understanding conflict dynamics and yet practical and manageable steps so that a reader can be far more confident that they can assess, and then make an effective contribution, to such situations. For those of us who lack confidence in this important area this work is something of a lifeline.

Phil Waugh, Senior Pastor, Springwood Baptist Church, NSW

A must-have book
Death and taxes are not the only certainties in life. Conflict ought to be added to that short list. Those leading communities or organisations need to be well prepared to manage conflict well if they are to be fruitful in their work. Alan Kelshaw's wisdom and background as a lawyer, and engagement with the PeaceWise movement in Australia, has enabled him to write this must have book for Christian leaders. Leaders who create a culture where conflict is dealt with in a

way that enriches the community which they lead are giving that community an extraordinary gift. Every Christian leader, or future leader, needs to read this book.

Bill Rusin, Chair, Morling College Board, Sydney , former Principal, Covenant Christian School, Belrose, NSW, former Deputy Chair, Christian Education National, Sydney.

Professional and pragmatic

We all know that conflict is normal, and inevitable, in almost every area of life. Time and time again I have, sadly, seen the enormous personal cost of poorly handled conflict. So, it is amazing that so many churches fail to take even elementary steps to equip their leaders with tools and skills to help them when the inevitable arises.

Navigating Community Conflict addresses that particular need by giving leaders a solid basis for understanding the various aspects of conflict and, at the same time, the book works like a 'workshop manual' for those in the midst of a conflict. You can skip straight to the part that is most needed at the time.

Alan's experience uniquely equips him to speak into these various realms. He brings together a professionalism in the materials and concepts presented, and also provides pragmatism in the way it can be effectively implemented. Holding these two aspects together is no simple feat. However, the book does both admirably! This book should be among the resources for any Christian community that seeks to honour God's name even in the midst of conflict.

Pete Davies, Regional Minister, Baptist Association of NSW & ACT Former Director Church Health, Baptist Association of NSW & ACT Conflict Trainer, PeaceWise, Australia

A principled and practical resource

Navigating Community Conflict is a principled and practical resource addressing a critical aspect of Christian leadership. It is informed by thoughtful reflection on Scripture, judicious engagement with the relevant literature on leadership and conflict resolution, and years of personal and professional experience. I warmly recommend it and pray that it will do great good within the communities that are served by those who read it.

David Starling, Chief Academic Officer, Morling College, Sydney

**For further endorsements, see the book's website:
www.navigatingcommunityconflict.com**

NAVIGATING COMMUNITY CONFLICT

WHAT CHRISTIAN LEADERS NEED TO STAY STEADY AT THE HELM

ALAN KELSHAW

ARK HOUSE PRESS

ARK house

Ark House Press
arkhousepress.com

Cataloguing in Publication Data:
Title: Navigating Community Conflict: what Christian leaders need to stay at the helm
ISBN: 978-0-6452569-2-5 (pbk) | 978-0-6455535-0-5 (ebk)
Subjects: [BUS110000] BUSINESS & ECONOMICS / Conflict Resolution & Mediation; REL074000 RELIGION / Christian Ministry / Pastoral Resources; [REL071000 RELIGION / Leadership;
Other Authors/Contributors: Kelshaw, Carolyn;
Figures designed by Cocoon Creative | cocooncreative.com.au

Design by initiateagency.com

An invaluable guide to an increasingly important issue

The inability to successfully manage conflict is one of the primary reasons leaders step away from their roles and organisations, like churches, flounder. Consultants and leaders around the Western world agree that for unavoidable reasons organisational conflict is on the increase.

Alan Kelshaw's *Navigating Community Conflict* is written especially for those with leadership responsibility enabling them to chart a careful course through the complexities of conflict. Alan is eminently qualified to map out the territory of interpersonal and group tension having served in leadership and consulted with a wide range of churches and organisations over a significant period.

I have appreciated his wisdom and insight on many occasions. The book itself is easy to navigate with foundational sections and practical guidelines. The principles and applications all arise from wisdom that is well tried and tested. While there are unique elements in every conflicted situation, *Navigating Community Conflict* provides the essential frameworks, guides and tools to enable leaders to assess and respond to their own particular church and organisational challenges. This book is timely and an important contribution. I highly recommend it.

Tim Dyer
Trainer and Consultant in Conflict Management
The Johnmark Extension

A priceless resource

Alan Kelshaw has provided a wise, thorough, and practical resource for all who have suffered, are suffering, or will suffer the pain and hurt of destructive conflict in communities of Christ's people. Such conflict is inevitable. The commitments and skills of leadership during such times are not. They must be learned and practiced.

The biblical grounds, HELM framework, case studies, key perspectives, and reflection exercises, provided in Alan's book and accompanying resources, are priceless for all who long to live in peace with others. I for one will be purchasing this book and recommending it to leaders, friends, and colleagues.

Rod Thompson, Minister, Springwood Presbyterian Churches, NSW
Former Principal, Laidlaw College, Auckland, New Zealand

A comprehensive guide

This excellent book provides a comprehensive guide to navigating community conflict. Alan Kelshaw draws out the submerged threats within ourselves and in communities that can derail the best of intentions. He focuses wisely on bringing a reconciling spirit and 'understanding the weather'. He uses practical examples to powerful effect which help draw the reader into addressing the challenges they face with confidence. The HELM framework will provide a valuable tool for leaders seeking to keep their perspective when conflict looms or breaks out.

Peter Shaw, Chair of Praesta Partners: an international coaching organisation
Visiting Professor of Leadership Development at Higher
Education Establishments in the UK, Canada and Australia
Author of 30 books on aspects of leadership

A perfect blend of a biblical foundation matched with a whole ocean of tools

Navigating Community Conflict is the book leaders don't know they need - but they do! In the cauldron of conflict, the knee-jerk reaction is almost always the wrong one, and risks deep personal hurt as well as the situation escalating rapidly out of control. Kelshaw has provided the perfect blend of a biblical foundation for how leaders can rightly think about conflict, matched with a whole ocean of tools to help them actually deal with it well - and also to know when to get outside help. This is a wonderful gift to Christian leaders everywhere and deserves to be used widely.

Bruce Burgess, Founding Director, PeaceWise, Australia

A practical step-by-step approach with concrete strategies and resources

In the rough seas of community conflict we need an experienced companion and a practical guide to a safe harbour. Alan Kelshaw's *Navigating Community Conflict* provides both and points us to our Lord, our ultimate Companion and Guide, whose Word is the lens through which we are invited to reframe conflict, ourselves, others and a way forward. Leaders will find encouragement to stay steady at the helm and see 'conflict as an opportunity for personal and community transformation, Godly growth and organisational well-being.' Kelshaw's practical step-by-step approach to various types of conflict, and his concrete strategies and resources offer us peace in the midst of the storm of conflict.

Ellene Ford, Dispute Resolution Consultant, former, Barrister-at-law

A resource to equip, challenge and encourage

When the storms of conflict threaten your organisation, remain steady at the helm with Alan Kelshaw's book, *Navigating Community Conflict*. Alan provides a biblical framework for understanding community conflict and guiding leaders based on Christian truths. Jesus' followers need to do more than just resolve conflict – they are called to reconcile through confession and forgiveness. This book equips you to address both the material and relational issues that arise in group conflicts. You will be resourced, challenged, and encouraged to live out your Christian faith as you lead your organisation through conflict.

Ted Kober, Senior Ambassador, Ambassadors of Reconciliation,
Billings, Montana, USA

A book to use in my leadership class

Alan Kelshaw brings together everything you want in a coach for leading a Christian community through conflict. He is biblically astute, emotionally intuitive, deeply experienced, strategically informed, and committed to community. I will be using this book in my leadership class at Regent College.

Mark Glanville, Associate Professor of Pastoral Theology,
Old Testament Scholar, Regent College, Vancouver

The LORD Is Peace.
Judges 6:24

Let the peace of Christ rule in your hearts
since as members of one body
[Christ's community]
you were called to peace.
Colossians 3:15

Have salt in yourselves,
and be at peace with
each other.
Mark 9:50

...those who promote peace
have joy.
Proverbs 12:20

I dedicate this book
to all those who have suffered pain
and hurt when faced with poorly
navigated conflict in a
community of
Christ's people.

CONTENTS[1]

PART 1: PRINCIPLES

PART 2: STRATEGIES

PART 3: RESOURCES
PLUS BONUS CHAPTERS

Accessed via the book's website: navigatingcommunityconflict.com
Password: ncc1234#

---

[1] For a detailed table of contents of this book, see Part 3, Resources, 16.9(e).

HOW TO USE THIS BOOK

Your concern:	Suggested action:
If you want to be proactive and be equipped ahead of time to navigate a conflict in your community when one arises: ⟶	Read this book from cover to cover
If you have a conflict brewing in your community and need to act immediately: ⟶	Read: • chapters 6 and 7; and • any other chapters in Part 2, and on the book's website, which have chapter titles relevant to your context.

> **To access the bonus chapters along with the Part 3 Resources on the book's website navigatingcommunityconflict.com enter the password: ncc1234#**

HOW THIS BOOK IS STRUCTURED

Preface	A personal journey
Introduction	*Why* read the book? *What* is its purpose? For *whom* is it intended? *When* is it relevant? *Where* is it different?
Part 1: Principles	
Chapter 1	Foundational theological beliefs about conflict.
Chapters 2-5	Individual and group self-awareness about conflict in general and the internal drivers which impact leadership responses in particular.
With this understanding about conflict in place, the following two chapters, 6 and 7, form the heart of this book.	
Chapter 6	A biblical framework, under the acronym HELM, for stable, strategic, leadership throughout times of conflict.

Part 2: Strategies	
Chapter 7	The HELM biblical framework applied across an extensive, prioritised series of strategies for leading throughout a community-wide conflict.
Chapters 8-11 draw on chapters 6 and 7.	
Chapters 8-11	The HELM biblical framework applied across four prevalent types of conflict in Christian communities.
Chapters 12-15 provide additional practical insights on leading well.	
Chapter 12	The practice of on-going biblical peacemaking in a community.
Part 3: Resources [See the book's website]	
Chapters 13-15	The context for working with outside professionals, the media and lawyers during conflict.
Chapter 16	Practical resources set out under the HELM biblical framework provided in chapter 6 along with other resources which may be useful.

LIST OF FIGURES

ABBREVIATIONS

NIV: New International Version
ESV: English Standard Version
NRSV: New Revised Standard Version

FOREWORD

I once heard a senior politician, who happened to be a committed Christian, say that he was glad he was not a church minister as church politics is much dirtier than the 'real thing', the stuff he was dealing with on a daily basis. It gave me pause for thought.

There is some truth in what he said, even though the political world is all pretty ugly and strife riven. From my own experience both in leading churches, and leading not-for-profit organisations, I have seen and experienced conflict first hand. It's never easy. And I do not think I always saw it as 'an opportunity to reflect on God's character in community and bring him honour' as Alan Kelshaw extolls us to do in this fine book *Navigating Community Conflict: what Christian leaders need to stay steady at the helm*.

In both churches and Christian not-for-profit groups, I have observed that there is intrinsic difficulty when conflict fractures relationships in a community which is ostensibly dedicated to love and being a witness to the world. The odds are stacked pretty high on keeping the peace, and dealing with any conflict in discrete and 'loving' ways. But churches and to some extent, Christian not-for-profit organisations, also breed huge loyalties and traditions which mean the values and feelings go deep. And when they are threatened it is often shocking how thin the veneer of love and niceness goes.

Leadership in such a context is extremely challenging. Church leadership is never just the pastor and elders in leadership, but their family and friendships forged over years. It means a whole sense of communal identity interwoven in one particular place. It is our most sacred investment as love has been poured into lives and relationships. I have met many ministers and other Christian leaders over the years who have suffered terribly when conflict has rent their position from under them, or their authority has been challenged by forces and impacted family networks. Many of them have lost livelihoods, even marriages and the future faith allegiance of their children under the impact of such an onslaught. Some leaders never recover and take bitterness to their graves. Yes, church politics (and even Christian not-for-profit politics) can be very ugly. And exceedingly painful.

So I am grateful for the depth of study that Alan Kelshaw has undertaken in putting this book together.

What a wise resource for such a crucial area of Christian organisational life. It is actually more than just tips but a handbook, replete with the most helpful of biblical principles, charts, questions, prompts, online links and telling case studies. As he says, the wisdom comes out of his own lived experience and the discovery that there was nothing he could find to help when he needed it. So he has brought together the principles needed to understand dealing with conflict and made it so accessible. So this work has been forged in the fire. It is masterful work.

I personally found his analysis of the rubric of conflict – including the personal dimension we all bring to it – with our desires and 'idols of our heart' particularly challenging to think about. It made me reflect on some of my own experiences, and what idols I had brought to the situation. Also of great significance was including a way to examine contextual factors – be they group think, social environmental influences, as well as the impact of leadership styles. Most helpfully the HELM model is a strategy for charting what needs to be considered to work through a conflict to a resolution which allows a community to move in a healthy direction. It is a model that I think is brilliant in its breadth and depth. It is profoundly God-honouring and faithful to God's heart.

This book could, I believe, save so many churches and Christian organisations from damaging, time and resource-draining impasses. Even better, it may prevent some of the splits and pain that can follow. The questions at the end of each chapter are an excellent resource for leaders to both self-check and to guide their teams into healthy conflict resolution. It would be an ideal gift to give each graduating ministerial candidate, each new chair of a Board and indeed every person taking on leadership roles in Christian organisations. And it has advice for other areas of life where conflict can quickly erupt. I hope it gets wide usage and application.

Rev Tim Costello AO
Exec Director of Micah Australia
Former CEO of World Vision Australia

PREFACE

This book sets out to equip Christian leaders to provide stable, strategic, biblical leadership throughout conflict from beginning to end. It arises from profound personal experience. Some years ago, I became an involuntary protagonist in a conflict in my church. I was chair of the governance group at the time. This conflict caught me totally by surprise. It polarised our community. Feelings ran high.

My decisions *as a leader* were blunted. Strong reactions welled up within me, stirring emotions I had not felt as a leader before. The typical cool-headed thinking and decision-making I valued as a follower of Jesus, and as a lawyer, were muted with confusion, disappointment and frustration. I had not encountered anything like this in my life thus far. Nor had our church faced such a substantial conflict in its 50-year history.

Questions flooded in:
- How could this happen?
- Why now?
- How would the hundreds of godly, committed people in this church respond?
- How would my family and friends, many of whom attended this church, react?
- What would be the impact on our witness within and beyond the local community?
- How could the leaders work together to avoid a potential tsunami?

- What would be the effect on achieving the church's vision and purpose?

The conflict instantly absorbed our attention, blurring our strategic leadership focus. I resigned as chair of the governance group, although I remained a member. There were many meetings, often called at short notice. We were in uncharted waters, reacting to unique and highly charged circumstances. It was daunting and preoccupying.

We wanted to act honourably and appropriately under Christ, but we had few documented guidelines to inform us. As I later reflected on this time, I realised how invaluable it would have been if I, and my fellow leaders, had had the benefit of some kind of guiding framework, arising from biblical thinking, to help us shape our leadership responses.

I believe such a framework could have reduced our sense of ambiguity and steadied us in our attempts to remain faithful to our leadership calling. It could have channelled us more efficiently towards strategically balancing our own needs, the needs of the community and the pressing need to address the conflict. I had in mind a framework that covered:
- relevant biblical principles for leading in conflict situations;
- pertinent practical strategies arising from these biblical principles; along with
- readily accessible resources.

I imagined augmenting this framework with research on the nature of conflict, critical priority questions leaders should be asking in these situations and other related material.

And, of course, I wanted all this integrated and handed to me on a platter!

A niggling impetus to do something about this took hold and refused to go away.

Around this time, I attended our denomination's annual conference. As one does, I sat in my seat, minding my own business, listening to the keynote speaker. Suddenly his words arrested me. Drawing on Proverbs 3:5 and 6, he spoke of 'the power of a single move'. If we step out and meet the *need*, God will provide the plan. He observed we often find our cause in the greatest disasters of our life. He challenged us to take on something bigger than ourselves, bigger than our culture and comfort, and see where it goes. By losing ourselves in God, we can do more than we think we can. With these challenging words, my spirit quickened: I sensed the Lord prompting my mind and heart to act on that niggling impetus to address the need for this resource myself. Thus this project began.

My subsequent literature review did not reveal quite the kind of ready-reference guidebook I envisaged. Undeniably, many others have written books addressing the issue of Christians in conflict. However, I did not find anything specifically intended to provide comprehensively, in the one place, all I would have loved to have had at my fingertips with integrated principles, strategies and resources around *leading well* throughout the turmoil of conflict.

As I began to research the biblical principles to underpin this work, I discovered 'new treasures as well as old' (Mt 13:52) in the storeroom of God's word. These discoveries gave me great hope. They encouraged and strengthened my faith. They convinced me conflict is never terminal. To my surprise and excitement, the principles arranged themselves around the acronym HELM. Here was a coherent, biblical framework: exactly what I had desired for our church leadership team!

I outline this HELM framework in Chapter 6. The framework shapes the strategies set out in Part 2. An acronym such as HELM begged to be extended. Therefore, I have used the image of navigation throughout this book to describe the process of leading when addressing conflict. I fully acknowledge many others have used this image before me. In fact, during my theological research, I found previous authors had used navigational terms to describe governance and leadership as far back as biblical times. I am convinced it remains a natural and compelling metaphor for leadership today, especially during conflict.

Thus, I hope and pray this book will equip leaders to stay steady at the HELM — to indeed provide stable, strategic, biblical leadership throughout conflict in their community from beginning to end; leadership which will result in the community remaining organisationally safe, hopeful, healthy and relational throughout this challenging time.

INTRODUCTION

This chapter addresses:
- Why read this book?
- What is this book's purpose?
- For whom is this book intended?
- When is this book relevant?
- Where is this book different?

Why read this book?

Read this book if you want to be the leader who will remain steady at the helm while navigating conflict graciously, confidently and biblically.

It is your companion on that journey, and it is full of hope.

Christ calls us to belong to communities of his people. Primarily that call is to link to his body, the church (Rom 12:4-8; 1 Cor 12:12-14, 27). Alongside this core relationship, however, Christ's kingdom purposes find rich expression in other communities which seek to faithfully serve him, such as Christian missions, para-church organisations, schools and charities.

If you are a leader in any of these contexts, you have my immense respect. You exercise your responsibilities within enormous complexity. Our society is complex. Our communities are complex. We are complex beings. We have complex personal histories. Conflict, when it erupts, has a nasty habit of intensifying this complexity. And erupt it undoubtedly will at some point in the life of your community, often when you least expect it, and never when it's convenient.

In 2000, the authors of a national USA survey of over 14,000 churches concluded that seventy-five per cent (75%) of them had experienced tensions identified as 'conflict' in the previous five years. Twenty-five per cent (25%) identified the conflict as 'serious'.[2]

Nationwide research into Australian churches in the 1990s concluded:

> '44% of leaders feel conflict has been evident in their congregation in the past two years made up of:
>
> - 25% where it is easily resolved;
> - 16% where it can only be resolved with much effort; and
> - 4% where there appears to be no clear solution'.[3]

Unfortunately, my own experience as a consultant and mediator in Australian churches, and the Christian not-for-profit sector, suggests these findings remain current. Conflict arises in every Christian community, no matter what country. It is never a question of if, but when and where.

Before you are tempted to give up and immediately abandon your leadership role, remember two things:
- First, while conflict in Christian communities is inescapable, it is to be expected (and some say necessary!); and
- Secondly, this book will equip you and your leadership team to provide stable, strategic, biblical leadership so you can help your community heal.

Assuming you still have at least one foot on the deck, let's explore two questions together – when conflict erupts, *What will you do?* and, *Who will you be?*

This book is designed to help you make healthy choices in *both* these areas. When conflict erupts in your community, you will find yourself faced with its unexpected and confronting consequences. These may include:

- people resigning, leaving or becoming detached;
- factions developing around a 'cause-to-fight-for';
- malicious letters circulating, including to the press;
- judgmental emails and social media comments disseminating; and
- casual gossiping.

So, first question: What *will* you do? Will you intervene? Ignore the problem? Manage the conflict yourself? Seek independent outside assistance? Whatever you choose to do, you will not only experience the consequences of the conflict, you will also be responsible for the wellbeing of your community – *from beginning to end.* Consultants, mediators, or staff from the head body of your denomination or professional association may come and go. However, as the leader, you must remain on duty. Will you survive? Will your community survive?

And most importantly, the second question, when conflict erupts: *Who* will you be?

Wherever the centre of a conflict lies, be it among the leaders themselves, in a large or small section of the community, or an isolated few, strong feelings will inevitably impact the way you lead. Conflict draws out deep emotions and responses which, under normal circumstances, would probably embarrass us. It's a human thing! You may become confused or preoccupied or lose sight of your overall responsibilities. Regardless, will you be one of those who can manage their feelings, examine their heart, and carefully and prayerfully consider their responses?

> **Why read this book?**
> Read it to be equipped to make choices about *what you will do* and *who you will be* when conflict erupts. Read it to be the leader equipped to heal a community broken by conflict. Read it as a guide to enable you to live out the injunction that all of God's people are *'called to peace'* (Col 3:15 emphasis added). And read it to be the leader who courageously remains on board with a steady hand on the helm, providing stable, strategic, biblical leadership, holding a secure course to safety.

What is this book's purpose?

The purpose of this book is, therefore, to engender stable, strategic biblical leadership from beginning to end throughout chaotic, conflicted situations in churches and other Christian communities.

Three presuppositions give rise to this purpose.

This kind of leadership is imperative

First, from the earliest hint of conflict to its ultimate resolution, strategic biblical leadership during times of conflict is *imperative*. As Peter Steinke observes:

> The people who are most in a position to enhance the health of a [community] are precisely those who have been empowered to be responsible, namely the leaders. They are the chief stewards, they are the people who are willing to be accountable for the welfare of the system. They set a tone, invite collaboration, make decisions, map a direction, establish boundaries, encourage self-expression, restrain what threatens the integrity of the whole, and keep the system's direction aligned with purposes.[4]

This kind of leadership is possible

Strategic biblical leadership during times of conflict is *possible*. Equipped with a framework of biblical principles, leaders can indeed, thoughtfully and prayerfully, lead well throughout any conflicted situation to bring about a positive outcome.

This kind of leadership is transformative

Strategic biblical leadership during times of conflict is *transformative*. It creates an environment that deprives conflict 'of its destructive tendencies and turns it into an opportunity to find lasting solutions to serious problems, to experience significant personal growth, to deepen relationship, and, best of all, to experience and demonstrate the love of God in a new and life-giving way'.[5]

The radiant hope at the heart of this book is that as leaders apply the principles of scripture and employ the holistic strategies which arise directly from them, they will thrive, and their communities flourish. Leaders need the courage of this hope to act boldly in times of conflict as they:

- learn the disheartening facts of the conflict;
- negotiate firmly held perceptions and unstated expectations;
- discover 'skeletons in the closet';
- uncover the issues-behind-the-issues;
- engage in difficult conversations;
- set a course; and
- seek to remain at the helm even when they feel they are losing their nerve.

What is this book's purpose?
This book provides maps, charts and channel markers so leaders can reset the rudder of their discernment and, with God's help, pilot a course that leads their community out of the fog of confusion and to a safe harbour for his honour and glory.

For whom is this book intended?

If you are still reading, clearly, this book is intended for you! It is for anyone in a leadership role in a church or other Christian community. It is for those who aspire to be good stewards of conflict. It is for any leader who determines to navigate conflict well so their community can flourish. But who do we include, and what do we mean when we talk about 'leaders'?

Leaders are those who influence or seek to influence others through the nature of their relationships. Walter Wright captures this well. Leadership, he says, is 'a relationship in which one person seeks to influence the thoughts, behaviors, beliefs, or values of another person'.[6]

The nature of these relationships may be *formal* or *informal*.

Churches and other Christian communities such as para-church or mission organisations, schools, not-for-profit groups and charities which seek to serve Christ, achieve their purpose through legal structures. Thus, most such groups will have people whose influence – whose leadership – is exercised through *formal* relationships shaped by their *governance* responsibilities on a Council, a Board, a Diaconate, a Governance Committee, or as a Warden or Trustee.

Usually, there will also be *executive* employees whose leadership influence is also exercised through formal relationships. Executive roles may include Ministers, Rectors, Executive Directors, Presidents, Chief Executive Officers, and School Principals. They sit in a formal relationship with their governance group, their staff and their community to achieve shared purposes.

If you are someone who exerts influence – who leads – via formally appointed governance or executive relationships, this book is intended for you.

Others may exercise influence over specific areas of the organisation's shared purposes via formal relationships of accountability to the executive leadership. People in these roles include:
- those exercising spiritual oversight, such as an elder; and
- those exercising management oversight, such as a senior manager, team leader, or as the chair or coordinator of committees, task forces, working groups etc.

If this description fits you, this book is intended for you as well. It will likewise assist you in exercising strategic, biblical leadership when negotiating conflict in your current context.

Perhaps you are someone who holds no formal role in your community but can influence others through your *informal* relationships and networks. You are the person who leads from the 'foot of the table'. Sometimes your unofficial leadership will be 'for the better' – it will be positive and constructive; however, sometimes, it may be 'for worse' – it may be negative and destructive.

You will also find this book helpful. It will assist you to exert your informal leadership influence 'for better', understand how to support your formally appointed leadership, and contribute to your community's healing.

Moreover, this book will assist trusted outside professionals who engage with a community during a conflict. Those of you who are denominational leaders, Executive Officers with a peak body, Christian consultants, mediators and lawyers, can significantly influence – and even lead – the course of events. This book will be a welcome companion on your journey as well.

> *The book's intended audience includes formal and informal leaders within Christian communities:*
> - Governance groups;
> - Executives;
> - Spiritual leaders;
> - Management leaders;
> - Influencers; and
> - Outside professionals

When is this book relevant?

This book is relevant when conflict erupts in the community under your care. Every dispute arises from a unique combination of facts, circumstances, perceptions, expectations and personalities. Conflict is as varied as the human condition itself.

The book aims to assist any leader facing tumultuous and unruly conflicted situations as diverse as:

- when there is a public and acrimonious breakdown in the relationship between founding members of a Christian school;
- when a group of disgruntled members of a not-for-profit group garner support to terminate the employment of their Chief Executive Officer;
- when church leaders argue their differences in doctrinal beliefs via disparaging letters disseminated amongst their community;
- when a board fails to agree on the fundamental purpose and direction of a respected organisation in a changing market environment;
- and so it goes...

This book does not, however, set out to provide advice on, or assistance to, leaders facing conflict arising from:
- sexual misconduct and abuse cases[7];
- incidents involving children;
- criminal conduct; and
- necessary intervention by an outside body or group.

The required formal responses expected of leaders in these situations are not covered in this book because it will be *essential* for them to seek external legal, police, insurance or other professional advice. Leaders will also need to consult any relevant existing policies and procedures to guide their responses. (If your organisation has not developed policies and procedures to address matters such as those outlined above, make it a priority to do so after seeking appropriate external professional advice.)

> **When is this book relevant?**
> This book is relevant when a rising tide of conflict threatens the equilibrium of your community. It is relevant when leaders determine to stay steady at the helm, to the glory of God.

Where is this book different?

Certainly, there is a wealth of material available to help Christians address conflict. However, this book is different arising from its specific weaving together of the following emphases:

(a) Its emphasis on *leading* throughout the duration of conflict from beginning to end.

Many books set out to provide a comprehensive examination of conflict resolution models. I commend them to you. This, however, is not one of the focus areas of this book.[8] Rather, the emphasis here is to assist leaders to *remain in their leadership role throughout the whole duration* of any conflict.

(b) Its emphasis on assisting leaders to think and act within *a deliberate biblical framework.*

Without a doubt, books written about conflict for the Christian community are normally consistent with biblical thinking. They have much to offer and I have referenced many within this book. In addition, biblical truth may be evident in wise secular literature. Given all truth is God's truth, wherever it is found, I reference it where applicable.

What this book attempts, however, is to foreground key biblical principles overtly. It does so by developing a framework around the acronym HELM, designed to give leaders ready access to biblical thinking as they shape their leadership responses during conflict.

(c) Its emphasis on *biblically integrated practical* strategies and readily accessible leadership resources.

This book integrates practical leadership strategies for leading through and engaging with conflict within each aspect of the HELM biblical framework. It does the same for a wide range of leadership resources.

(d) Its emphasis on assisting leaders across *all* Christian communities.

Most books addressing Christians in conflict do so in the context of the church alone. The audience of this book includes both formal and informal leaders of churches and other Christian organisations as outlined above under the sub-heading *'For whom is this book intended?'*

(e) Its emphasis on *leadership health* during conflict.

Another point of difference is a focus on helping leaders understand, both individually and as teams, the powerful forces inherent in conflict events likely to impair their capacity to lead well throughout conflict events. Along with this information, the book also provides searching questions for individual and team self-reflection.

(f) Its emphasis on applying the biblical framework across the *most prevalent types* of conflict.

The book applies the biblically grounded stay-steady-at-the-HELM framework across the range of most prevalent conflict categories which I have addressed as a lawyer, mediator and consultant. The purpose of doing this is to illustrate the efficacy of the framework across a range of different contexts.

It is my hope that by weaving all these emphases together in one place, leaders will have at their fingertips a guidebook to help reduce ambiguity, and provide steadying guidelines as they seek to remain faithful to their calling. It is my belief this book is well placed to strengthen leaders in their efforts to be strategic in balancing their own needs, the needs of the community and the pressing need to address the conflict.

Where is this book different?

Its difference arises from the specific weaving together of the following emphases:

- Its emphasis on *leading* throughout the duration of conflict from beginning to end;
- Its emphasis on assisting leaders to think and act within *a deliberate biblical framework;*
- Its emphasis on *biblically integrated practical* strategies and readily accessible leadership resources;
- Its emphasis on assisting leaders across *all* Christian communities;
- Its emphasis on *leadership health* during conflict; and
- Its emphasis on applying the biblical framework across the *most prevalent types* of conflict.

Stories

Please note, the stories included in this book are a compilation of imagined and highly modified factual situations. Any resemblance to real-life circumstances, therefore, is purely coincidental. It would be unwise to make connections, draw conclusions or be tempted to revisit any historical conflict in your world.

A note on using the resources

It is fully acknowledged that the resources provided in Part 3 on the book's website are not exhaustive and other tools may be relevant.

It is also fully acknowledged that God is greater than human resources, processes and constructs even where they arise from biblical principles, research or extensive observation and experience. The God of the impossible, even in the midst of seemingly intractable and extensive conflict, can convict and prompt any of us toward confession, repentance and reconciliation and resolution of our issues.

A note of caution
(or what lawyers call a disclaimer)

Many conflicts involve legal considerations. Sometimes these are incidental and readily addressed. On other occasions, they give rise to complex arguments and require attendance at court. For many years I acted as a lawyer (solicitor). However, I have not practised for over a decade. I no longer hold a practising licence and cannot provide legal advice. The book, therefore, does not provide legal advice.

The material in this book, and on the book's accompanying website, is of a general nature only. It is not a substitute for obtaining legal advice which is specific to navigating a particular conflict in your community and the individuals and circumstances involved. Neither the author or the publisher accept any liability for any loss you suffer in relying on the material in this book or on the website. You release both the author and publisher from any liability in respect of any claim and indemnify us from any loss arising from the use of these materials by you, your community or group.

Further, the contents of this book are not intended to provide leaders with specific advice on any individual conflict situation. The book aims simply to offer suggestions for leaders of maturity, faith and discernment to stay steady at the helm while they consider their context. So, seek further advice as necessary and, then, resolve to take the most relevant actions in the circumstances.

Summary of terms

No book written by an ex-lawyer would be complete without a section defining terms! Unless it is clear from the context that another meaning is intended, the following definitions apply:

'CEO'	the Chief Executive Officer of a community, or a person known by a similar title
'conflict'	has the meaning as stated in section 2.1 below, and includes 'tensions', 'disharmony', 'problems', 'dispute', 'discord', to avoid undue repetition.

'community conflict' or similar	has the meaning of conflict arising in the community: • as a whole; • in a section or involving a group; or • between individuals connected to the community
'emotions'	has the meaning defined in section 4.2 as 'whatever in our behaviour is instinctive, automatic, defensive, reactive, even mindless' and includes 'feelings'
'interests'	has the meaning of the motivations, the values, needs, concerns, desires and limitations which lie behind the presenting issue(s)
'leader', 'leaders' 'leadership group' 'team'	has the meaning provided in this chapter (under the heading 'For whom is this book intended') and includes all the individuals or groups who have the power to guide and influence responses to conflict
'manage'	to become involved in leading the parties to a conflict in a process toward resolution of their relationship breakdown and the particular issues in dispute
'navigate' 'navigating'	to maintain strategic leadership over the whole community while leading throughout a conflict without neglecting the community's constitutional objects/purposes
'principles'	a statement which is accepted as a true and trustworthy guide; the way God wishes us to go out and live life
'support person'	someone who provides emotional and practical support to a person involved in a conflict, a friend, colleague, family member, workplace representative or lawyer; however, the person chosen will not normally be an advocate, provide formal advice, nor have a personal interest in the outcome of the conflict

'values'	'the stated or assumed beliefs, commitments, ethos, and qualities that govern everything that the organisation does'[9]

Now you know where we're heading, let's turn to Part 1. This provides you with an understanding of conflict and the principles which will empower you to steer a course to a safe harbour.

---

2   Dudley, C., Zingery, T., and Breeden, D. *Insights into Congregational Conflict* (Hartford, CT: Faith Communities Today, Hartford Institute for Religious Research, 2007) https://faithcommunitiestoday.org/wp-content/uploads/2019/01/Insights-Into-Congregational-Conflict.pdf, p.1.

3   Kaldor, Peter, Bellamy, John, Powell, Ruth, Hughes, Bronwyn, Castle, Keith *Shaping a Future: Characteristics of Vital Congregations*, NCLS Research, Sydney, 1997, p. 131.

4   Steinke, Peter L., *Healthy Congregations: A Systems Approach*, Herndon, VA: Alban Institute, 2007, p.xi. (Copyright © the Alban Institute. Reproduced with permission of the Licensor through PLSclear.)

5   Sande, Ken, *The Peacemaker: A Biblical Guide to Resolving Personal Conflict*, 3rd Edition, Baker Books, 2004, p. 16.

6   Wright, Walter C., *Relational Leadership: A Biblical Model for Influence and Service*, Second Edition, InterVarsity Press, Illinois, 2009, p. 8.

7   For an excellent book on this topic, see McKnight, Scot and Barringer, Laura, *A Church Called Tov: Forming a Goodness Culture That Resists Abuses of Power and Promotes Healing*, Tyndale Momentum, 2020. The book explores ways of identifying, naming and addressing toxic church cultures especially in the area of sexual misconduct and abuse, and how to develop cultures of health and goodness.

8   I am not suggesting conflict resolution models are unimportant. They are vital. Indeed, my research unearthed a wide variety of approaches for resolving conflict individually and in community. However, they are not the focus of this book.

9   Wright, *Relational Leadership*, p. 102.

PART 1

PRINCIPLES

Part 1 will equip you with an understanding of:

- The foundational beliefs which underpin this book
- Core biblical and research perspectives regarding:
  - the origins and growth of conflict individually and communally
  - the characteristics of conflict
  - the power and benefits of a biblical response
- The complex factors which significantly influence our responses to conflict as leaders, individually and as a group
- The principles required to be considered by leaders in a conflict situation to bring honour and glory to God

NAVIGATIONAL CHART - BIBLICAL FOUNDATIONS OF CONFLICT 1

> This chapter provides the foundational beliefs, drawn from the Bible, which lie at the heart of this book.

The story of the Bible concerns God's initiative to resolve, for eternity, the breakdown in relationship between himself and his creation. Wonderfully, through Christ's atoning work on the cross, we may now be reconciled to God and invited to form a new humanity. This new humanity is most fully expressed when it is lived out in Christ-honouring communities led by men and women who also seek to honour Christ. Flowing from these understandings, the following beliefs underpin this book.

1.1 *Conflict is elemental*

Conflict was an elemental force in human relationships from the outset of creation. We see it playing out after Adam and Eve reached for something they thought was a good thing, but which God had warned them not to touch. Once they realised what they had done, they were ashamed. Adam blamed Eve, and Eve blamed the serpent. Then, in a classic flight response, they both hid from God (Gen 3).

We see its progress with chilling clarity in the next generation, in the conflict between their sons, Cain and Abel (Gen 4). Cain's covetous heart did not get the good thing he wanted. This made him 'very angry', and 'sin came crouching at [his] door' (v.7). Sadly, ignoring God's warning, he failed to 'master it'. Instead, 'sin sprang to life' (Rom 7:9) as Cain played out another classic response to conflict – fight. He attacked and murdered Abel (Gen 4:3-8).

In the presence of this elemental force inherent in human relationships, it is not the *conflict* itself but how we choose to *respond* which determines whether sin springs to life. Thus, for Adam and Eve, shame bred blame, and blame bred flight; for Cain, covetousness bred anger, and anger bred fight.

1.2 *Conflict is endemic*

Conflict is not only elemental; it is also endemic. We still ignore God's warnings. These cycles of conflict, evident in the first communities, continue, to a greater or lesser extent, down the ages, in our responses to our creator God, and between all of us humans (Rom 7:7-12).

The New Testament writer, James, is clear about this endemic nature of conflict. You hear echoes in his observation that: 'You desire but do not have, so you kill. You covet, but you cannot get what you want, so you quarrel and fight' (4:2). Likewise, the apostle Paul notes the underlying human condition that exerts a constant gravitational drag towards conflict: it is not only that '... all have sinned and fall short of the glory of God' (Rom 3:23) he says, but also that: '...you were alienated from God and were enemies in your minds because of your evil behaviour' (Col 1:21).

No one who seeks to serve God through Jesus is immune. The potential for conflict is ever-present. We could argue followers of Jesus, of all people, are at the most significant risk, since the opportunity for conflict increases exponentially, as we:
- 'struggle ... against the powers of this dark world and ... the spiritual forces of evil in the heavenly realms' (Eph 6:12; see also 4:27);

- contend with the pull of the desires of the flesh, our 'sinful nature' (Gal 5:16-21);
- negotiate 'the world' and all its influences on us (1 Jn 2:15-16);
- rub shoulders together in families, casual groups, or formal purpose-driven communities (Mt 19:1-9; see 1 Cor 1); and
- respond to the ongoing challenge to change, in the ways we live together as individuals (Mt 18:3), and as catalysts for broader social change in our society (Mt 5:13).

Paul also knew conflict well from experience, so well, that he hesitated to visit the young Christians in Corinth. He was afraid that: 'when I come I may not find you as I want you to be, and you may not find me as you want me to be. I fear that there may be discord, jealousy, fits of rage, selfish ambition, slander, gossip, arrogance and disorder' (2 Cor 12:20).

And with those searing words, he succinctly identifies the behaviours which have bred cycles of conflict in all communities since sin came into the world.

If conflict is an elemental force in human relationships and endemic across time and communities, we will inevitably face it sometime. Being aware of this reality can be helpful. It makes sense of the ongoing cycles of conflict in our lives. It can reframe our shock and discouragement into a more realistic assessment of who we are. It can free us to learn how to navigate effectively through conflict as part of everyday Christian living. With this comes hope.

1.3 *Christ is the ultimate answer to conflict*

Understanding conflict, navigating the seemingly irreconcilable, and leading through it well, is intrinsically gospel work. It calls us constantly back to the hope we find in Christ.

Christ is central to resolving the conflict between the creator and humanity. His reconciling work on the cross is the ultimate answer to resolving this conflict. As the apostle Paul says: 'For God was pleased to have all his fullness dwell in him [that is, Christ] and through him to reconcile to himself all things [and that includes us, humans!] ... by making peace through his blood, shed on the cross' (Col 1:19-20).

Christ is also the answer to our conflict with our fellow humans. Relationships break down. Issues divide and separate. As we draw near to Christ and allow his nature to shape our responses, as we follow his way of reconciliation, we can be restored to once again live at lasting peace with one another. Finding peace with God opens the door to finding peace with our neighbour. Paul exhorts us to 'let the peace of Christ rule in your hearts, since as members of one body you were called to peace' (Col 3:15). His reconciling work on the cross is the ultimate answer to living in relational peace with our fellow humans.

1.4 God's word provides a trustworthy navigational chart for every conflict

In responding to conflict, we may think of the word of God as being like a navigational or nautical chart. Such a chart is:

> ...one of the most fundamental tools available to the mariner. It is a map that depicts the configuration of the shoreline and seafloor. It provides water depths, locations of dangers to navigation, locations and characteristics of aids to navigation, anchorages, and other features. The nautical chart is essential for safe navigation. Mariners use charts to plan voyages and navigate ships safely and economically.[10]

Whether we are cresting a wave of joy, or being swamped by anxiety and uncertainty, God's word is our map for a safe passage. It locates areas of danger in our lives, individually and collectively. It provides aids to navigation and guides us to sheltered anchorages.

The Apostle Paul says 'all scripture is God-breathed and is useful for teaching, rebuking, correcting and training in righteousness, so that the servant of God may be thoroughly equipped for every good work' (2 Tim 3:16). Each of these God-initiated purposes is relevant when navigating conflict. God's word is not dry, abstract theory, but living truth. It maps out the safe passage to peace.

Conflict provides an opportunity for everyone, leaders and followers, to learn and experience biblical peacemaking principles. Doing so will better equip the community to reflect the character of Jesus Christ in embodying the coming together of seemingly irreconcilable perspectives. Embracing biblical peacemaking enables everyone to work toward outcomes that honour God and unify the community. Addressing conflict is core ministry in Christ's name; it is, without equivocation, the work of the gospel.

1.5 *Navigation is an apt biblical metaphor for leading throughout conflict*

The image of navigation to describe leadership activity is not new. According to research, it has been used for centuries. The Apostle Paul uses the Greek word, *kyberneseis*, in 1 Corinthians 12:28. Although often translated 'gifts ... of guidance'[11] or 'gifts of ... administrating',[12] it is also the same word used for 'pilot' (Acts 27:11) and 'sea captain' (Rev 18:17). No matter its context, as David Starling observes after examining the literature of the time: '...readers and listeners in Paul's time would have still been aware of the nautical background of the term when it was used to refer to leadership roles in non-nautical contexts'.[13]

Margaret Mitchell, who has also researched the image, notes that its use in the writings at the time shows a substantial link between discord and peace. She recognises 'the central place which the metaphor of the ship captain and his task to keep a ship afloat play in literature on factionalism and concord...'.[14]

This book continues in that tradition!

1.6 *Unity demands a reconciling spirit*

The psalmist celebrated: 'How good and pleasant it is when God's people live together in unity!' (Ps 133:1) Jesus' prayed that his disciples would live in unity: 'Holy Father, protect them ... so that they may be one as we are one' (Jn 17:11). He also prayed that his followers, throughout the ages, would live in unity: 'I pray also for those who will believe in me through their message, that all of them may be one, Father, just as you are in me and I am in you' (Jn 17:20-21).

Nevertheless, the tenor of Jesus' teaching was realistic. He experienced and anticipated conflict, both among his followers and in the society at large. Rather than teaching for the absence of conflict, he offered a way to live and be amidst conflict. He taught and modelled *a reconciling spirit* willing to move towards the goal of unity persistently. 'First go and be reconciled' even before you enter into worship, he teaches his followers in Matthew 5:24; prioritise reconciliation over court action as a matter of self-protection, he tells them in Luke 12:58.

Leroy Goertzen takes us into the mystery and paradox of God's redemptive purposes, concluding that the tone of scripture suggests that 'unity demands conflict'. He observes: 'the healthy unity that Scripture points to as the experiential goal for its people, is one made more sure and precious through conflict'. Then to amplify the point, he quotes another Christian leader who said: 'The mark of community – true biblical unity – is not the absence of conflict. It's the presence of a reconciling spirit.'[15]

There is no conflict-free community. What we aim for is a reconciling spirit willing to move towards unity constantly.

1.7 *Christian communities play a vital role*

The thrust of scripture shows that God's new humanity is to be lived in community. Given conflict is inevitable within communities, conflict is of communal concern.

Paul believed that in God's economy, *everyone* connected to the community is to assist in resolving conflict. He challenged the *whole* Corinthian community, both its leaders and members, to address their many substantial conflicts. (See 1 Cor 5; 6:1-11; 16:15f.) Jesus himself challenged both the alleged guilty party (Mt 5:23, 24) and the perceived innocent party (Mt 18:15) to both go and address their conflict.

1.8 *The Holy Spirit is present throughout every conflict*

There are no circumstances when we are alone. And that includes when responding to conflict. Have you ever considered what prompted Jesus' great promise, '...that if two of you on earth agree about anything they ask for, it will be done for you by my Father in heaven. For where two or three come together in my name, *there am I with them*'? (Mt 18:19 italics added) It is arresting and liberating to realise that Jesus spoke these words in the context of conflict.

It is because the Holy Spirit remains present, alive and powerful in us, that Paul can throw out the challenge: '...if someone is caught in a sin, you who *live by the Spirit* should restore that person gently' (Gal 6:1, italics added).

These words from Jesus and Paul reassure us that the Spirit's presence will be with us, especially as we courageously step out to resolve conflict. The Holy Spirit always accompanies us.

1.9 *All truth is God's truth, wherever it is found*

The one who is all truth (Jn 14:6) has given us his word to illuminate our unique human predicament. It provides the healthiest and most holistic way forward in times of conflict.

The one who is all truth has also created all human beings in his image (Gen 1:27). Therefore, it will not surprise us that all humans carry the capacity to reflect on truth and advance it. We can benefit greatly from this 'common grace' when it is evident in material dealing with conflict developed by people who do not identify as Christian.

> ***In summary, the foundational beliefs on which this book is written include:***
> - Conflict is elemental;
> - Conflict is endemic;
> - Christ is the only lasting answer to all conflict;
> - God's word provides a trustworthy navigational chart for every conflict;
> - Navigation is an apt biblical metaphor for leading through conflict;
> - Unity demands a reconciling spirit;
> - Christian communities play a vital role;
> - The Holy Spirit is present throughout every conflict; and
> - All truth is God's truth, wherever it is found.

These foundational beliefs help us to understand every conflict as an opportunity for the people of God to respond afresh to his call to be a new humanity. With these beliefs in place, we can now confidently turn to what the Bible says concerning the origins and growth of conflict in our lives.

---

10 https://oceanservice.noaa.gov/facts/nautical_chart.html; National Oceanic and Atmospheric Administration (NOAA).

11 So NIV.

12 So ESV.

13 Starling, David I, *UnCorinthian Leadership: Thematic Reflections on 1 Corinthians*, Eugene, Oregon: Cascade Books, 2014, p. 6.

14 Mitchell, Margaret M., *Paul and the Rhetoric of Reconciliation: An Exegetical Investigation of the Language and Composition of 1 Corinthians*, 1st American Edition, Westminster/John Knox Press, Kentucky, 1992, p. 163.

15 Leroy Goertzen, *Understanding, Managing & Redeeming Church Conflict*, p. 33; the quote is from 'An Interview with Bill Hybels', "Standing in the Crossfire," *Leadership* 14:1 (Winter 1993) p. 14.

UNDERSTANDING THE WEATHER - ORIGINS AND RESPONSES 2

Gerard had been involved in Pandama Christian Mission almost from its inception. He was part of the furniture – well known, liked, loyal, diligent and hospitable.

Over thirty years, he had filled many roles – played the piano at the weekly mission chapel service, interviewed candidates for mission service, ferried people to and from the airport, led groups to mission conferences overseas, and served on the governance board.

For the past five years, Gerard has been the board chair. Recently, the mission's long-standing and much-loved director had retired. The board immediately formed a search committee to find a replacement. Nearing retirement himself, Gerard saw serving on this committee as one final opportunity to contribute and leave a positive legacy. Once the board appointed a new director, he too would step down and take a well-earned break.

Gerard not only volunteered to stand for the committee, but he also let it be known to the committee members that he sought to be chair. This would be in addition to his role as chair of the board.

Ilona, who had similarly served as a board member for some years, was also elected onto the search committee. To Gerard's dismay, she spoke against his nomination for chair at the new group's first meeting.

She believed it was not appropriate for the same person to hold the vital role of chair in both contexts. How could the committee be accountable to the board in such circumstances? What if the committee needed to consult the board for guidance? Gerard would hold too much power. The other board members were confused. They had all served together for many years and knew each other well. Surely, they could trust each other to work things out as they went along. Nevertheless, Gerard remained convinced God would have him carry out the role and remained unwavering in his aspiration.

What should the committee do? Is this a simple difference of opinion between board members to resolve by a vote? Or is this a conflict to manage? If it is a conflict, where did it originate, how did it escalate, and what might be its hallmarks?

And what, if anything, do we do about conflict as Christians? Can there ever be a successful outcome?

The creator God saw all that he had made, including humanity, and knew it was very good. Tragically, this good was soon spoiled. In families and communities, between individuals and within groups, pride, selfishness and greed took hold. The resultant painful tensions and personal estrangements not only echo through the biblical narratives and world history, but even now reverberate in our own families and communities, families and communities like Gerard's – even, or perhaps inevitably, in communities that seek to follow Jesus. It is no surprise to anyone in leadership that when it comes to conflict, the issue is not *whether* it exists within our community but *where* it is lurking and *when* it will surface.

In his ministry, Jesus frequently encountered conflicts:
- between members of the society in which he moved (Lk 12:13-15; Jn 4:1-26);
- with the religious and political system with which he contended (Mt 21:12-17; Mk 2:23f);
- among the disciples (Lk 9:46-48; 22:24ff); and
- between his followers (Lk 10:38ff).

Similarly, the writers of the New Testament consistently experienced conflict in their wider societies and cultures. Many were with Jesus when he negotiated and addressed conflict. They were themselves leaders who needed to steer their faith communities through conflict. This background and experience, combined with the guidance of the Spirit, qualifies them to assist us today. Their teachings describe a God-honouring approach when leading through conflict. Their insights and instruction are pivotal to our thinking.

As we embark on our journey, our priority is to have a sound understanding of what conflict is, where it originates and how it plays out individually and communally – and whether there is any hope of a remedy!

2.1 *Defining conflict*

The media frequently uses the term 'conflict' where the story involves violence. So, a headline may refer to 'Conflict in the Middle East', or 'Conflict Between Bikie Gangs'. While military or physical violence will have the hallmarks explored in this book, few of us experience conflict on this scale. Most of us are more likely to experience conflict as deep, personal, internal struggles where emotions run high.

This more common experience of conflict ranges across the broad spectrum of human interaction. We daily encounter differences of opinions, strongly expressed desires or unwelcome actions. These are usually with those with whom we have a pre-existing relationship.

This relationship may be with a particular individual or with a group. Something is communicated; it is misunderstood or runs counter to the other person's desires or the group's desires. While this does not *necessarily* lead to conflict, we recognise this is where it starts: a negative thought is spawned; a retaliatory response occurs; frustration, disappointment, anxiety sets in. Inflamed emotions trigger actions and reactions. The escalation progresses. And before we know it, we are deep in interpersonal conflict affecting us and those around us.

One writer defines conflict of this nature as 'a difference of opinion or purpose that frustrates someone's goals or desires';[16] another as 'conflict equals differences plus tension'.[17] Here is my definition for this book:

> ***Key definition:***
> Conflict =
> → emerging *differences* over opinions or actions
>   → which threaten the *desires* of an individual, a group, or both
>   → arousing negative *emotions*, and
>   → prompting antagonistic *behaviours*.

To represent it visually:

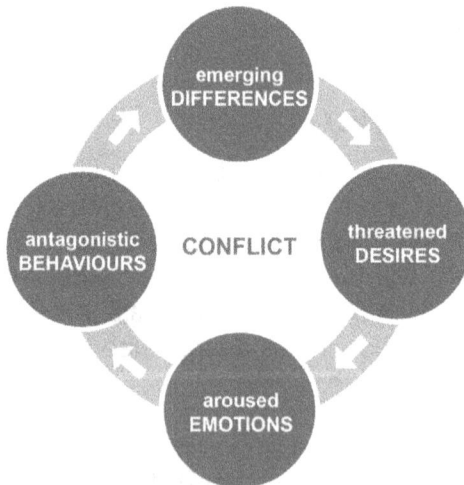

FIGURE 1: DEFINITION OF CONFLICT

2.2 *The origins of conflict*

Ken Sande gives further voice to those daily irritants which can trip us up, observing that conflicts arise from:

- 'misunderstandings resulting from poor communication';
- 'differences in values, goals, gifts, calling, priorities, expectations, interests, or opinions';
- 'competition over limited resources'; and, without pulling any punches, he names the uncomfortable reality,
- 'sinful attitudes and habits that lead to sinful words and actions'.[18]

These do not *necessarily* lead to conflict. Sometimes people address concerns in ways that avert conflict via what may be called 'redemptive conversations'. That is, people deal with their differences as peacemakers. So, what is going on when such irritants *do* lead to conflict?

Think of layers. On the surface, relatively easy to observe and identify are the 'presenting issues'. They are the many and varied polarising concerns that irk our sense of justice and beg to be proactively faced and wholeheartedly addressed. These become the solution-driven stuff of conflict resolution, grist for the mill for mediators and consultants.

Below the surface are the much less readily observed and identified heart matters – the 'issues-behind-the-issues'. This is the profoundly personal, internal cauldron, where struggles and tensions fire our emotions. As we will see soon, it is when these matters of the heart develop secretly over time and begin to drive us that the threat to our desires becomes untenable, and those daily irritants mutate and erupt into conflict. For there to be any seriously lasting solution in a conflicted environment, this deeper layer also needs to be acknowledged, faced and addressed.

> *Key perspective:*
> When leading through conflict, leaders do well to prioritise understanding the power of the underlying heart matters that drive conflict. They are at play in their hearts, in the hearts of the protagonists and throughout their community.

So, what is the discernment we need for this? There are clues to help us. What might they be?

2.3 *The desires of our hearts*

From a biblical perspective, James provides the most helpful indicator in the context of conflict. He pens his letter having observed several clashes between people in the communities to which he is writing. His conclusion? The harmful influences which fuel conflict arise when our *'desires' demand satisfaction at any cost.*

> *What causes fights and quarrels among you? Don't they come from your* desires *that battle within you? You* desire *but do not have, so you kill. You covet but you cannot get what you want, so you quarrel and fight* (Jas 4:1-2 emphasis added).

Earlier in his letter, he spells out his beliefs about such 'desires':

> *...each person is tempted when they are dragged away by their own evil desire and enticed. Then, after desire has conceived, it gives birth to sin; and sin, when it is full-grown, gives birth to death...* (Jas 1:14, 15).

Our hearts are the incubators of our desires. These desires can gain traction leading to either negative or positive outcomes. On the one hand, there are some desires where the possibility for adverse outcomes is not altogether surprising. It doesn't surprise us that the desire 'to get rich', left unchecked, may lead 'to ruin and destruction' (1 Tim 6:9). Nor does it surprise us that the 'pleasures' of sexual desire, left unchecked, may lead to 'adultery', 'greed' and 'wandering' from the faith (2 Pet 2:13-15). James sums up the adverse outcomes of our unchecked desires by saying:

> *...if you harbour bitter envy and selfish ambition* in your hearts, *do not boast about it or deny the truth... For where you have envy and selfish ambition, there you find disorder and every evil practice.* (Jas 3:14, 16 emphasis added)

On the other hand, there are some desires where the possibility of adverse outcomes can be surprising. For example, it may surprise us that our positive and satisfying desire to see and experience God (Is 26: 8, 9; Heb 6:11) and find satisfaction in him (2 Sam 23:5), left unchecked, may lead to alienating pride and arrogance. Similarly, it may surprise us that the honourable desire to lead God's people (1 Tim 3:1), left unchecked, may lead to cultish outcomes.

It is important to recognise that Proverbs observes a 'longing fulfilled is sweet to the soul' (13:19). James points out that his readers desired a 'good and perfect gift' with its genesis in God (1:17). In and of themselves, our original desires may be positive and beneficial, with the potential to produce much good fruit (1:18).

We might ask, therefore, what is going on here?

Even when the consequences seem negative, even patently sinful, desire usually has something legitimate at its root. Behind the desire to amass personal wealth, might there not be a genuine, though corrupted, yearning for security? Behind a desire to express angst through assault, might there not be an authentic, though skewed, impulse for justice? Does it surprise us that, having created us in his image, God has planted in our hearts desires which reflect his good intentions for us? There is wisdom in bringing this compassionate understanding to our leadership in conflicted situations.

So why would James call his readers' desire for a 'good and perfect gift', *evil*? (1:14) The problem was that they had been, in fact, 'deceived' by their desires (1:16, 22, 26). Moreover, they had allowed these desires to escalate, to be left unchecked, to take control within their hearts, driving destructive squabbling.

James is not the only writer in the New Testament to uncover and lay bare the hidden issues-behind-the-issues that corrupt and precipitate conflict, even though the original desire had been for something good. The word of God leaves nothing hidden. In story after story, it refuses to paper over the human tendency to be deceived by 'the thoughts and attitudes of the heart'.[19] As illustrated in the table below, scripture narrates, with penetrating honesty, how people with otherwise intrinsically good and reasonable desires end up in conflict.

The incident	The surface layer, the presenting issue(s)	The godly heart posture, the good thing which the person, the group, might have desired	The below the surface layer: the destructive heart desires behind the issue(s) which led to conflict
The man who asked Jesus to intervene and divide his inheritance (Lk 12: 13-15)	Money from a deceased estate	A fair and equitable distribution of the assets available	'all kinds of greed'
Paul and the Corinthian church (1 Cor)	Differences over theology, tensions with Paul, an absence of leadership in the church	A healthy community where people could speak openly, be heard and make lasting agreements	'Some have become arrogant... proud'
Brothers and sisters in conflict with God, themselves and each other (Jas 4: 1-2, 16)	The way they carry on their business	Meaning and purpose in the person's chosen vocation; reasonable income for supporting their family	'quarrels and fights ... you boast in your arrogant schemes', 'bitter envy', 'selfish ambition'
Jesus' disciples arguing with each other (Mt 18, Lk 9: 46ff)	Which of them would be the highest on the pecking order or hold the greatest influence in the next kingdom	Inclusiveness, appropriate significance, being recognised	Desiring to be 'great' or prominent; to be the favourite; stubbornly not caring, not listening, not forgiving

Let's make this personal. Imagine someone, maybe even yourself, with a keen desire to:

- develop a special ministry;
- hold a position with influence for good in the community;
- be loved, listened to, respected; and
- contribute to your community's future direction...

These are beneficial objectives. They are good and worthy things! We may even believe God wants us to have them. But, what if we don't get them? When faced with the disappointment of unfulfilled good desires, why does one person end up painfully and unexpectedly in conflict while another remains calm and peaceful?

Which person am I, as I negotiate the daily desires of my heart?

Am I someone who sees the object of my desire as the *only* pathway to deep meaning and personal happiness? Do I choose to believe this deception? Ignoring the consequences, do I take matters into my own hands; set out to get what I want in my own strength at any cost? Do I exalt myself and privilege my desire over anything or anyone else?

Or, am I someone who deliberately recognises *God* alone as the pathway to meaning, submits my desire to him and trusts him, not only for the outcome but also for the process of attaining it? Whether my desire is fulfilled or not, do I choose to honour God?

Let's unpack this choice further.

2.4 *Responding to our desires by exalting ourselves*

New opportunities and revitalised hope are potent forces in our psyche. When something comes across our path which seems to offer such things, it is customary to want to take hold of them. However, when our desire to do so morphs into an exalted sense of entitlement that drives and influences our responses, this may be a red flag. Are we developing an unhealthy allegiance to our desire? Is it beginning to look like the only path to meaning and happiness? What is the state of our trust and faith? Are we drifting away from God? Indeed, might this desire have unseated God from his rightful place in our lives at a heart level?

This is familiar territory. All of us will have faced situations where a good and worthy thing comes into view, and our desire for it intensifies. We believe it would be beneficial for us and, if we are leaders, maybe for the communities under our care. We convince ourselves God wants this for us. We dwell on the possibilities. Perhaps some questions surface. Someone raises a doubt. Achieving the objective is delayed. We feel aggrieved. Our sense of entitlement or calling is frustrated. We rebuff the objections.

We talk to others about our grievances. We progress our claim but with more robust language. In our heart, we consolidate our allegiance to the good thing, demanding it as our right – then judge those who stand in our way. If they continue to thwart our desire, we punish them by withdrawing friendship or lashing out angrily. They respond stridently and publicly. We feel isolated, wounded, disillusioned. We hit back. We are... in conflict.

The idols of our heart

We have talked a lot about our heart, this seat of our emotions, the core of our being. What are we dealing with when we reflect on the nature of the human heart? Are our hearts good? Are our hearts evil? Aleksandr Solzhenitsyn nails it:

> If only it were so simple. If only there were evil people somewhere insidiously committing evil deeds, and it were necessary only to separate them from the rest of us and destroy them. But the line dividing good and evil cuts through the heart of every human being. And who is willing to destroy a piece of his own heart? [20]

Ouch! We are so unwilling to destroy that piece of our own heart that scripture identifies as 'idolatry'. The prophet Ezekiel speaks of this in terms of 'setting up idols in (our) hearts' (Ezek 14:3).

Heart idols, or 'idols of our heart', the term we will use here, is a strange concept to the 21st-century ear. It is, however, a highly relevant insight for individuals in conflict and those intent on leading their community well through conflict. It is another clue to identifying the potential beneficial or harmful impact of those below the surface currents stirred by conflict. It may also shine an unsettling light into our hearts as leaders, an uncomfortable thought we'll come to shortly.

David Powlison affirms the biblical link between insatiable desire and idolatry, pointing out that 'the New Testament merges the concept of idolatry and the concept of inordinate, life-ruling desires. Idolatry becomes a problem of the heart, a metaphor for human lust, craving, yearning, and greedy demand.'[21]

Martin Luther provides further insight: 'whatever your heart clings to and relies upon, that is your God; trust and faith of the heart alone make both God and idol.'[22]

In scripture, the concept of 'idols' often refers to the worship of deities represented literally by stone, wood carvings and other forms drawn from creation. However, as we have already noted about the prophet Ezekiel, the scripture also uses the concept of 'idols' metaphorically.

Thus, we find the record of some of the elders of Israel petitioning the prophet to inquire of God concerning a specific community issue. The prophet retires to consider their request. On his return, the elders 'sit down in front' (Ezek 14:1) of him, ready to hear his inspired response. However, instead of providing an answer to the presenting issue, the prophet goes straight to the heart issues. He recounts what God has told him: 'Son of man, these men have set up *idols in their hearts* and put wicked stumbling blocks before their faces' (14:3, italics added). God had looked into their hearts and what he saw were leaders who had deserted him to worship their desires.[23] The actual issue was internal, a problem of their hearts and minds. They had displaced worship of the one true God for something else.[24] There was no point in dealing with the presenting problem when the real issue was the-issue-behind-the-issue!

We see the concept of idols also used metaphorically in the concluding words of 1 John: '(d)ear children, keep yourselves from idols'. Whatever the precise thought John had in mind, the truth is he wants his hearers to keep away from 'God-substitutes', to turn from actively worshipping false gods, whatever they might be and wherever they might find them.

More specifically, the metaphorical use of idolatry is in play when scripture speaks about *greed*. A glance at any dictionary will explain why the Bible condemns greed as idolatry – greed is, quite simply, the desires of our hearts gone rampant.[25] The insatiable appetite created by greed commandeers our love, our beliefs, our worship.

God is the God who is. There is no other true God. And it is precisely because this is so, he has commanded: 'You will have no other gods before me' (Ex 20:3). This exclusivity encompasses both kinds of 'gods', literal material representations, as well as metaphorical idols of the heart. God is described as a 'jealous' God, like a bird that jealously protects its eggs from predators, his eager desire for our wholehearted worship displays his commitment to guarding his life-giving relationship with his followers. God knows full well it is only when we offer wholehearted allegiance in worship to him as the one true Lord of all things that we can become fully human as he intended.

> **Key perspective:**
> Any desire that rules even part of us acts like a god in our lives. It requires our loyalty. It holds out the hope of ultimate satisfaction and fulfilment. It requires us to sacrifice things or people to achieve it. It takes the rightful place of the one true God in that area of our lives. We give our worship over to feeding it. It becomes, in the language of scripture, an idol, an idol of the heart.

How and why good and worthy desires can result in adverse outcomes

When we are caught up in the storm of conflict, our worthy desires can quickly become destructive if they have morphed into idols of our heart. Whilst such idols are notoriously difficult to identify, we can recognise a pattern emerging as we reflect on those times when we have left our desires unchecked.[26] It is not unlike becoming aware of the weather around us when a storm is brewing.

Stages in the pattern of unchecked desires:	The weather pattern of unchecked desires:	The outcome of unchecked desires:
My heart responds positively to something worthy	A refreshing breeze catches my attention. What I am wanting is splendid; something worth achieving, worth celebrating, most definitely, indeed, something: →	'I desire it'

My desire remains unmet	The breeze stiffens. I dwell on the excellence of my desire; it becomes a craving for its perceived benefits. I may believe this is something I need or deserve to be happy or fulfilled, and so it works its way deep into my heart. I justify and legitimise my craving. If it remains unmet, I may feel disappointed, bitter, depressed, frustrated, anxious, even enraged. I really, really want this, indeed: →	'I insist on it'
My insistence comes to nothing	By now, clouds are building. My desire begins to assume the role of a god in my life and insists on being met. It consumes me. Fear of losing it begins to dictate my attitudes. When others ignore my insistence and thwart my desire or don't meet my expectations, I attribute all sorts of nasty motivations to them. They are uncaring, lazy, ungodly, wrong, controlling, harsh, selfish ... I embrace the idol in my heart. I let it play god. Now, when I think about those who thwart my desires, in my mind, if not with my words and actions: →	'I condemn them'
My hopes and expectations remain thwarted	The storm erupts. Continuing to dwell on the issue, I move, consciously or unconsciously, into fight or flight mode – I actively argue, defend, gossip; or passively withdraw friendship and intimacy, turning away and losing interest. Idols always demand sacrifices. The idol in my heart demands someone suffer for failing to satisfy my insistence that my desires and expectations be met. So in obedience to it: →	'I penalise them'

When an otherwise healthy desire shifts into something we insist upon having, when fear of losing what we want drives us to condemn and penalise others, it is sure evidence that our desire has escalated to the status of an idol of the heart, a false god.

There is a paradox here.[27] The process of exalting ourselves and escalating our desires, in truth, pitches us into a downward spiral:

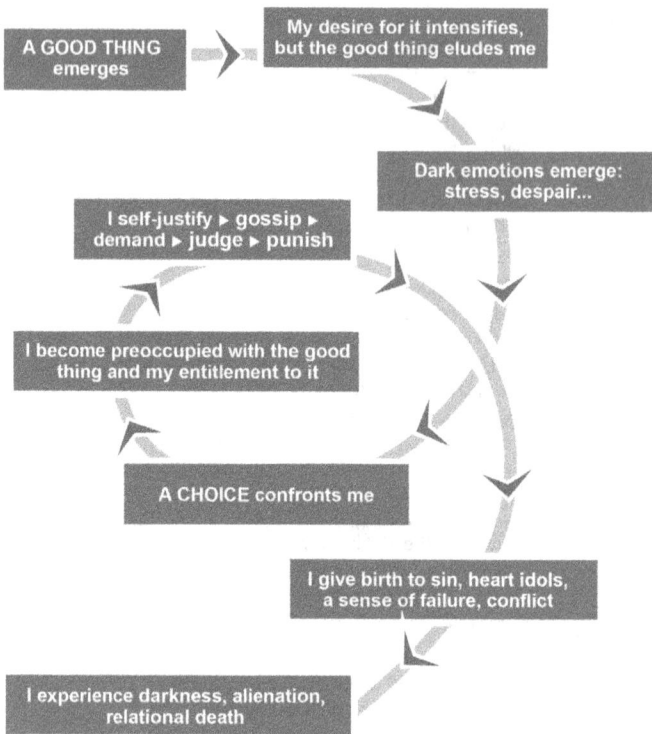

FIGURE 2: PROGRESSION OF A HEART DESIRE – SELF-EXALTING

This slide downwards does not bring honour to anyone. It exalts neither God nor ourselves. We forget God is our provider. We forget who we are to be. And we forget what we are called to do. Indeed, when we become preoccupied with our desires, God is invariably all but left out. As Alfred Poirier observes, our desires *distort* what we see. 'They magnify some things while minimizing others. Unfortunately, it is God who often gets minimized.'[28] And thus, depressingly, our good and worthy desires culminate in adverse outcomes.

2.5 *Responding to our desires by honouring God*

So, what are we supposed to do when the *good and worthy thing* we desire eludes us? What do we do with the loss and the grief we experience when this occurs? Is there an alternative trajectory, and why would we bother seeking it anyway? Where, if anywhere, does God fit in all this, and does it matter? While we could draw from many scriptures here, James' focus is helpful. He encourages us to remember that God does not leave us bereft when we exalt and honour Him. He has promised, there is no good thing that he withholds. Rather, he:

Lavishes good gifts upon us:

- He gives 'wisdom' (1:5, 3:17), rewards (1:12), 'grace' (4:6);
- He gives us 'birth through the word of truth' (1:18);
- He speaks to us through scripture (1:18, 4:6);
- He 'shows favour to the humble...' (4:6); and
- He answers our prayers as we earnestly seek him (5:16-18).

Secures our identity as:

- The 'firstfruits' of his creation (1:18);
- 'Peacemakers' (3:18); and
- Those who come 'near to God' (4:8).

Brings us to maturity as we:

- 'persevere' (1:12);
- 'listen to the word [scripture]...and do what it says' (1:22);
- 'ask God' and 'resist the devil' (4:2, 7);
- examine our 'motives', our' friendship with the world', our 'proud' hearts (4:3, 4, 6);
- 'purify' our 'hearts, 'confess' our 'sins' (4:8; 5:16);
- 'submit' ourselves to God (4:7); and
- 'grieve' our sinful attitudes and behaviours (4:9).

Remembering God does not leave us bereft, but lavishes greater gifts upon us and this can be a turning point. It allows us to get to trust God as we accept and grieve our loss. Here is the other side of the paradox. When we accept and grieve our loss, that is, when we lose our life for kingdom purposes, we will gain it. This step is the pathway to an upward spiral instead:

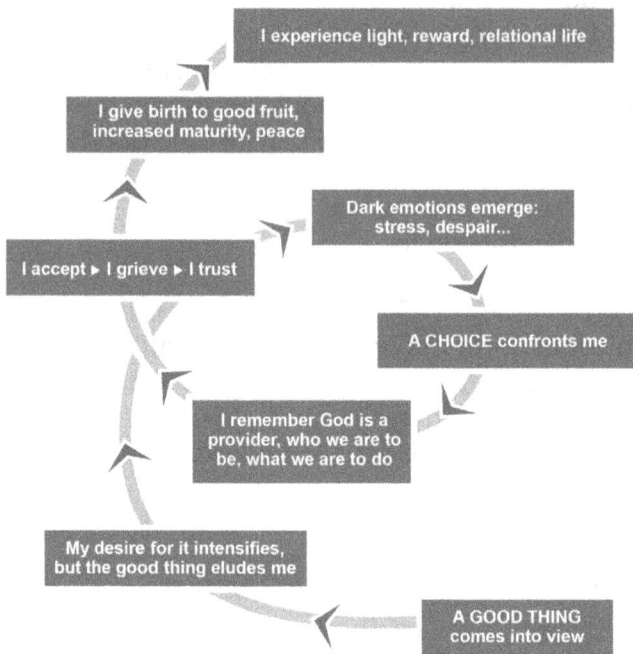

FIGURE 3: PROGRESSION OF A HEART DESIRE – GOD-HONOURING

It is important to note here that the choice to accept we may not receive what we desire, and grieving its loss, *does not* mean it was not necessarily a 'good and worthy thing' in the first place. Nor does acceptance and grieving necessarily imply we condone what others may have done to us. It is not saying: 'It is ok that I do not have this good and worthy thing'. It is actually saying the opposite: 'It is not ok that I do not have this good thing. But that is the reality of my situation. God is enough; even in this, I accept that. I choose to protect myself by putting appropriate boundaries in place. I choose to forgive the one who has hurt me.'

What acceptance *does do* is free us to receive the alternative good and perfect gifts God offers. It gives us the grace to let go what we desired and respond in a godly manner. It offers us peace amidst our feelings of disappointment and frustration. Acceptance declutters our inner world so we can ask ourselves some challenging questions:

- Where is God in the situation?
- Is he aware of me?
- Has he seen my pain and confusion?
- Can I trust him?
- What might he do to resolve the situation?
- What might he be trying to show me?
- What might I do to resolve the tensions?

We may conclude the answers to these questions are resoundingly in the negative. At best, there may be ambiguity and uncertainty. The challenge for us here is to trust God and his timing, with the most pressing question being: *Is God sufficient?*

Trusting God, resting in his plan and providence for the outcome allows us to keep our emotions in check and realistically engage with our questions. It provides the opportunity to learn, to gain further perspective on the events. It allows us to live as God designed us to live by responsibly having mastery over our desire, rather than letting our desire have mastery over us.

The psalmist is helpful here. He is quite clear it is taking *'delight in the Lord'* that brings fulfilment to 'the *desires of [our] heart'* (Ps 37:4 italics added). Taking delight in the Lord, notwithstanding uncertain and perhaps unfavourable circumstances, is a sure sign of our maturity in Christ. It holds our desires in the proper perspective.

> **Key perspective:**
> Recognising our need to take 'delight in the Lord' is vital for every follower of Christ, for every believer who ends up as a protagonist in a conflict. It is as critical for leaders, perhaps even more so, given the responsibility of leaders to model maturity and invoke it within their communities.

The book of Acts records two situations that could have been highly conflicted but weren't. Why? Because leaders did not allow the good and worthy things sitting behind the presenting issues in their communities to become destructive heart desires, that is 'idols of their hearts'. The following table summarises the incidents, sets out the presenting issues, identifies the good thing behind them and the potential idols that could have emerged for the leaders.

The incident	The surface layer, the presenting issue(s)	The good thing desired	Potential idols of the heart for the leaders
The daily distribution of community relief (food) (Acts 6:1-7)	Ethnic discrimination and sense of rejection	Justice and equity for those in need	Favouritism Greed Covetousness
The Council at Jerusalem (Acts 15:1-35)	Gatekeepers of Jewish law and religious rituals viewed the new Christian way as illegitimate without these Jewish practices	Faithful adherence to their centuries-old understanding of God-given law	Legalism Pride Obstinacy

In each of these situations, the leaders remained humble and took the initiative to respond with maturity. In the first situation, they convened a community meeting to gain justice and equity for those in need. They carefully listened to the concerns, redefined their roles, and articulated a reasonable process for resolution. There were immediate outcomes for the local community with a flow-on impact to the broader community. The meeting affirmed the priorities of the existing leadership and established another group of leaders, people 'full of the Spirit and wisdom'. They authorised and empowered these new leaders to meet the community's legitimate local needs and concerns (Acts 6:1ff). Their reputation, influence and effectiveness spread throughout the district (6:7).

In the second situation, leaders appointed representatives and humbly sought outside help to address the simmering conflict about Jewish rituals (Acts 15:22). They raised the sights of the protagonists on what it meant to be faithful in this new Christian way by testifying to God's powerful ongoing work. Again, there were immediate outcomes for the local community with a flow-on impact to the broader community. The local believers were encouraged and strengthened in their faith. They adopted a much more culturally attuned missional approach with non-Jewish people coming to faith (15:19). And everyone left with a blessing of peace.

Our desires are formidable forces. Yet, consciously, prayerfully and trustfully, handing them over to God opens the door for God to lavish greater gifts upon us, secure our identity and bring us to maturity. Releasing our desires opens us to the best gifts – the gifts that empower us to be all we can be; to be fully human. To take this approach to address our heartfelt desires exalts and honours God, makes us wise and lavishes benefit upon us. As the psalmist says: '[the Lord's] favour lasts a lifetime; weeping may stay for the night, but rejoicing comes in the morning' (30:5).

If only, as Aleksandr Solzhenitsyn laments, it was all so simple!

2.6 *Desires and idols in the hearts of leaders*

Individual leaders are simply not immune from deceptive desires which may develop into idols of the heart. Yes, of course, there are the usual human hopes and dreams, but the very context of leadership magnifies a host of legitimate and worthy desires for such things as:

- trust and respect;
- loving and mature relationships; and
- accomplishing the work of one's calling.

Leaders know the potential for far-reaching negative consequences when they do not achieve these good things. That there is significantly heightened potential for such desires to escalate into controlling demands does not surprise us. It is easy to imagine:

- A leader craves respect. Respect is not shown. The leader lashes out instead of humbly and gently seeking to understand the underlying causes and relational problems.
- A leader values his colleagues' opinion of him. His colleagues, however, never affirm him or his contribution. As a result, the leader loses confidence, becomes fearful and reduces his efforts in the group instead of going to his colleagues to address his concerns.

- A leader pursues a gifted person to head up a vital ministry. She declines. The leader shuns her rather than maintaining a mature collegial relationship.

Further, it is not only the individual leader at risk of good desires escalating into heart idols. A leadership group is also at risk, collectively. Such a group heart idol might present as:
- arrogance and indifference, instead of showing humility and loving engagement;
- legalism characterised by cold, dispassionate behaviour, instead of pastorally caring for the community;
- seeking power and privilege '...lording it over those entrusted to [them]...' (1 Pt 5:3), instead of showing respect and the fruit of the Spirit;
- pride evidenced by being fractious or controlling, instead of showing unity and trust; or
- tightly held governance traditions, instead of flexibility, love and dependence on God.

> **Key perspective:**
> When good desires become destructive and develop into a collective idol of the heart in a leadership group, a detrimental, even ruinous mindset may grow. This mindset can become entrenched in the communal outlook, culture and decision-making processes of the group.

Have you ever considered whether controlling desires or heart idols such as these might have developed in your leadership group? If you suspect this could be so, you may be grateful for the unvarnished honesty of biblical narratives. They not only confirm the existence of collective heart idols, but they also indicate you are not alone. Furthermore, they show us what kinds of obsessions can develop into idols of the heart of a group. The following table summarises the incidents, sets out the presenting issues, identifies the idols revealed by their behaviours, along with the alternative posture characterised by humility and maturity they could have exhibited had they trusted God.

The incident	The surface layer, the presenting issue(s)	The controlling heart desires, or idols, which developed and the associated behaviours displayed by the group	The godly heart posture, characterised by humility and maturity, the leaders could have exhibited had they trusted God
The elders of Israel collectively enquire of the prophet Ezekiel (Ezek 14:1-11)	A significant community concern	a god-substitute (We are not told the specifics of the heart issue. It was sufficient, however, for God to refuse to respond to the community concern.)	Wholehearted worship of the one true God; repentance; avoid putting stumbling blocks in the way of the community; seeking God's answer to the particular issue
An argument among Jesus' disciples (Mt 18, Lk 9:46-48)	Which of them would be the greatest in the kingdom of heaven?	power, privilege, self-advancement	Exhibiting all the qualities of godly greatness, namely: humility, welcome, being a servant, being open to change their orientation, pastorally caring like a shepherd, addressing conflicts, and practising ongoing forgiveness
The Pharisees (Mt 23)	Their systemic practices and attitudes	insisting on respect, approval, prominence, security or being right, traditions[29]	Showing the qualities of justice, mercy, faithfulness, servanthood, humility and transparency
The church at Corinth (1 Cor)	Conflicts among themselves and between them and the Apostle Paul	obstinacy, divisiveness, quarrelsomeness, jealousy, arrogant, dominant, boastful	Looking up to those leaders who have 'devoted themselves to the service of the Lord's people.' (16:15); that they 'agree with one another' and that there be 'no divisions among [them]' (1:10); that they see conflict as an opportunity (1 Cor 10: 31)

When our desires for good and worthy things are not met, and we respond in ways that don't please and honour God, is it an indicator that our identity as a person comes from a place other than God? Am I saying to myself: 'I need this good thing, and I am afraid if I don't get it, I won't be ok?' Instead, what happens if

I remember I am a child of the King, adopted and precious in his sight?[30]

We have explored a definition of conflict. We have also looked at its origins in the below the surface desires of the human heart, which can control us if they take on the status of idols. We have considered this at play in the hearts of individuals in the communities under our care. We have acknowledged this potential in our hearts as leaders. We have recognised this can also play out in the collective 'heart' of a whole group. What now? Are our communities stuck? Are our leadership groups doomed? Are we as leaders impotent? The biblical response is a resounding *'no'!* There is a remedy!

2.7 *The remedy for our sinful desires, the idols of our hearts*

For the Christian, the wonderful news is that Christ has gone before us in experiencing all facets of conflict – its desires, its escalation, its emotions. By entering this world and experiencing its strife, tensions and conflict, he understands. Notwithstanding evil and sin in the world, he perfectly reconciled his divinity and humanity without succumbing to that sin. By his death and resurrection, individually and collectively, we can be reconciled to him.

We have seen that scripture teaches that conflict starts, not with my brother or sister and their (wrongful) actions, but within me! I must look at my own heart, motives, longings, and whatever else resides in my heart *before* looking at the broader circumstances of the origins of the conflict (see Mt 7:3-5). Once we know what is ruling our hearts, we will begin to identify the source or sources of that conflict. In remedying our ungodly desires, we need, with God's help, to recognise, repent and replace these influences in our lives. We are called to replace the current spirit with a 'new heart and a new spirit' (Ezek 18:31), 'a pure heart, ...a steadfast spirit' (Ps 51:10).

First, we must *recognise* and name our good and worthy desires, and where they have taken control of us as heart idols. We do this by considering the principles outlined above along with the clues or indicators we have described. We might also ask ourselves the questions listed at the end of this chapter.

Once we have identified and named these sins and come to a place of conviction, the invitation is, for us secondly: to *repent* to '...confess [our] sins' (Jas 5:16), that is 'wash [our] hands... and purify [our] hearts' (Jas 4:8) and, once again, '...fear his name' (Ps. 86:11). This invitation is addressed to each of us individually. It is also an invitation to a leadership group. In the incident described by Ezekiel, the elders needed collectively to turn away from their idols and renounce all that went with them (14:6).

God's vision for leaders involved in conflict is for them, individually and collectively, to turn their backs on all such ungodly desires. Instead, God's vision is for them to turn in dependence to him, seek his face and trust his word. It is an opportunity to give up our small desires, depend on God, and discover his lavish gifts. The whole process involves dying to ourselves again and again. This is the pathway to resurrection; it is only through death that genuine life re-emerges.

> **Key perspective:**
> The ego stripping nature of repentance is challenging in the context of a polarising conflict between brothers and sisters in Christ. Humbling ourselves, however, is a command and a hallmark of our maturity. Sadly, as we know from history, Christian leaders have been slow to address their culpability, even slower to repent of their sin and slower still to reveal their repentance to their community.

The great news is that when we do repent '...he is faithful and just and will forgive us our sins and purify us from all unrighteousness' (1 Jn 1:9). Jonah understood the consequences of choosing not to repent. From the depths, he acknowledged 'those who cling to worthless idols forfeit the grace that could be theirs'.[31] When Jonah was at the bottom of the sea, he addressed the hardness – the idols – of his own heart. He realised the consequences of disobedience.

The third step in remedying the controlling desires of our hearts is to *replace* the idol with actions and behaviours, characterised by humility and maturity which honour God. We rejoice that there is a better way, a way where we can rest in Christ and the benefits he promises.

Difficult as it may be for us to ensure we honour God and let go of our heartfelt controlling desires, our heart idols, the irony is that He has promised:

> For the Lord God is a sun and shield;
> the Lord bestows favour and honour;
> no good thing does he withhold
> for those whose walk is blameless. (Ps 84:11)

2.8 *Summary*

Most desires that build up in our minds and manifest themselves at the centre of our conflicts in Christian communities, begin as good and worthy. However, when we don't receive the 'good thing' (we may even believe God intends it for us!), the problem is not usually the desire itself. Instead, it is about what we have done with that desire. Have we submitted the desire to God, accepted we might not receive what we wanted and may need to grieve its loss, and be able to continue to delight in Him? Or have we harboured the desire, allowing it to take root and hold a level of rule or mastery over us?

The scale of influence our desires have over us drives the likelihood of conflict. Recognising and naming our desires and evaluating how they have affected our behaviours and responses in the situation is one of the keys to identifying the issue-behind-the-issue. If we have let the desire rule us, we need to repent of our sin and reconcile any broken relationships. These realities are the same for anyone, including leaders and groups of leaders.

Questions for reflection and discussion

Searching questions help individuals and groups recognise and name hidden forces and heart idols driving a conflict.[32] Ask the following questions initially of yourself, using 'I', then as a group, using 'we'.

1) *What is the good thing I sincerely desired but didn't get?*
   For each good thing on the list:
   What is worthy and right about it?
   What are the potential dangers of wanting that thing or outcome too much?

2) *What do I fear I would be deprived of by not getting the good thing I desire?*
   (This loss might include a role, respect, reputation, security, a relationship, control, failing, one's health.)
   Or, complete the statement: *In this conflict, I'm afraid that...*

3) *What do I crave?* (This craving might include peace, acceptance, money, being needed, control, success, love, comfort, safety, perfect children, an identity image, vindication, justice.)
   Or, complete the statement: *In this conflict, all I want is...*

4) *How do I judge, threaten, or avoid those who stand in the way of getting what I want?* (These judgements might include thinking of others as unworthy, hopeless, wrong, mistaken; gossiping about them; treating them with condescension.)
   Or, complete the statement: *In this conflict, my thoughts about the other party are...*

5) Review the various potential 'idols of the heart' in an individual leader outlined in section 2.4. What heart issues do you think you harbour as a leader?

6) Review the list of potential 'idols of the heart' in your leadership group as a whole in section 2.6. What heart issues do you think your group harbours?

We have looked at the origins and growth of conflict in the heart of an individual and the corporate heart of a leadership group. We will now broaden our perspective to consider the origins and growth of conflict in a Christian community.

---

16 Sande, *The Peacemaker*, p. 29. The definition used by PeaceWise in Australia.
17 Schrock-Shenk, C. Introducing Conflict and Conflict Transformation in Shrock-Shenk, C. and Ressler, L. (eds.) *Making Peace with Conflict: Practical Skills for Conflict*

Transformation (Scottdale, PA: Herald Press, 1999) p.23 as quoted by Alastair McKay in How Does the church handle conflict in its midst, and what challenges does it face in handling conflict constructively? http://www.bbministries.org. uk/images/PDFs/Articles/How_does_the_church_handle_conflict_in_its_midst_ BBweb.pdf [Accessed 12.4.21], p. 3.

18 Sande, *The Peacemaker*, p. 29.

19 Heb 4:12. Hence the need for scripture to be applied to the situation to discern and judge whether these 'thoughts and attitudes' are honouring to God or not.

20 Solzhenitsyn, Aleksandr, *The Gulag Archipelago 1918-1956.*

21 Powlison, David, "Idols of the Heart and 'Vanity Fair'," The Journal of Biblical Counselling, Volume 13, Number 2 (Winter 1995): p. 36 and quoted by Tim Keller in *Gospel in Life*, Zondervan, 2010, p.39.

22 Rosner, Brian S., "Idolatry" in New Dictionary of Biblical Theology, ed. T. D. Alexander and B. S. Rosner (Downers Grove, Ill: InterVarsity Press, 2000), p. 571.

23 The prophet has previously linked the presence of idols to the provoking of God's jealousy. Ezek 8:3. See Ex 34:14.

24 Calvin, in his commentary on these verses, says, '...for God has erected the seat of his empire in our hearts: but when we set up idols, we necessarily endeavour to overthrow God's throne, and to reduce his power to nothing.' Commentaries on Ezekiel Lect. XXXVIII, p. 44.

25 Col 3:5, Eph 5:5.

26 The background thinking in this section has been informed by and adapted from *The Peacemaker* by Ken Sande (Copyright © 1991, 1997, 2004 Baker Books, a division of Baker Publishing Group) and in conversations with Wendy Konemann counsellor, teacher and mediator.

27 I am grateful to Wendy Konemann for much of the thinking lying behind the information summarised in figures 2 and 3. The background thinking in these figures has also been informed by Ken Sande from his book *The Peacemaker,* p. 100ff.

28 Poirier, Alfred, *The Peacemaking Pastor: A Biblical Guide to Resolving Church Conflict*, Baker Books, 2006, p. 55.

29 Arising from these idols of the heart, Matthew 23 records the actual behaviours which were exhibited, namely, laziness, hypocrisy, wickedness, exhorting themselves, demanding respect, greed, self-indulgence, rituals.

30 See section 5.1(f) for a further discussion on the desires and idols in the heart of a group of leaders.

31 From the 1984 version of the NIV, Jonah 2:8. The current version translates the verse as: 'Those who cling to worthless idols turn away from God's love for them'. The ESV renders the verse: 'Those who pay regard to vain idols forsake their hope of steadfast love'.

32 The questions provided here are mostly taken from *Peacemaker Mediation Manual*, Peacemaker Ministries, www.PeaceMakerMinistries.org Spokane Valley, WA, 1998, 2006 p. 49f, used by permission and reworked for this context.

A BREWING STORM - THE RISE AND RISE OF CONFLICT 3

In this chapter, we look at:
- the nature and effect of conflict in Christian communities;
- the sources of conflict in Christian communities;
- how conflict usually unfolds in Christian communities;
- early warning signs; and
- whether community conflict is necessarily bad.

We have looked at the nature and origins of conflict in our personal lives. What about the nature and origin of conflict in a *whole* community? One author aptly describes it this way:

> ... *conflict makes a church* [or any community] *feel as if it's being swept along by a raging flood. And often it is that way. But if the church* [or community] *can discover the various and sundry tributaries that feed into the conflict, they can turn flood waters that destroy into a river that gently but powerfully moves them downstream.*[33]

These 'tributaries', to which we now turn, are common to Christian and secular organisations alike. That said, we experience something unique wherever people intentionally gather in Christ's name to seek his purposes.

Eugene Peterson offers insights into this uniqueness:

> When Christian believers gather in churches, everything that can go wrong sooner or later does. Outsiders, on observing this, conclude that there is nothing to the religion business except, perhaps business – and dishonest business at that. Insiders see it differently. Just as a hospital collects the sick under one roof and labels them as such, the church collects sinners. Many of the people outside the hospital are every bit as sick as the ones inside, but their illnesses are either undiagnosed or disguised. It is similar with sinners outside the church. So Christian churches are not, as a rule, model communities of good behaviour. <u>They are, rather, places where human misbehaviour is brought out in the open, faced, and dealt with</u>.[34]

This last statement is a significant truth to carry into this chapter as we explore these tributaries. It articulates the biblical hope that the remarkable and radical authenticity of the Christian community can transform conflict into an opportunity for us to become the people God intended us to be.

3.1 *Nature and effect*

Churches and other Christian communities which gather around a common spiritual purpose experience conflict as particularly intense. So much is personally at stake because of our faith. Our faith is how we make sense of this world and the next and our place within each. We commit to our faith. Not only does it provide lasting meaning for us, but we act on it. We invest much of ourselves and our resources in our faith and in our faith community. If we are not secure in our faith, any challenge to it may become a threat to our identity and sense of well-being – an atmosphere to brew a conflict if ever there was one.

All this underscores the need for leaders to take a profoundly Christ-honouring approach when leading through conflict. Such an approach is even more essential when we remember that disputes occur within the framework of the far-reaching spiritual realities of the powers of darkness and the pull of the flesh, which we outlined in chapter 1.2.

In the light of this, consider the following potential spiritual consequences of conflict unique to a Christian community:

- cause people to seriously question or even stumble in their faith;[35]
- affect Christ's reputation in the broader community (see 1 Cor 6:1-11);
- trigger deep emotions linked to a deeply held faith commitment;
- challenge people to change course as the gospel confronts their behaviour and positions (Mt 18:3);
- frustrate, and even disenchant people in the community, based on too high a view of how Christian community should function;
- reveal erroneous beliefs which enable dysfunctional behaviour, beliefs such as:
  - tolerance is equivalent to Christian peace
  - mature Christian communities don't have conflict
  - nothing good can come out of conflict
- disclose immature biblical and theological literacy when people use God or the bible to shut down discussion or judge others:
  - 'they're unbiblical'
  - 'by their fruit you will know them'
  - 'they're in league with the devil'
  - 'they're fundamentalists', or
  - 'God has said to me...' as the final limiting and polarising argument;
- grieve the Holy Spirit (Eph 4:30[36]).

Key perspective:
The unique characteristics of conflict in Christian communities mean there is much more involved and at stake than in secular contexts. Yet, Christian communities, and their leaders, have the empowering guidance of the Holy Spirit and the entirely sufficient truths of scripture to assist them in responding.

Not so uniquely, conflicted Christian groups may share the following characteristics in common with any other human group in conflict:

- polarised relationships between leaders, colleagues, even friends;
- injured reputations, careers and personal finances;
- self-absorption;
- exhausted morale;
- loss of focus on shared purposes and strategic outcomes;
- skewed understanding about what the organisation values;
- damage to community finances;
- disregard for succession planning;
- inadequate or non-existent conflict resolution processes;
- dysfunctional people perpetuate the conflict for their own psychological needs;
- past grudges and hurts re-emerge;[37] and, if not resolved, conflict continues to recur as an ongoing cycle.[38]

Whatever our role in a church or Christian organisation, whether leaders, paid staff, volunteers, members, or adherents, conflict calls out something in each of us. Once we become aware of a conflict, we respond with flight, fight, freeze or (as some suggest) fawning. Even a choice to play down the problem, not engage, nor participate in its resolution, is still a response. Therefore, as leaders, we must manage our reactions even as we wrestle with how best to handle the dispute.

Indeed, as a leader, the experience of conflict will intensify our reactions to decisions made by the leadership group. At times, we will be in alignment with the group; at other times, we will be at significant variance. But, at all times, as the people of God, how can we be wise about how we manage ourselves – who will we be; what will we do?

While the downside of poorly handled conflict is significant, what might be the consequences when conducted in a God-honouring manner? Imagine the opportunity, for yourself and your community, to:

- acknowledge God's holiness, redemptive actions and presence;

- bring glory and honour to God;
- exhibit the enduring fruit of the Spirit;
- learn and grow to be more like Christ;
- serve one another;
- act with justice;
- testify to Christ at work;
- experience deepened personal relationships;
- find new clarity around community beliefs, values, mission, and strategic direction;
- gain fresh motivation to find lasting solutions to organisational predicaments;
- re-establish effective communication channels;
- realign resources to improve ministry effectiveness; and
- break debilitating historical cycles of attitudes, behaviours and conflict.

Conflict, well-handled, can be the pathway to this kind of growth in a community. It provides an opportunity for people to demonstrate love, unity and dependence on God. Just imagine.

> **Key perspective:**
> Both the positive and negative consequences of conflict in Christian communities are always more profound, more widespread and more enduring than most leaders realise or imagine.

3.2 *Origins of conflict in Christian communities*

Chapter 2 discussed how an individual or a leadership group might develop a 'heart', which may or may not align with God's kingdom purposes. Similarly, a Christian community can also unwittingly develop a collective character, a subconscious mindset, a shared identity that can be considered its 'heart'.

This 'heart' may exhibit itself as warm and inviting, single-minded and strategic. On the other hand, even simultaneously, it may be inflexible in its determination, formal in its processes and closed in its thinking.

There are moments when you shake your head, as a leader, in dismay at the obscure origins of a conflict in your community. It may be insightful at such times to reflect on the young church Paul founded in the nouveau-riche Greek city of Corinth. Multiple issues threatened the viability of this fledgling Christian community. They included factionalism, class divisions, spiritual superiority, theological differences, various obsessions, unethical conduct and leadership failure. The Apostle spent most of his first letter courageously addressing these matters.

Not only did this create a complex ecosystem in the church, but each separate issue was itself complex. What a nightmare for anyone in leadership! Can we nevertheless glean from the letter what might have been at least one of the issues-behind-the-issues? Were the conflicts being fuelled by something concealed within the communal 'heart' of the whole Corinthian church or of a powerful sub-group within it? Paul zeroes in on an elite group and observes the state of their heart: 'Some of you have become arrogant... I will find out not only how these arrogant people are talking, but what power they have' (1 Cor 4:18, 19).

This arrogance – Paul says '...you are proud!' (1 Cor 5:2) – led to their failure to address a significant sexual issue in the community. In boldly identifying this character trait, Paul put his finger right on the nub, the cause of the problem. Here was the issue-behind-the-issue; deep in the shared heart of the most influential section of the community lay an attitude of 'arrogance' and 'pride', and it was infecting everything.

The potent combination of this underlying heart issue and a vacuum in godly leadership spawned numerous internal conflicts – clashes with the Apostle himself and tensions between various groups within the community. Paul highlights the power of the heart issue to impact everyone with his classic rhetorical question: 'Don't you know that a little yeast leavens the whole batch of dough?' (1 Cor 5:6) Knowing his letter would be read aloud at one of their meetings, Paul names their heart issue of pride to bring it into the light and address it.

To help them re-focus, Paul first points them toward Christ. He reminds them:

- They have been 'sanctified in Christ' (1:2);
- That Christ has extended them 'grace' (1:3, 4);
- They have been 'enriched in every way' in Christ (1:5);
- Because of what Christ has done, they 'do not lack any spiritual gift' (1:7); and
- '...the message of the cross' is indeed the 'power of God' at work in them (1:18).

Having exhorted them to re-focus on Christ, Paul challenges the church in two directions: one, that all members of the community submit to those who have... 'devoted themselves to the service of the Lord's people' (1 Cor 16:15); and two, that all the members of the community address their dysfunction. They are *all* responsible to 'build up the church' (1 Cor 14:12) and indeed become who God wants them to be as a community of faith. This can be possible as they:

- clarify their purpose (3:8, 9, 16; 12:31);
- address their behaviours which dishonour Christ (5:2-5, 6:1-11);
- build unity within the community (12:24-26); and
- love one another (13).

> **Key perspective:**
> Heart issues are alive in every Christian community. Those which become God substitutes – idols of the heart – can infect the whole. Problems of the heart give birth to and drive the presenting issues.

The following are a few examples of sometimes bizarre, sometimes understandable, community heart idols I have come across in consultancy and mediation contexts (perhaps they are not unfamiliar to you!):

- entrenched worship traditions and rituals ('No modern songs around here, thanks!');
- rigid processes ('We've always done it this way!');
- pandering to the undue influence of strong personalities[39] ('If so-and-so disagrees, forget it!');

- harbouring past hurts ('We'll never get over what they did to us!'); or
- mistaken beliefs ('Conflict is wrong and we must avoid it!').

Whenever a substantial conflict occurs in a Christian community, it has its genesis in the hearts of the people involved, irrespective of their position. As these individual heart idols mutate into a group consensus, they translate into behaviours and responses which do not honour God, or anyone involved. Without exception, the same principles as discussed above concerning individual ungodly heart desires[40] apply in the resolution of the heart idols of a community or group – namely, remembering, self-reflection, acknowledgement of sin and repentance before God.[41] Even the confession of just one individual involved in a conflict can spark community repentance and begin to disperse the fog of conflict.

3.3 *How conflict usually unfolds in Christian communities*

A lot is going on when a destructive conflict erupts in a community. A rich mix of ingredients boil up a potent brew. Recognise this?

- An issue develops (in a relationship, or over some matter, probably both) arising from a different understanding of the opinions or actions of another person or group:
  ⟶ the 'issue' component

- As the heart desires of an individual, or group, are irritated and threatened, the finger-pointing blame-game starts:
  ⟶ the 'you' component

- A series of responses and behaviours escalates, impacting everyone:
  ⟶ the 'us' component

- Assorted underlying desires and influences which I, and any group of which I am a part, bring to the situation, intensify the conflict:
  ⟶ the 'me' component

- Leaders either ignore the problem or intervene with (either mediocre or wise) judgment and processes:

   ⟶   'the leadership' component

- The community reacts, swept along by the variable winds and powerful currents of the unfolding events and conversations:

   ⟶   'the community' component

- The sovereign purposes of God and his desires for and influences on the people and events are impacted for good or ill:

   ⟶   the 'God' component

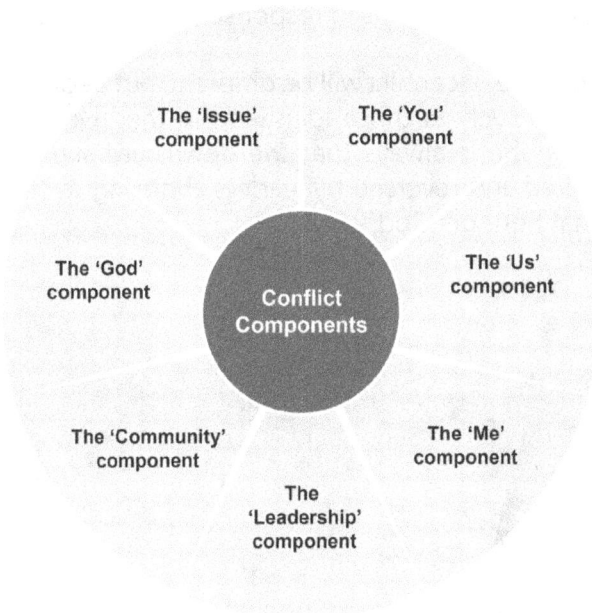

FIGURE 4: COMPONENTS OF A CONFLICT

Most of us would probably agree that the process to resolve community conflict must certainly include addressing the 'issue', the 'you', and the 'us' components. Yet, interestingly, the 'me', the 'leadership', the 'community' and the 'God' components are often not considered, or not considered sufficiently, even in Christian contexts of conflict resolution.[42]

We have explained the importance of understanding the 'me' component, the critical heart issues driving the conflict. Throughout this book, we will discover that the significance of the character and actions of the 'leadership' during conflict cannot be underestimated. We will also appreciate that no person is an island, and the effects of conflict on the 'community' should also be considered. Further, and most importantly, we will explore what it means to let God *be* 'God' during conflict.

The emotional roller coaster of conflict

Hand in hand with the various components of a conflict will be a roller-coaster of emotions. People begin to question their sense of safety and stability as they experience the community reeling through dips and upswings in response to the unfolding events.

Every experience of conflict will be different, but people may often feel emotions such as those identified in the inverted parabola below. The hope is always that the downward slide into chaos may be halted and reversed by leaders choosing to respond in a manner that honours God.

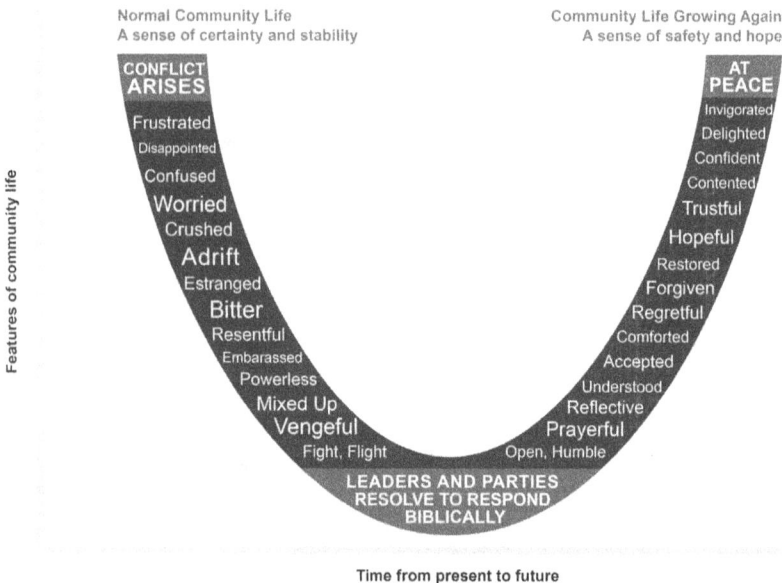

Normal Community Life
A sense of certainty and stability

Community Life Growing Again
A sense of safety and hope

CONFLICT ARISES

AT PEACE

Frustrated
Disappointed
Confused
Worried
Crushed
Adrift
Estranged
Bitter
Resentful
Embarassed
Powerless
Mixed Up
Vengeful
Fight, Flight

Invigorated
Delighted
Confident
Contented
Trustful
Hopeful
Restored
Forgiven
Regretful
Comforted
Accepted
Understood
Reflective
Prayerful
Open, Humble

Features of community life

LEADERS AND PARTIES
RESOLVE TO RESPOND
BIBLICALLY

Time from present to future

FIGURE 5: CONFLICT'S EMOTIONAL ROLLERCOASTER

3.4 *Early warning signs of conflict in a community*

Even though they develop over time, conflicts, like storms, can take us by surprise. The astute leader, like a keen weather watcher, will be alert to early indicators. These may include:[43]

(a) **Organisational challenges** such as:
- confusion over community identity and purpose or mission (e.g., there may be a mission statement, but people are unaware of it);
- muddled understanding about governance (e.g., individual governance members act as lone rangers rather than operating as a team);
- unclear linkage or relationship between the governance group and senior leadership (e.g., the group becomes over-protective of the leader, resulting in legitimate concerns being ignored; alternatively, the group becomes under-protective such that the leader's faults are publicised);
- avoidance of problems (e.g., not seeking outside assistance promptly);
- lack of healthy processes (e.g., inadequacies in staff performance reviews);
- changing the organisational structure without having addressed underlying concerns; and
- a pattern of regular change-over in crucial leadership roles.

(b) **Community factors** such as:
- people coalescing into factions and cliques;
- changes in communication and friendship patterns;
- a vacuum in leadership when a founder or other long-serving leader leaves;
- leaders failing to meet stated or unstated expectations;
- reduced attendance and participation;
- a decline in offerings or voluntary donations – financial issues;
- more complaints and rumours than normal; and
- change in language (e.g. people use 'spiritual' language as a weapon).

(c) **Relational challenges** such as:
- significant people harden or polarise their positions; and
- people withdraw from one another or lose energy for commitment.

(d) **Personal challenges** such as:
- changes in behaviours and responses of senior leaders; and
- blaming leaders for current difficulties.

(e) **Emotional indicators** such as:
- elevated anxiety; and
- fear, triggering over-reaction and loss of perspective.

(f) **Spiritual elements** such as:
- people blame others while ignoring their own culpability;
- immaturity due to ungodly motivations and behaviours;
- idolatry; and
- sin.[44]

(g) **External factors** such as:
- a downturn in the broader economy leading to community hardship; and
- social changes in the wider community resulting in uncertainty about the future.

> **Key perspective:**
> In most situations, there will be 'warning signs' that conflict may be brewing. 'Conflict is always a complex interaction of cultural, structural, spiritual, and theological forces.'[45]

Taking note of these early warning signs will alert leaders to the potential for conflict within their communities. Such awareness may also offer the chance to act pre-emptively to head off conflict. Unfortunately, at other times, despite our best efforts, conflict will erupt anyway. What then?

3.5 *Is conflict in Christian communities necessarily bad?*

Given the devastation wreaked by conflict, it is not surprising many Christians see any form of conflict as inherently wrong, unfitting or sinful. Indeed, when tainted by sin, conflict can cause significant hurt and distress to those involved. Leroy Goertzen, however, confirms what we have earlier observed – conflict is consistently and inescapably part of everyday Christian life. Encouragingly, he does so in a way that holds out great hope:

> *...faithfulness to the Gospel makes some form of conflict necessary and therefore inevitable. Necessity and inevitability presume a sense of purpose – one not easily deciphered. However, in the providence of God, conflict serves his purpose.*[46]

Stoesz and Raber recall a sharp disagreement between two directors in a board meeting where reconciliation was unlikely. Despite this, when one of the protagonists was asked to pray, he used words to the effect: '*Thank you for those who differ with us. They help us in ways those who always agree with us never do'.*[47]

His prayer recognises it is not *conflict* in and of itself that is the problem. Conflict may end up along the continuum of being a 'good' thing (which engenders healthy, God-honouring outcomes), or a 'bad' thing (which gives birth to sin's chaotic disintegration). The determining factor in this outcome is our *response*. Conflict itself, therefore, may be considered neutral.

Like temptation, conflict presents us with life-maturing choices around response and perspective. How we choose can strengthen the good of all involved, or it can pander to our shared fallen nature. How telling it is that when Jesus warned '...unless you *change*... you will never enter the kingdom of heaven' it was in the context of a dispute. (Mt 18:3 – emphasis added) We observe Jesus did not give this teaching to outsiders who did not know Him. No, he gave this teaching to his disciples – followers who already believed in him and who had 'entered' his kingdom. They had already made significant choices away from their previous life orientation. Faced with conflict, Jesus was asking them to change once again, to select a different response to the natural inclination of their sinful nature.

To follow Christ is to 'sign up' for personal, ongoing, transformative change. To follow Christ through conflict is to remain open to even further life-stretching change, including being prepared to reconsider our cherished perspectives on reality. An impossible task, we might ask? Certainly, the process will be daunting without prayerful thought and reflection, careful listening to different perspectives and asking oneself and others hard questions. Remaining open to this kind of change is likely to call us to repentance, to grant forgiveness, to give and receive apologies and open the way to personal reconciliation. These are all aspects of the deep, abiding 'change' which comes as we respond to the Spirit, both individually and collectively '...so that [we] may be mature and complete, not lacking anything'. (Jas 1:4)

God teaches that in his providence, everything in our lives, including conflict, unfolds within his sovereign purposes.[48] Thus, rather than seeing conflict as unfavourable and inherently 'bad' or unproductive, it is far more helpful and biblical to see it as an *opportunity*, a unique life circumstance to use constructively.

Such a biblical response is undoubtedly the ideal. Amid the maelstrom of conflict, however, it is a constant challenge for any of us to hold these perspectives consistently. Therefore, embrace the advantages of recognising conflict as an opportunity.

> *Key advantages* of recognising conflict as an opportunity include:
> - character development;
> - deeper personal understanding;
> - new appreciation for others;
> - growth in relationships;
> - fresh, innovative outcomes; and
> - renewed energy and purpose.

3.6 *Summary*

Leaders seeking to lead their communities well through significant conflict will do well to be keenly aware of the nature and effect of conflict in their communities. They will benefit from a clear understanding of the many sources or tributaries that lead into conflict and how it is likely to unfold.

The astute leader will be cognisant of unhealthy organisational practices and changes in community behaviour which act as warning signs of potential conflict. Reframing conflict as neither good nor bad but rather as an opportunity, will empower leaders to remain focused on their task.

Questions for reflection and discussion

1) Describe, briefly, the character of your community.
2) List the downside characteristics of an actual or potential conflict in your community.
3) Reflect on what might be the benefits.
4) What heart issues do you think your community displays? Review the examples of 'sometimes bizarre, sometimes understandable community heart idols' in section 3.2. Do you find any resonances in your community?
5) Review the 'early warning signs' in section 3.4. How would you describe, albeit tentatively, anything listed there which may be triggering a current dispute you are facing?

In the following two chapters, we explore influences which impact leaders, first individually and then collectively, as they respond to conflict and decide how to navigate through it for everyone's best interests.

33 Speed Leas, article, *Rooting Out Causes of Conflict: When you get to the bottom, church conflict may have several sources* http://www.christianitytoday.com/pastors/1992/spring/92l2054.html

34 Peterson, Eugene H., *The Message New Testament with Psalms and Proverbs*, (Preamble to James), Copyright © (1995). Used by permission of NavPress, represented by Tyndale House Publishers, a Division of Tyndale House Ministries. All rights reserved. (Emphasis added.)

35 The potential for 'stumbling' in the faith and conflict are often connected. See Ezek 14:3ff, Mt 18:6ff, Mk 9:42, Rom 14:13, 20, 1 Cor 10:32.

36 I note the verses which follow refer to bitterness, rage, anger, brawling, slander and malice.

37 Psychiatrists observe that trauma from conflict we have experienced in the past, if not dealt with, slides into the trauma of a subsequent conflict intensifying this trauma and leading us to respond to the current conflict in ways more than the reality of the situation warrants. See Karl Lehman, *Outsmarting Yourself: Catching Your Past Invading the Present and What to Do about It* – 2nd Edition, Libertyville, Illinois: This JOY! Books, 2014, pp. 14-16.

38 Rev Les Scarborough, Consultant with John Mark Ministries, Sydney, Australia, in his work with over 100 conflicted churches observes that 'if a conflict is not resolved healthily, then the conflicted cycle will repeat itself in 4-5 year cycles.'

39 Be particularly alert to the influence of matriarchs, patriarchs, or founding members of your community. They may be positive, however, there may be concerns.

40 See chapter 2.

41 We note there is a clear challenge for group self-reflection and evaluation in the hearers' response to the issues addressed in Mt 7:1-5, 18:15-20 and Gal 6:1.

42 The 'God', 'me', 'you' and 'us' components of a conflict were originally developed by Bruce Burgess of PeaceWise in Australia as a distillation of Ken Sande's Four G's of peacemaking ('Glorify God', 'Get the log out of your own eye', 'Gently restore' and 'Go and be reconciled') which Sande develops in the four parts of his book, *The Peacemaker*.

43 The information listed in the seven headings is a synthesis of material found from the following sources: Tim Dyer, consultant, supervisor and trainer, John Mark Ministries in Tasmania; Steinke, *Congregational Leadership*, p. 15ff; Barthel, Tara Klena & Edling, David V., *Redeeming Church Conflicts: Turning Crisis into Compassion and Care*, Baker Books, 2012, p. 120, 135ff; Rev. Dr Ian Duncum, Church Consultant, Sydney, Australia; Leas, *Moving Your Church Through Conflict*, p. 13 quoted by Goertzen, *Understanding*, p. 71; and my from own general experience.

44 Speed Leas states: 'Although many books on the psychology of conflict omit this category, in my experience, it's a principle cause of church dustups'. *Rooting Out Causes of Conflict*, Christianity Today, 1997.

45 Van Yperen, Jim, *Making Peace: A Guide to Overcoming Church Conflict*, Moody Publishers, Chicago, 2002, p. 46.

46 Goertzen, *Understanding*, p. 29.

47 Stoesz, Edgar and Raber, Chester, *Doing Good Better! How to be an Effective Board Member of a Nonprofit Organization*, Good Books, Intercourse, PA, 1997, p.97.

48 See Ps 139:1-18; Prov 16:1, 9, 33, 19:21; Mt 10:30-31; Rom 5:3-4.

SUBMERGED THREATS - AN INDIVIDUAL LEADER 4

In this chapter, we consider:
- **seven significant influences which shape the meaning an *individual* leader attributes to conflict events;**
- **the influence of the internal emotional world, especially anxiety, on an individual leader's automatic reactions to conflict (instinctive norm); and**
- **the influence of an individual leader's will on their capacity to purposefully respond to conflict.**

Have you ever wondered what drives your instant, involuntary responses to conflict? And why your responses may vary markedly from, and between, your colleagues and the antagonists? It is not an infrequent conundrum for many groups and organisations and one which faced the church leaders in the following story.

The church's governing group council convened for its regular monthly meeting. Following the usual opening devotion, Denise, the chairperson, normally asked whether there were any urgent items to be added to the agenda. Rarely was anything raised.

This time, however, one member spoke immediately. He wished to raise the matter of a conversation he had overheard after the service the previous night. He said he had witnessed the Associate Minster, Lyall, complaining loudly to several people about Steve and his capacity to do his job as Senior Minister.

Present at the meeting as required by his role, Steve was caught off guard. Incensed, he instantly exploded. Denise tried to interrupt. However, Steve would not be silenced. Feeling betrayed, he in turn angrily vented his frustrations about Lyall across a flood of issues.

Whether they liked it or not, a serious conflict now sat squarely in the lap of this governance group. Let's meet its members and eavesdrop on some of their instant, internal and external, involuntary responses to this unfolding conflict.

Donald, a long-time director, came from a dysfunctional family. He was led to faith through the church's youth outreach. In the meeting now, he began to sweat and clench his fists. He wanted to curl up under the table and hide. Steve's anger had triggered memories of his belligerent alcoholic father. Thoughts and questions tumbled through his mind:

> *This church is a haven for many people. This council has always been my safe place. Conflict will destroy all this! People will be anxious. They will take sides. The church could split.*

Gerald, who runs his own consultancy business, had been delegated to lead the church through its most recent strategic planning process. He was deeply proud that much of the plan had been his idea. Gerald had also overheard Lyall's ill-considered conversation. However, now in the meeting, he was shocked and disappointed by the Senior Minister's graceless overreaction. Grappling with the implications, he thumped the table and said:

> *A conflict like this will undermine the strategic plan's success – Steve's eye will be off the ball. We can't let it be derailed now! Not after all the effort we've put into it. We have to fight on every front to make sure the plan isn't jeopardised!*

The treasurer, **Belinda**, had held this role in numerous different churches. She had moved around the country in her highly responsible position with a national accounting firm. Her shoulders sagged as she absorbed the information. Her chest felt tight. Her heart raced. She felt paralysed and couldn't speak. An exhausting sense of *deja vu* swept over her as she thought:

> *Not again. Not another church. The rumour mill will be at work. This will seriously affect the budget bottom line. We may not be able to pay staff. Why had she ever put up her hand to be treasurer again? Would she never learn?*

Lee Wu was a respected overseas-born member of the church's substantial ethnic community. He had been looking down at the table throughout Steve's outburst, fidgeting with his papers. Now he looked up, smiled gently and when there was a gap in the discussion, observed:

> *This church does not have conflicts. It never has. These minor tensions will soon blow over. We must show ourselves to be a cohesive council. We must show the church we are pouring oil onto these small waves.*

Aaron, although still a student, had shown excellent leadership promise. The governing group had recruited him as the church's youth representative. Still at university, he was over-awed by the combination of experience and articulate personalities in the room. Nevertheless, he swallowed, took a deep breath, and spoke up:

> *Steve, there's a lot going on for you. And there seems to be a significant breakdown in the relationship between you and Lyall. Hearing about Lyall's outburst has clearly taken you by surprise, as it has us all.*

He turned to Denise:

> *Would it be helpful to take a brief coffee break to settle ourselves before we talk this through any further?*

Denise, a partner in a city legal firm, was experiencing the familiar adrenalin rush associated with gearing up for a court battle. Her mind had been racing:

> *How far would Lyall go with this? Would he sue the church? How would they protect their reputations? What rights does he have? Has Steve neglected his staff? Are our human resource policies sufficiently robust?*

At Aaron's prompt, she deliberately and consciously pulled herself back and addressed the meeting:

> *This situation has taken you by surprise Steve, so, of course, you are reeling. We all are. Yes, there seems to be a lot going on, and it looks like Lyall is also distraught.*

> *We obviously need to consider our next steps. Thanks for this sensible suggestion, Aaron. Let's take a brief coffee break. While we do, could we ask ourselves: 'What do we need to hear from God in this?' We'll reconvene in fifteen minutes.*

> *Steve, spare me a moment please.*

We will return to this meeting later. In the meantime, we observe that all leaders, just like this group, bring their multifaceted selves to every occurrence of conflict – their personality, beliefs, values, character, pre-existing heart idols, along with life experiences from early childhood to the present day.

These are powerful influences, layered with meaning and feelings. They are the source of the specific and distinctive meaning leaders give to the facts and circumstances of a conflict event. This meaning triggers an associated range of automatic, unconsidered emotional reactions – the leader's reflexive, preferred 'instinctive norm' in response to conflict.

Such unconsidered reactions usually elicit ill-considered behaviours. It is not surprising that leaders often live to regret these. As the Bible confirms, ill-considered anger 'does not produce the righteousness that God desires' (Jas 1:19,20). Lack of awareness regarding the powerful influence exercised by these automatic responses can quickly derail a leader facing conflict. Their capacity to lead can be significantly compromised if they give thoughtless rein to their instinctive norm.

Many years ago, I attended a course entitled *Journey of the Heart*, run by counsellor and friend, the late Rev Peter Pereira.[49] As part of the course, Peter used an excellent diagram to illustrate:

- how our involuntary reactions to life events arise from the meaning we place on them;
- how this meaning is often unconsciously based on earlier life experiences, especially trauma, along with other defining influences; and
- how, by being aware of this, we can consciously choose alternative responses.

I have adapted Peter's diagram to assist our discussion. I use it here to illustrate the impact of the powerful, multi-layered forces which influence a leader's responses to conflict. I also use it to show how, by being aware of these, a leader can consciously choose alternative responses.

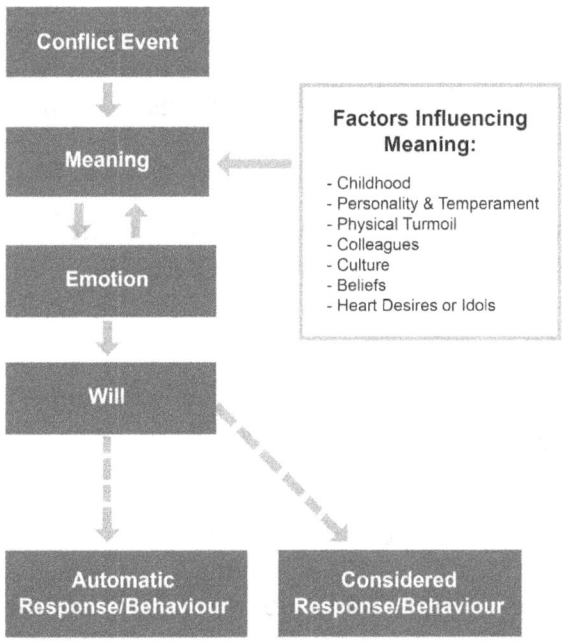

FIGURE 6: RESPONDING TO CONFLICT — THE INDIVIDUAL LEADER

The purpose of this chapter, therefore, is to arm you, as an individual leader, with sufficient self-awareness and insight to:

- understand the factors which directly influence the meaning you are likely to place on a conflict;
- manage your emotions so that they do not rule you;
- choose a considered path to respond in a way that draws on the wisdom of Christ and honours God; and
- astutely discern, with mature Christian empathy, how these forces also drive the responses of others.

It is worth noting, of course, that a considered choice is not necessarily a natural or easy one. For the followers of Jesus, a considered choice is complicated by the spiritual complexity we outlined in section 1.2 and the pressure of those desires of our hearts which we addressed in chapter 2. That is, we:

- struggle against spiritual forces;
- contend with desires of the flesh;
- negotiate 'the world';
- rub shoulders with others who disagree with us; and
- respond to the challenge to change.

So, as we unpack the powerful influencing factors that determine the meaning we place on conflict, we are greatly encouraged to draw deeply on the wisdom of God. As the psalmist reassures us, he is 'our refuge and strength, an ever-present help in trouble' (46:1).

4.1 *Influences on the meaning individual leaders attribute to a conflict event*

(a) Early childhood experiences

An ancient Hebrew proverb says: '(s)tart children off on the way they should go, and even when they are old, they will not turn from it' (Prov 22:6).

Research confirms that 'early childhood is the time when the building blocks for all later development and intellectual growth are set in place...'.[50] This works both positively and negatively:

'how we learn to handle conflict determines the positive or negative role it has in constructing our feelings, our intellect, and our personality'.[51]

Our childhood observations and experiences of how our family of origin and significant others managed conflict, shape the patterns we develop in coping with it, the meaning we place on it, and our emotional responses to it. These become part of us. We take them into life. The memories generated, with the meaning and feelings they evoke, and the trauma experienced, always lie just below the surface.

It is not surprising then, as new conflict situations arise, these latent memories, along with the emotions and meaning we unconsciously attribute to them, instinctively kick in. We react accordingly. These become recurring patterns. They unquestionably influence the individual leader's responses to conflict, for better or for worse.

Where we have not received early training and modelling to resolve conflict well, our capacity to lead a community through a conflicted situation will be significantly compromised. As a result, we are likely to be plagued by defensiveness, uncertainty, doubt, fear, even cowardice.

On the other hand, where we have been taught early in life how to resolve conflicts productively, we are more equipped to take the initiative to lead those in our care through conflict with confident hope.

> **Key perspective:**
> Childhood experiences significantly shape our reactions to conflict – our preferred instinctive norm – and the meaning we place upon them. Compromised learning around addressing conflict as a child will usually result in compromised instinctive reactions when faced with conflict as an adult. Conversely, productive early role models and guidance typically lead to instinctively healthier responses as an adult.

Of course, none of us has learned to manage our reactions to conflict perfectly. While laying down new pathways for our initial responses to conflict can be a troubling process, it is possible. Wonderfully, we are not left to do this on our own. We have the power of the Holy Spirit to help us. As Ezekiel reminds us, God promises that '...I will give you a new heart and put a new spirit in you' (36:26).[52]

(b) Personality

Personality type influences our patterns of thinking and responses. It does so in a whole variety of life circumstances, including conflict. Personality type works in tandem with our early childhood experiences to shape the meaning a leader may attribute to a conflict event. This all influences the development of the leader's instinctive, default conflict resolution style.

As you are undoubtedly aware, psychologists have attempted to categorise and describe personality traits and behaviours via various standardised assessment tools. Your organisation may use such tools as part of its leadership recruitment and review processes. Common examples include:

- Myers-Briggs Personality Type Indicator (MBTI);
- Belbin Self-Perception / Team Role Inventory (BSPI / BTRI);
- Dominance, Influence, Steadiness, Compliance/ Conscientiousness (DISC) Profile; and
- Fascination Personality Test.

These tools do not pretend to be an exact science in predicting how we will respond in any given situation. They can, however, alert us to our likely reactions and suggest where our strengths and vulnerabilities lie. They may flag where a change in approach is warranted. Importantly, they may provide insights into our preferred conflict resolution style. The research behind these tools can help us understand ourselves and our impact on others (why others respond to us as they do), as well as understand others and their impact on us (why we respond to others as we do).

> **Key perspective:**
> When responding to a conflict event, a Christian leader will be better equipped to bring honour to God by understanding their personality and preferred conflict resolution style. As Jim Van Yperen soberly observes: 'your conflict style is the arena where you will tend to sin most often – against God, others and yourself'.[53]

Van Yperen has developed his own *Conflict Response Style Assessment tool.* He claims it is a tool which 'by better understanding yourself – what you are thinking and why – you can learn new ways to anticipate, prevent and correct negative conflict response patterns, replacing these with redemptive habits of reconciliation'.[54]

Taking time to explore our preferred conflict resolution style prayerfully, can enliven our relationship with our Lord, allowing him to reveal to us where we are most vulnerable. It can foster insight and wisdom to help us more deeply understand ourselves and the meaning we may, rightly or wrongly, be attributing to the conflict. Further, it can strengthen our leadership capacity and expand our contribution to leadership discussions.

(c) Physical turmoil

When humans face a threat (whether real or imagined) such as conflict, a complex array of involuntary physical reactions are galvanised. These are yet another influence on how we respond instinctively to conflict, the meaning we place upon it (is it really dangerous or not?), and our capacity to carry out our leadership obligations.

We are familiar with the surge of adrenaline that puts us immediately on guard and triggers classic flight, freeze, fight or fawning responses. A whole range of spontaneous physical changes occur. These include:
- our breathing, sweating, blood pressure and heart rates increase;
- our lungs and nostrils open wider, our pupils dilate; and
- our muscles become tense.

To complicate matters further, conflict activates each facet of the brain, provoking powerful interactions to send us urgent messages. Briefly:

- the brain stem, from where our essential vital signs originate, initiates the bodily changes listed above;
- the limbic system, the feeling side of the brain, instantly both alerts us to the perceived current danger and stirs subconscious memories of past threats, awakening intense feelings; and
- the neocortex, the cognitive part of the brain, connects us to our five senses to inform our initial response to the situation.[55]

Overall, there is a reduction in the ability to solve problems. Instead, the mind locks onto *our* position and the potential danger the *other* poses.[56]

These involuntary physical reactions are so common they have generated two ubiquitous pieces of advice for anyone in the first moments of conflict: *Take a deep breath; remove yourself from the situation.* Even a cursory search shows these pieces of advice referenced in everything from popular psychology to scholarly works, and for a good reason. To be able to respond well to conflict, our brains and feelings need time to normalise. Taking a deep breath and going for a walk, even briefly, buys us that time. It is sound advice. No wonder James emphasises the importance of being, '...slow to speak and slow to become angry...' (Jas 1:19).

> **Key perspective:**
> Being aware of how the typical complex changes in our brain, indeed throughout our whole body, influence us when facing conflict events is very practical. It helps us better understand our reactions and pause to clarify whether the meaning we are placing upon the conflict is valid.

When parties to a conflict belong to a community, others around them will also experience physical turmoil in response to an escalating conflict. Gaining insight into what is happening, realising that this is natural and inevitable, may save leaders a lot of grief.

Conversely, ignorance in these matters can leave leaders exposed and utterly mystified when conflict blind-sides them. Leaders used to functioning well at a high level under normal circumstances, may look back later, baffled by their lack of balanced cognitive function in response to conflict in their community. They may be mortified by their flawed decision-making, or embarrassed by their emotional outbursts.

(d) Our colleagues

If you are an individual within a group of leaders, you may find your unconscious response to conflict, and the meaning you attribute to it, influenced by the mindset and behaviour of your colleagues.

We have observed that conflict intensifies complexity and emotions. Team discussions about how to address a conflict are sure to display this. We may observe surprising changes amongst our colleagues. One or another member may, for example:

- use more emotive, judgmental, even pejorative language than usual – or conversely, become more considered and thoughtful in their use of language;
- display a lack of empathy for those in conflict – or conversely, suddenly show unusual insight;
- fail to take the lead when hitherto they have done so – or conversely, rise to the occasion from obscurity to make a startling contribution;
- act with atypical thoughtlessness – or conversely, proceed with a level of care not previously exhibited; or
- uncharacteristically withdraw, or refuse, collegial support – or conversely, unexpectedly offer, or welcome, such support.

The influence of our colleagues' mindset and behaviour upon us may be empowering – we feel confident to make a positive contribution and choose healthy and constructive responses to conflict.

Alternatively, the influences may be so stressful they undermine our confidence – destabilising our capacity to respond well when conflict occurs. We may, for example, retreat, becoming intimidated and anxious, afraid to speak up – a classic flight response. Or we may become forceful and bombastic, fearful of not being taken seriously and determined to prove our worth, interrupting others, overriding their opinions—a classic fight response.

So, assuming no danger to life and limb, what might be happening in our inner world that means our colleagues' influence upon us can lead to fear? Could it be that we are letting the heart idol of wanting to be well thought of in the court of public opinion rule our contribution to the group? The result, we either overreact or withdraw. Both responses spell a failure of leadership. Neither response honours God. Have we in reality substituted fear for trust in God alone?

The book of Proverbs invites us to consider that the 'fear of man will prove to be a snare, but whoever trusts in the Lord is kept safe' (29:25). The biblical antidote to fearing others is to confess our fear, and the potential heart idols which may cause it, before Christ, seek his forgiveness (1 Jn 1:9), and re-prioritise to 'trust in the Lord with all [our] heart and lean not on [our] own understanding...' (3:5). As Psalm 27 reiterates: 'The LORD is my light and my salvation; whom shall I fear?' (v.1, emphasis added).

> **Key perspective:**
> Being able to proactively discern the influence upon us of others within the group can lead us back to dependence upon God, and free us to fulfil our leadership responsibilities.

(e) Our culture

Cultural dynamics are another influence on the meaning an individual places on a conflict event, and their instinctive norm when responding to it. Culture, like people, will have elements that distort God's good intent for his creation, elements that foster God's good intent and elements that are neutral.

In western culture, some responses to conflict which distort God's good intent include:
- preoccupation with personal rights and self-interested justice;
- a determination to win at all costs;
- demonising and punishing one's opponent;

- avoidance of relational issues;
- low personal responsibility and accountability;
- suppressed emotions which often explode into harmful behaviour; and
- all summed up, of course, as a strong focus on self.

Cultural distortions are also evident in dealing with conflict within and between different ethnicities and nationalities. In many Asian cultures, for example, the dominant cultural importance of saving face can present as conflict avoidance or minimisation with a statement such as: 'No, there is no conflict here; there are only "tensions" which need to be "accommodated!"'. Moreover, in some cultures, direct questions indicate genuine interest and concern, whereas, in others, such questions are interpreted as a form of attack.

The dynamics of subcultures also shape how people unthinkingly deal with conflict. We see this in intergenerational differences. We can observe it in the different approaches taken by denominations, traditions of spirituality and places of employment. Significantly divergent attitudes between people in rural, regional and city environments may result in noticeably different instinctive responses to conflict. Some rural communities traditionally view conflict as harmful and damaging, convinced it is essential to take steps to avoid or remove the problem. People in city businesses, on the other hand, may relish the combative possibilities of conflict and view avoidance as a form of weakness.

Different educational experiences will also influence a person's automatic responses to conflict. Overall health, and particularly medical conditions (diagnosed or undiagnosed), may also have a bearing, this likelihood being magnified when there is a mental health issue.

Whether cultural influences are harmful, positive or neutral in their impact on a conflicted situation, the wise leader will deliberately and proactively weigh up which elements in their culture bring honour to God and which ones distort the biblical call when responding to conflict.

The power of the gospel is that Christ transcends human culture. His message is counter-cultural and cross-cultural. The authors of scripture were inspired to write for all God's people, whenever they were born and in whatever culture they find themselves.

When the Apostle Paul addressed the Corinthians' conflicts in his first letter, he contrasted the power of the cross with the world's cultural wisdom (1 Cor 1:20). He indicated that Jewish culture demanded signs and the Greek culture sought wisdom. What Paul preached, however, was the powerful folly of the cross (1:22-25). The principles and values proclaimed through this message are aimed to form a new humanity, a new culture which honours God. Paul points the way for us, as leaders, by confirming the gospel transcends all human culture.

> **Key perspective:**
> The influences from our culture and its many subcultures on the meaning an individual leader places on a conflict event and upon their instinctive response to it often go unrecognised. The wise leader will be alert to their powerful undercurrents, identifying those elements which distort God's good intent for his creation, those elements which foster God's good intent and those elements which are neutral.

(f) Our beliefs

The way we interpret our faith will also shape the meaning we place on a conflict event and our instinctive norm. Our core beliefs and values allow us to make sense of the world around us. For the Christian, these cornerstones of life are fundamentally informed by scripture and reinforced by associated symbols and community practices. We may invest heavily in their maintenance. We commit energy, time and our limited financial resources to our chosen faith communities. When conflict arises in this context, we can readily construe it as a threat to our beliefs about ourselves, our identity, our place in the world and the faith perspectives we value.

> **Key perspective:**
> What we believe has practical consequences in our lives and communities. A patchy, superficial, or even a flawed understanding of Christian beliefs and values can propel leaders towards less than God-honouring responses to conflict.

Such flawed understandings may arise when we hold on to certain faith interpretations too tightly, allowing them to replace genuine trust in God. In such instances, our beliefs can themselves, surprisingly, become idols of our hearts. In turn, this impacts the meaning we place on a conflict event and how we respond.

(g) Our sinful heart desires or idols

The meaning an individual leader will place on a conflict may be further influenced by sinful heart desires or idols, that were explored in sections 2.3 to 2.5. This in turn may well impact our decision-making and lead to responses that do not honour God and for which the only remedy is repentance and forgiveness.

These, then, are some of the significant influences that shape the meaning an individual leader attributes to a conflict event.

So, what?

(h) The meaning we place on conflict

This multitude of powerful influences will almost instantly and unconsciously craft the meaning by which any person interprets a conflict. We are, after all, *'meaning making machines'*. To quote one author who discusses this concept:

> *We are meaning making machines. We hear things, see things, filter it through our experiences, judgments and assumptions to make sense of the world around us and give it meaning. In short, we tell ourselves a story. Then we believe it. From our point of view, it is the absolute truth. Given this certainty, we then decide what to do next.* [57]

We are equally meaning making machines when it comes to conflict, as we can see by what happened for each of the church governing group members as they faced the conflict between Steve and Lyall.

The governing group has had this conflict thrust upon it. Each leader, including Steve and Lyall, 'hears' and 'sees' the conflict. Each leader promptly filters the conflict through their own experiences, judgements and assumptions. These are the powerful influences, layered with meaning and feelings discussed in this chapter interacting with the desires of their hearts, their potential heart idols, discussed in chapter 2. They make sense of the conflict. They are the source of the specific and distinctive meaning each person gives to it. In short, each leader tells himself or herself a story about the conflict. Then they believe it. From each person's point of view, it is the absolute truth.

Given this certainty, each leader is forming an opinion on what to do next. The meaning each leader attributes to the conflict is firing a complex range of automatic, unconsidered emotional reactions. Here are people reacting reflexively, with their unique preferred 'instinctive norm' instantly in play. We see their emotions translating into involuntary concrete behaviours – some of which are perplexing to others and even to themselves!

Let's analyse the responses of three of these leaders in more detail.

Donald (a long-term director)

Influencing factors:	family of origin: an abusive father, imperative to hide for self-protection
Internal emotional response:	panic, fear, sadness, defencelessness
Desires of the heart:	self-preservation, being in a safe environment and creating this for others
Concrete external response:	sweats, becomes fidgety, locks fists in lap to control the impulse to hide
Meaning: (the story he tells himself)	conflict is terrifying and dangerous; I won't be able to feel safe here any longer, nor will the congregation

Gerald (business owner)

Influencing factors:	personality style, dominant western culture
Internal emotional response:	anger, shock, indignation, determination
Desires of the heart:	preserving his legacy, maintaining authority
Concrete external response:	thumps fist on table
Meaning: (the story he tells himself)	this conflict is about to disrupt our plans and nullify the successful investment I've put into them; it will put my reputation and authority at risk, as well as the group's

Belinda (church treasurer)

Influencing factors:	paralysing physical responses triggered by memories of previous experience
Internal emotional response:	fear, overwhelmed, weariness
Desires of the heart:	financial health for the church, not to have to deal with yet another church's finances undermined by rumours
Concrete external response:	muteness
Meaning: (the story she tells herself)	conflict creates rumours which spread like wildfire and devastate the financial viability of a church

Can you identify the various factors influencing each of the others under the headings listed, that is, Aaron (the student), Lee Wu (the member of the church's Chinese community) and Denise (a legal partner and chair of the council)?

The meaning each council member places on the conflict, and their response to it, is crafted by deep memories and perceptions. Although entirely understandable, are these meanings grounded in the truth of the situation? Aaron looks around the table and is perplexed by the atypical responses of people whose capability he usually finds awesome. Like us in similar contexts, he is unaware of their history. He cannot see the instant tsunami of feelings, cultural norms and expectations, personality traits, heart desires and physical turmoil flooding and shaping the meaning they are attributing to the conflict. Some of them may be sufficiently self-aware to understand why they are responding as they are. Others may be completely mystified.

This story shows how understandable it is that conflict simply means *threat* for many people. It threatens the safety and stability of their community, their core beliefs and values, indeed their very identity. This perception is, however, profoundly impoverished. It misses the bigger picture and undermines hope. According to God's word, irrespective of its source or context, conflict is a fresh opportunity to reflect God's character in a community and bring him honour – in short, to be fully human, as God intends.

> **Key perspective:**
> As leaders, we live and work within the sphere of many influences which shape the meaning we are tempted to place on a conflict. Sometimes our interpretation will coincide with reality. Often, it won't. The important thing is that we *first* recognise these powerful influences exist, suspend drawing conclusions *and* always seek the truth about what is happening. Having done this, we can then form a meaning related to the facts and circumstances of the specific context.

The story that opened this chapter brings to our notice another crucial influence upon an individual leader's response to conflict, namely, the world of emotions.

4.2 The influence of the internal emotional world on an individual leader's automatic reactions to conflict

We noted the flood of emotions – anger, fear, shock – experienced by many people in our story. Emotions accompany all the ups and downs of everyday life. Conflict intensifies them. It almost instantly draws out strong, unfamiliar feelings. As we've seen, these feelings unconsciously, but directly, drive behaviour. As one definition astutely highlights, emotion is: 'whatever in our behaviour is instinctive, automatic, defensive, reactive, even mindless'.[58]

> **Key perspective:**
> Conflict disturbs and unsettles our soul. It draws from us emotions which potentially give rise to reactive behaviours, which are often not characteristic of a person's typical behaviours or Christian values.

Research has shown that when our emotions are stirred, particularly if we feel our survival or reputation is under threat, the logic and creative aspects of our brain diminish. In effect, our brain becomes partially hijacked or overridden by our emotions. This is precisely what happens when conflict erupts, especially if we construe the dispute as a matter of personal survival or the maintenance of our good name.

Is it any wonder we are left vulnerable to automatic, defensive, over-reactions; to confusion, distraction, diminished speech capacity and reduced memory function! But there is a high cost associated with failing to recognise and manage our emotions and vulnerability. We may experience:

- spiritual drift (confusion, doubts, questions);
- physiological consequences (headaches, muscle tension, illness);
- relational effects (aloofness, flattery, tetchiness); or
- psychological impacts (self-preoccupation, moodiness, depression).

It is not altogether surprising many of us consider the emotional world to be irrational or harmful. Indeed, sometimes it seems more sensible to ignore our emotions and avoid facing them altogether.

Acutely sobering, then, is Walter Wright's assertion that: 'The primal task of leadership is to handle both our own and other people's emotions'. To drive his case home, he declares that: 'Managing emotion is twice as important as intelligence or competence in predicting effective leadership'.[59]

Why is this so? While many positive emotions may accompany the dreams and aspirations of leaders and their followers, Wright observes that there is a downside. People may become emotionally dependent on the expectations of leaders. Leaders may use the emotions generated to manipulate their community by promising hope and certainty when they are ill-equipped to do so. As Wright concludes: 'Effective leadership resists dependency and empowers followers to own responsibility for their choices and action'.[60] This is imperative when leading through conflict.

> **Key perspective:**
> Leaders who need to manage conflict within their community may experience profound and ongoing emotions, even where they are not a party to the conflict. Leaders who can identify their emotions, who purposefully take command of them and exercise good judgment, will help themselves respond in healthy ways and build trust and goodwill with the parties to the conflict and with their community.

Emotions are processed differently from our cognitive, or conscious, responses. They require us to stop, to take time, to listen and ask ourselves hard questions. They call us to immerse ourselves in God's word, inviting him to search our hearts. (See Ps 139:23) There is power in naming our emotions. Doing so means we take mindful hold of them rather than allowing them to take hold of us. Bringing them into the light reduces their power over us.

These practices empower excellence in leadership. They become particularly relevant when conflict flares. In the confusion of conflict, leaders who have been schooled only to respond rationally and analytically may suppress their emotions. Suppression is unproductive and likely to intensify the harmful spiritual, physiological, relational and psychological consequences mentioned above. The result? Compromised responses, high levels of anxiety and tarnished Christian witness.

Anxiety

It is worth considering this issue of anxiety more closely. I am grateful for the honesty of the ancient prayer in Psalm 139: 'test me and know my anxious thoughts' (v. 23). Jesus said: 'Be careful, or your hearts will be weighed down with... the anxieties of life...' (Lk 21:34). The apostle Paul in his letter to the Philippians instructed them: 'Do not be anxious about anything...' (Phil 4:6). It suggests anxiety is neither a recent nor an abnormal psychological phenomenon. Anyone who has had to negotiate community conflict will immediately recognise why Steinke identifies anxiety as *the* core emotion leaders need to address at such a time.[61]

Anxiety can, of course, have both positive and adverse effects. On the one hand, it can help us focus and galvanise us to act and change. Indeed, people don't change unless there is some level of stress. To be anxious in a negative sense, on the other hand, means to be choked by the cares of this world, to worry, be uneasy, to let yourself be distracted or pressured away from trusting God. This kind of anxiety may blunt our understanding, inhibit our capacity to listen or self-reflect and immobilise our usually competent responses. Moreover, negative anxiety is 'contagious', able to spread like an infection through a community.[62]

Referencing the church context (although just as relevant in other settings), Steinke observes that most people are primarily 'interested in relieving their own anxiety' – and leaders are not immune. When leaders focus on this, they do so at the expense of more important goals, such as 'managing the crisis or planning for a clear direction. Their primary goal is anxiety reduction, not congregational renewal.'[63] Effective leadership, he says, 'means to have some command of our own anxiety and some capacity not to let other people's anxiety contaminate us... our thinking, actions, and decisions'.[64]

By inviting God to 'test me and know my anxious thoughts', the psalmist opens himself to searching appraisal. He shifts his anxiety into the sovereign care of the living God. This shift is the antidote to our primary interest in relieving our own anxiety. It frees us to seek deliberately, with the Spirit's power, the higher purposes of conflict resolution and community renewal.

4.3 *The influence of the will on an individual leader's capacity to purposefully develop well-considered responses to conflict*

Thus far, we have argued that the specific meaning we place on a conflict event is likely to be unconsciously influenced by a range of life experiences and our unique make-up. We have noted how this can fire various automatic, unconsidered reactions and translate quickly into ill-considered emotional responses and behaviours. We should not conclude, however, that this progression is inevitable. In God's providence, we are not slaves to our history, bodies, circumstances, or emotions. We have the Spirit of God within us and his power at our disposal. And in fact, the Spirit gives back to us the capacity to maintain 'self-control'; it is one of the fruits which demonstrate that we 'walk by the Spirit' (Gal 5:16, 23).

If God empowers us to engage our will to act purposefully, then at the point where we need to decide whether to do so, we face what in biblical terms is called 'temptation' (1 Cor 10:13). Will we yield to destructive forces?[65] Or will we choose, with God's help, to exercise self-control by engaging our will to deliberately take command of ourselves and honour God alone?

Even when we disappoint ourselves by failing to maintain self-control, it is encouraging to know we can always return to being 'in step with the Spirit' through confession and forgiveness. Cleansed and restored to fellowship with our Maker, and with one another, we will be ready once again to lead with God's purposes as our priority.

4.4 *Summary*

These then are the influences, the meaning and the emotions which potentially affect individual leaders in working through how to respond to conflict in a God-honouring manner.

When individual leaders discern what is going on for others, while simultaneously maintaining an honest self-reflective stance, they are well-placed to respond to conflict thoughtfully. Such leaders can provide a God-honouring strategic and constructive alternative to destructive automatic, instinctive norms.

Questions for reflection and discussion

As you read this chapter and reflect on the questions below, you may identify patterns in your responses to conflict which fall short of the glory of God. So, take time to repent, receive Christ's forgiveness and allow your instinctive responses to be transformed by the Holy Spirit (1 Jn 1:9, Ps 103:3, 4).

1) Look back over the various influences identified in this chapter. Which has been the most significant influence on shaping your intuitive, automatic response to conflict, your instinctive norm?
2) Revisit section 4.1(e), 'Our culture', and ask:
    (a) Which characteristics of my country's dominant national culture am I most likely to exhibit? How do they affect my response to conflict? What do I need to do about it?
    (b) Which of the sub-cultures listed is most relevant either to me or my context? How do they affect my responses to conflict or my understanding of why others respond the way they do? What do I need to do about it?
3) If you haven't already done so, identify the various factors influencing each council member under the headings listed in section 4.1(h). Looking in from the outside, what do you think could be influencing Lyall and Steve?
4) Describe your own intuitive, automatic, instinctive conflict resolution style. How does it connect to your past experiences of conflict, beginning with your earliest years?
5) What are you most anxious about for yourself when faced with conflict? What does this tell you? How are you going to manage that anxiety?
6) What are you most anxious about for your leadership group when addressing conflict? What does this tell you? How can you raise your concerns with the group?
7) In what or whom are you trusting as you deal with your anxiety?
8) Under what circumstances do you find it most difficult to choose a God-honouring path? Why do you think this is the case?
9) What, if anything, do you discern God wants you to bring to the attention of your leadership colleagues?
10) What does God want to bring to your attention through your leadership colleagues?

You may find it helpful to journal your responses to these questions, compose a prayer, or both. Then, resolve to address any concerns.

In this chapter, we have explored the influences which impact and likely impede an individual leader's responses to conflict. We have observed these influences are also at play within a leadership group. Can you imagine what is going to happen once the council returns from their coffee break? In the next chapter, we turn our attention to the influences which potentially drive the responses to conflict of a *whole leadership group*.

---

49 I am indebted to Peter for much of the background thinking used in this chapter. He taught the basic concepts I have drawn on at a church in Blaxland near Sydney, Australia, in the early 2000's.

50 From *The Handbook of Conflict Resolution: Theory and Practice*, Third Edition, Peter T. Coleman, Morton Deutsch, Eric C. Marcus, Editors, Jossey-Bass, San Francisco, 2014, *The Development of Conflict Resolution Skills: Preschool to Adulthood*: Sandra V. Sandy, p. 431f.

51 Ibid.

52 See also 2 Cor 5:17; Eph 4:22-24.

53 Van Yperen, *Making Peace*, p. 164.

54 For this resource, and others, see *Tools for assessing your conflict resolution style*, Part 3, Resources, 16.2(b).

55 Boyd-MacMillan, Eolene and Savage, Sara, *Transforming Conflict: Conflict transformation amongst senior church leaders with different theological stances*, The Foundation for Church Leadership, York, United Kingdom, 2008, p. 18f.

56 Ibid.

57 Paraphrased from Riana Avis, March 4, 2015, http://thebaobabway.com/

58 Peter L. Steinke article *Changing Emotional Systems* Alban Institute www.alban.org/conversation.aspx?id=2354 p. 1.

59 Wright, *Relational Leadership*, p. 62.

60 Ibid, p. 63.

61 Steinke, *Congregational Leadership*, p. 3, 8.

62 Ibid, p. 10. (Copyright 2006 © by the Alban Institute. Reproduced with permission of the Licensor through PLSclear.)

63 Steinke, Peter L., *Twenty Observations about Troubled Congregations* https://alban.org/archive/twenty-observations-about-troubled-congregations/

64 Steinke, *Congregational Leadership*, p. xii. (Copyright 2006 © by the Alban Institute. Reproduced with permission of the Licensor through PLSclear.)

65 As explored in section 1.2.

SUBMERGED THREATS - A GROUP OF LEADERS 5

In this chapter, we look at:
- six significant influences which shape the meaning a leadership group *collectively* attributes to conflict events;
- the influences of a leadership group's *collective* internal emotional world on the group's automatic reactions to conflict (instinctive norm); and
- the influence of the group's *collective* will on its capacity to purposefully respond to conflict.

Whenever any group of leaders meets, every individual contributes an assortment of the kinds of influences identified in chapter 4. Even before that first coffee break, this is melding into a group personality or corporate culture. Unsurprisingly, it will have a significant influence on how the group responds to conflict *en bloc*.

In addition to this, other internal and external elements peculiar to the group leadership context, such as the group's customary conflict resolution style, decision-making norms, beliefs, history, and community expectations, contribute to this culture. They shape how the leaders operate together.

As in chapter 4, the diagram used by the late Rev Peter Pereira in his course entitled *Journey to the Heart*, adapted for the discussion here, will usefully illustrate the powerful, multi-layered forces which influence a group's collective response to conflict.

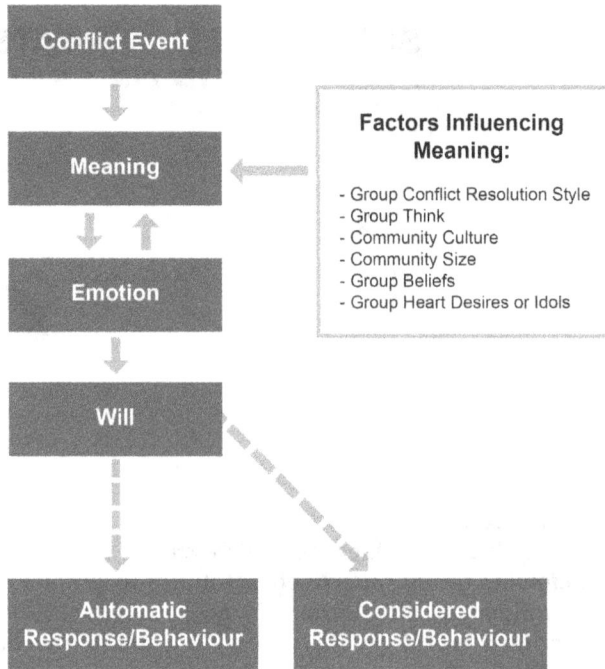

FIGURE 7: RESPONDING TO CONFLICT — THE LEADERSHIP GROUP

The purpose of this chapter, then, is to shed light on how a group of leaders might gain insight into:

- the factors directly influencing the meaning it places on a conflict event;
- identifying and managing its collective emotions; and
- purposefully choosing a path that honours God, facilitating healthy leadership.

5.1 *Influences on the meaning a leadership group collectively attributes to a conflict event*

(a) Group conflict resolution style

As we have noted, all leaders in a leadership group bring their *individual* instinctive responses to conflict with them into the room. These contribute to a distinctive norm that characterises the group's *collective* approach to conflict. Consciously or unconsciously, the group will default to this approach as its preferred conflict resolution style, impacting how it leads its community through a conflicted situation.

It is just as vital for a leadership group as it is for an individual to be aware of its intuitive *communal* style in responding to conflict.

It is hard for a leadership group to conceive they might be conducting themselves, perhaps unwittingly, in a manner destructive to the community under its care. It is even harder to admit to it. The following suggestions may help you identify the approach your group usually takes in responding to conflict.

Attack conflict resolution style

Does your leadership group instinctively attack? Does it, for example:

- criticise others, shift blame away from the group, look for a scapegoat;
- act impulsively, look for a 'quick fix' to solve the situation;
- judge others out of black-and-white moral categories (they are 'sinful', 'evil', 'wrong', 'hypocrites');
- react angrily if anyone dares suggest the group has contributed to the situation; or
- catastrophise the conflict, believing it will shatter the community?

Escape conflict resolution style

Does your leadership group instinctively try to escape? Does it, for example:

- deny the reality of the problem;

- downplay the scope of the problem, reframing it in (deceptively) simplistic terms, default to being 'nice';
- underplay its capacity to address the problem;
- acquiesce to the loudest and most vocal protagonists;
- fail to act as one entity, as individuals splinter off, refusing to participate in relevant discussions and decision-making, resigning or leaving the community;
- nurture suspicion and mistrust through cynical responses and destabilising public communications;
- capitulate to fear; or
- ignore or minimise any contribution the leadership group brings to the situation?

Peacemaking conflict resolution style

Does your leadership group instinctively seek biblical peace? Does it, for example:

- seek what God desires in the circumstances, including confession and forgiveness leading to reconciliation;
- make decisions from principle, not impulse;
- think through the situation and its response in a considered manner;
- choose and displays a calm, composed, gentle and self-aware group disposition;
- recognise it may have contributed to the problem and own the consequences; or
- respond by implementing a God-honouring master-plan to lead through the conflict?

> **Key perspective:**
> Just as each of us has a preferred conflict resolution style, so will every leadership group have its preferred conflict resolution style.

It will greatly benefit a leadership group to identify its collective default conflict resolution style and determine if it will likely inhibit or promote God-honouring responses in a conflicted environment.

(b) *Groupthink*

How a leadership group thinks and reflects together will have a bearing on its decision-making processes, its collective 'will' when responding to conflict. Conflict heightens the potential for the deceptive pressure of 'groupthink' to manifest itself. The phenomenon has been defined as:

> *A mode of thinking that people engage in when they are deeply involved in a cohesive in-group, when the members' strivings for unanimity override their motivation to realistically appraise alternative courses of action... Groupthink refers to a deterioration of mental efficiency, reality testing and moral judgement that results from in-group pressures.*[66]

Sometimes groupthink occurs when members take their decision-making cue from the person who speaks first or loudest. Other groups may acquiesce to the arguments of the person with the greatest gift for persuasion. A group may be swept along by the impassioned pleas or strident opinions of a small number of articulate and like-minded members acting as a bloc. Thus, a group may be steamrolled or become overly confident, negative or trenchant. The result? Individual group members probably have not thought through the issues for themselves. The situation becomes a hotbed for disenchantment, a breeding ground for group heart idols (see section 2.6 and sub-section (f) below). Groupthink leads to loss of objectivity. It allows poor decision-making to go unchallenged as the intuitive norms of others dominate.

The role of the chairperson is pivotal in countering groupthink dynamics. It goes without saying, the person in this role has the responsibility and authority to ensure good decision-making. One way of doing this is to empower each group member to step up to their obligation to contribute to the discussion and ask questions. The thoughtful chairperson who involves everyone in the discussion, tables emotions and names truth, will reduce group anxiety, promote healthy, productive discussion and mitigate against the risk of groupthink.

> **Key perspective:**
> The chairperson who ensures all perspectives are heard encourages mental efficiency, fosters reality testing and good judgment, and thus reduces the likelihood of groupthink.

(c) Community culture

We said above in subsection (a) that it is just as vital, for a leadership group as it is for an individual, to be aware of its intuitive *communal* style in responding to conflict. It is equally crucial to be alert to your whole community's unexamined conflict resolution style.

Over time, arising from its history, stories, gifts, and worldview, every community develops its own personality and ways of relating. These habits and patterns define who they believe they are. They colour how others interact with them. A whole community will thus develop expectations and automatic, 'normal' responses around conflict. Have you ever stopped to consider what these are? Have you ever tried to identify and describe the 'typical' responses to conflict in your Christian faith community?

It's all too easy for a leadership group to merely accept the entrenched culture in their community without too much thought. This acceptance is fine if the responses are healthy. However, groups of people will, at times, develop toxic cultures characterised by instinctive attack or avoidance, or the insidious, passive-aggressive combination of both. This communal culture, and how a leadership group engages with it, is a significant external influence on the capacity of the leadership group to lead through a conflict.

Several authors have observed these entrenched cultural responses to conflict in the church context. Change the jargon, and their comments reflect any community, Christian or secular.

Speed Leas says:

> *...each church has unwritten rules about how it goes about disagreeing. In one church every squabble is immediately*

taken to the pastor for his adjudication. In another church, disputes are publicly avoided and handled by gossip. But, however the dispute is handled, it is not necessarily handled consciously. People have learned over the years how to handle congregational conflict, and they may not even be able to articulate exactly what they do.[67]

Alastair McKay observes the unfortunate and common belief amongst many communities that conflict must be avoided and peace sought at all cost. Referencing the British context, he notes:

a central problem in dealing with conflict within most of our churches is the prevailing culture of conflict avoidance and 'niceness'. It is common for people in churches to live by the unwritten rule that: "Thou shalt be nice. Always be nice".[68]

This problem is not confined to Britain nor churches.

> **Key perspective:**
> Every Christian community will, over time, develop a culture – an established pattern or norm regarding 'the-way-things-are-done-around-here'. This culture will significantly influence the response of leaders to community conflict.

Taking time to discern how your community responds to conflict from the outset will help your leadership group consider how best to equip the community for sound biblical responses. Can you re-imagine the culture of your community? When must you act on this? How can you work purposefully with those under your care to rupture entrenched and toxic responses to conflict, wherever they are found? Why have these developed? Where do fresh insights from the teaching of scripture need to be sown faithfully and obediently into the life of your community? What is your vision to foster a healthy culture of peace which honours God?

(d) Community size

The numerical size of a community may constrain how a leadership group attributes meaning to a conflict event.[69] How can this be?

In a small community that sees itself as 'family', the leadership group may unthinkingly accept the meaning either a matriarch or a patriarch (or both) attributes to specific events as irrefutable.

In moderate-sized communities, the leadership group's responses can be significantly influenced by the chief executive leader, such as a school principal, a pastor, or the CEO, due to their highly visible position in the organisation.

In sizeable groups, the governing board or council may become insular, unwilling to consult. Therefore, the meaning a leadership group places on a conflict event may be skewed by a certain arrogance, an overreaching sense of its power and importance.[70]

(e) Group beliefs

Leadership groups will also develop a shared belief system. This element of their corporate identity may evolve intentionally, via an agreed process, or unconsciously, through the interchange of ideas over time.

A well-considered and communally agreed belief system that aligns soundly with God's truth and nurtures the community will empower any leadership group. Its effect will be to build confidence in the group's leadership. This is outstandingly the case when it comes to successfully leading a community through conflict to renewed health.

An unconscious, unclear or ill-informed belief system, on the other hand, will have the opposite effect. Unfortunately, a few commonly-held but deeply-flawed beliefs infiltrate many a corporate belief system.

One is that conflict *must be avoided at all cost*. Clearly, wisdom dictates we should escape situations where we are in danger of attack or death. But trying to keep the peace at any price in the face of conflict which arises from the everyday stresses of living together in a community is inconsistent with Jesus' teachings. (See, for example, Matthew 5:21-26; 18.) These scriptures affirm the importance of facing conflict.

What is it that is deeply-flawed about the belief that conflict must be avoided at all costs? Its overall implication is that God is not sufficient in times of conflict, guaranteeing efforts to lead effectively throughout situations of conflict will run aground. There are several reasons for this:

- This belief inadvertently promotes a culture ripe for unhealthy behaviour. It 'plays into the hands of the most dependent people who can threaten to incite disharmony as a way to receive what they want'.[71]
- This belief will drive a leadership group to emphasise a superficial and false unity at the expense of the far weightier, eternally significant task of addressing underlying heart issues and restoring broken relationships.
- This belief is a denial of truth – where a community suppresses conflict, people are left exposed to its destructive power. Where feelings are not acknowledged, people suffer. Where communities ignore substantive wrongs, people are deprived of justice.

When leaders believe that conflict should be avoided at all costs, people are left aggrieved and distrustful.

A flawed understanding of the concept of 'servant leadership' can also compromise leadership during conflict. David Brubaker believes the term directly contributes to reluctance among leaders to acknowledge the presence and power of conflict and deal with it effectively. He comments:

> *While the intent of this language is to encourage service to others rather than the raw exercise of power, the practical result can be pervasive denial of the existence and distribution of power within the ... system. When struggles over power arise, conflict resolution can be delayed as all involved deny that the conflict has anything to do with power.*[72]

Flawed belief systems such as these are antithetical to a biblical understanding of leadership. They render leadership groups blind to the God-honouring opportunities inherent in conflict. As Paul warns, such responses will only shame Christ and discredit a community (1 Cor 6:5).

> **Key perspective:**
> A healthy, self-aware leadership group will actively consider whether it holds any flawed beliefs about conflict likely to compromise its desire to reflect the way of Christ while navigating through conflict.

(f) Group idols of the heart

The meaning a group of leaders will place on a conflict may be further influenced by heart idols, which have developed in the group. Heart idols in a group was an uncomfortable reality we addressed in section 2.6. We listed there some possible heart idols and then invited you and your group to reflect on them. If you haven't done so, take a moment to revisit that section and consider whether any of those listed heart idols have become characteristic of your group or team. Then reflect on the following *good things* which may mask heart idols and the possible behaviours which may reveal them:

- Good thing: desire to be effective in accomplishing the work entrusted to the group
  - Potential concealed idols: identity grounded in the need to be seen as successful; pride – a belief that only you and your group can do what needs to be done
  - Possible manifesting behaviours: impatience with anyone who gets in the way; an overinflated sense of the group's importance, arrogance.

- Good thing: desire to be respected and appreciated
  - Potential concealed idols: identity grounded in needing to be liked to be ok; egotism – a pretentious sense of status
  - Potential manifesting behaviours: favouritism to those who flatter; bullying towards those who critique.

When heart idols take root within a leadership group, they may be evident, subtly or overtly, in its formal and informal interactions. They will impact the meaning the group attributes to any given conflict.

> **Key perspective:**
> Group heart idols may combine with the heart idols of individuals to generate responses that do not reflect God's heart, fail to trust him and enable poor behaviour.

It will be difficult for a leadership group whose behaviours are being driven by heart idols to remain 'in step with the Spirit'. To do so will involve recognising, naming and confessing them, seeking Christ's forgiveness and offering forgiveness to others (1 Jn 1:9).

(g) The meaning a group places on a conflict

Leadership groups are also *'meaning making machines'*. The powerful influences we've discussed will instantly and unconsciously craft the meaning a group attributes to a conflict, just as they do for an individual.

Take, for example, one possible scenario when the governing group members return from their coffee break to discuss the conflict between Lyall and Steve.

Denise, Gerald, and Belinda carry power in the group. Between them, they have the responsibilities to chair the council, bed down the strategic plan and budget the finances to support it. They are experienced business people, used to getting their way. To them, this conflict means risk to the church's present and future interests – and to their time investment and reputation. Conflict is an unwelcome intrusion.

- Denise may default to her legal instinct to fight. She may argue for legal solutions to the conflict – to clear Steve from accusations she might consider Lyall had no right to make; to protect the church from potential disarray; and ensure the strategic plan's ongoing success.

- Gerald may also go into fight mode to protect the church's interests and his deep-seated desire for kudos. He may support Denise's legal approach by arguing Lyall be dismissed (a step he wouldn't hesitate to take in his own business) to show strength and shut the conflict down fast.
- The physical turmoil and temporary speechlessness the conflict has triggered in Belinda may explode into a knee-jerk attack on this distracting intrusion into her efficient and ordered world.

If:

- others on the council are used to acquiescing to the combined professionalism of these three powerbrokers;
- shutting the conflict down fast allays Donald's fears and comforts Lee Wu's cultural instinct to save face by minimising or covering up the conflict;
- Aaron's youth and inexperience make him afraid to offer a tentative alternative view which will contradict these people he holds in awe; and
- the rest of the group is uncertain what to do.

Then:

- groupthink will ensure the others automatically adopt the meaning their three influential colleagues attribute to the conflict; and
- the group will take actions from an automatic, instinctive attack norm.

In this instance, the churning assortment of *individual influences* combines with *groupthink* and a *dominant but unacknowledged conflict resolution style* to influence the meaning the council attributes to the conflict and its responses.

> **Key perspective:**
> This book contends that irrespective of its source or context, and notwithstanding these many influences, the biblically sound meaning to attribute to conflict is that it is *an opportunity to reflect God's character in community and bring him honour – in short, to be fully human, as God intends.*

We will examine a comprehensive biblical framework to assist such a council in chapter 6. In the meantime, let's look briefly at a possible alternative scenario for when the council returns from their coffee break to discuss the conflict between Lyall and Steve.

If:

- others on the council are prepared to step up to their obligations on the council as equals beside the three powerbrokers rather than being intimidated by them;
- Donald recognises his fears and puts them immediately before God;
- Lee Wu graciously puts aside his immediate cultural instinct in favour of slowing down to pray about the situation and consider the relevant biblical principles;
- Aaron is prepared to overcome his awe and speak up; and
- the rest of the group is ready to engage honestly despite their uncertainty.

Then:

- the group will address the issues constructively, with every member contributing their thoughts to the discussion; and
- the group will take actions from a considered, thoughtful and Christ-honouring position rather than any unconscious groupthink.

Whatever the meaning a person or group places on a conflict event, the emotions stirred are consistent with that meaning.

5.2 *Influences informing a leadership group's collective emotional world*

What we have explored, especially about meaning–making and emotions during conflict, are all amplified in the group context. That is, the meaning attributed to a conflict gives rise to a world of *collective* emotions. These can include anger, frustration and the anxiety we explored in chapter 4.

A not unrelated emotion to anxiety is fear. Conflict generates the perfect climate to unsettle the composure of a leadership group and allow all-out fear to take hold. When it does, it feels entirely real and justified:

- How will our management of the emerging conflict be received by the powerbrokers in our community (say, a foundation member, a well-respected elder, or a significant donor)?
- Will our decisions hold the community together or cause an uproar and split it apart?
- What if this conflict swamps us with a deluge of unresolved hurts from the past?
- How will we meet the community's significant mortgage obligations if our people stop giving?

Fear is contagious, and when it takes hold, it can easily infect a whole leadership group. You don't need me to convince you that this will have a highly unproductive influence on a leadership group's capacity to guide a community through conflict. Fear can come back to bite you, and that fear, in one area, can trigger a range of other fears.

Why is that over one hundred times, the Bible calls us not to be afraid? After all, fear cannot stop the fearful thing from occurring. Part of the point of the biblical call to not fear may lie in what fear does to the one, or the group, who is afraid. It can paralyse and undo us completely. A group captured by fear will quickly lose objectivity and self-awareness. Such a group is in danger of forgetting the truth about God's trustworthiness. A group that would typically answer the question, *Is God sufficient?* with a resounding yes, may find itself, in the context of fear, unsure.

> ### Key perspective:
> Whether a leadership group fears the power of others, fears their community, fears their inadequacies or fears the bank manager, in the end, all these fears reveal a failure to trust God's providence and his word.[73]

The collective emotional world of a leadership group, especially when it involves fear, has powerful consequences. When facing conflict, it is vital leaders ask where their trust lies and whether their fears are undermining their trust in God alone.

5.3 *The influence of the will on the capacity of a group of leaders to purposefully develop well-considered responses to conflict*

We have argued that a leadership group's specific meaning on a conflict event is likely to be unconsciously influenced by a range of individual and group factors. We have noted how this meaning can lead to a variety of automatic, unconsidered emotional reactions. These can quickly translate into ill-considered, even sinful actions, which may reveal a group's collective heart idols.

While all this is true, we reiterate we should not conclude that this progression is inevitable. In God's providence, leadership groups are not slaves to their dynamics and emotions, nor to community culture. God has given us the capacity to choose. We can purposefully engage our wills to choose a God-honouring response. As we open ourselves to God's empowering presence, so he develops within us the ability to maintain 'self-control' (Gal 5:23).

Of course, there will be times when we fail and lose control. Our God promises, however, to be our refuge, strength and ever-present help in trouble. Jesus gives the way for every leadership group to re-set! James describes it this way: 'Therefore, confess your sins to one another and pray for one another, that you may be healed'. When a Christian leadership group hits the pause button, prays, and leads a spirit-filled discussion, healing can occur, and the crisis will be addressed in a God-honouring manner.

5.4 *Summary*

Given the influences and realities we have identified, there will be pressure to lead through conflict in ways that do not honour God. Leaders are always faced with a choice. They can respond thoughtlessly and destructively out of their ingrained intuitive norms. Or they can move forward prayerfully and reflectively, with a gentle heart and a considered mind, towards mature and God-honouring leadership responses and decisions.

Discussing these factors as a group will assist all members to become more self-aware and strengthen their objectivity.

Questions for reflection and discussion

As you read this chapter and reflect on the questions below, you may identify patterns in your responses to conflict which fall short of the glory of God. So, take time to pray, repent, receive Christ's forgiveness and allow your group's instinctive responses to be transformed by the Holy Spirit (1 Jn 1:9; Ps 103:3, 4).

1) Look back over the various influences identified in this chapter. Discuss which ones most impact your leadership group's responses to conflict. What idols of the heart might be driving your group to exhibit these influences?

2) What causes your leadership group the most anxious and fear? How will you address this anxiety and fear in a biblically faithful manner?

3) What does God want to teach your group right now about its attitude to conflict and to leading it well? Discuss.

4) Section 5.1(f) provided two examples of 'good things' that developed into heart idols. As you reflect on the following examples, can you identify the concealed idols and the behaviours likely to reveal them?

- Good thing: desire to be supported by the community to achieve shared goals
  - Potential concealed idols: ....
  - Possible manifesting behaviours: ....

- Good thing: desire to maintain peace within the community
  - Potential concealed idols: ....
  - Possible manifesting behaviours: ....

- Good thing: desire to be ....
  - Potential concealed idols: ....
  - Possible manifesting behaviours: ....

So, to what does the Bible call leaders to do? What insight does it provide to the principles to be applied and the processes leaders might use? How might they lead as obedient stewards of their community to God's glory? We will turn our attention to these matters in the next chapter.

---

66 Irving L. Janis, *Victims of Groupthink,* Houghton Mifflin Company, 1972, p. 9.

67 Speed Leas, *Rooting out Causes of Conflict,* p. 6.

68 McKay, *How does the church handle conflict,* p. 4.

69 In the church context, Arlin Rothauge and Lyle Schaller and others have identified four categories of church sizes. A community described as a 'family church' is seen as one with adult attendees of between 1 and 50/70. A community described as a 'pastoral church' is seen as one with adult attendees of between 70 and 150/175. A church described as a 'programme church' is seen as one with adult attendees of between 150-350. A community designated as a 'corporate church' or 'resource church' is seen as one with adult attendees over 400. Leas, Speed B, *Moving Your Church Through Conflict,* Alban Institute Inc, 1985, p. 75. referencing Arlin Rothauge, *Sizing up a Congregation for New Member* Ministry, The Episcopal Church Center, 815 Second Ave., New York 10017 and Lyle Schaller, *Looking in the Mirror: Self-Appraisal in the Local Church,* Abingdon, 1984.

70 Leas, *Moving,* p. 75ff. Leas also outlines in further detail how conflict unfolds and may be addressed in light of the four sizes or categories of church congregations referenced in the previous footnote.

71 Steinke, *Twenty Observations,* https://alban.org/archive/twenty-observations-about-troubled-congregations/ p. 1.

72 Brubaker, David R., *Promise and Peril: Understanding and Managing Change and Conflict in Congregations,* The Alban Institute, Herndon, Virginia, 2009, p. 113. (Copyright 2009 © the Alban Institute. Reproduced with permission of the Licensor through PLSclear.)

73 See Ps 27:1; Is 8:12, 13; 1 Jn 4:18.

THE HELM - A BIBLICAL FRAMEWORK 6

In this chapter, we look at:
- **eight biblical principles for leading a community conflict from beginning to end**

Cast your mind back to the story of Lyall and Steve in chapter 4 and of the council's deliberations after the coffee break in chapter 5. What if, rather than defaulting to its instinctive norm, the group instead acknowledged the assortment of influences impacting its responses? What if it purposefully stepped back from reacting reflexively? What would it mean to think biblically instead; to deliberately choose a more mature approach? Members of the council would find themselves addressing the following, and many more questions:

- How should they handle this significant relational breakdown in their leadership team?
- As a church, how could they seek God in the situation?
- How could they bring healing to Lyall and Steve?
- How could they care for those who overheard the conflict?
- How could they limit the ripple effect of rumours innocently or maliciously initiated?

- What principles should guide them?

This chapter seeks to provide a cohesive biblical framework to assist such a council, the protagonists and the community to think biblically; to deliberately choose the more mature approach. It is the cornerstone of this book: the research behind what is set out here informs every attempt within these pages to guide a biblical approach to healthy, strategic leadership throughout chaotic conflicted situations.

The stay-at-the-HELM framework developed in this chapter concentrates on eight theological principles. Part 2 sets out practical ways to activate these in your community. As we consider these biblical principles in more detail, you may find some are 'old treasures' for you; some may be 'new' (Mt 13:52).

If fully embraced, I believe they will empower you to be a leader who, throughout conflict in your community:
- is confident in and true to your identity in Christ;
- finds lasting, biblically consistent solutions; and
- creates safe places and processes for issues to be addressed, individuals reconciled, and community health restored.

It is my sincere hope this framework, with its HELM acronym, will provide a straightforward mnemonic to recall key biblical principles. I think of it as the 'ready reference' I was missing on my journey; the steering mechanism to navigate conflict's wild weather.

It is – the **HELM.**

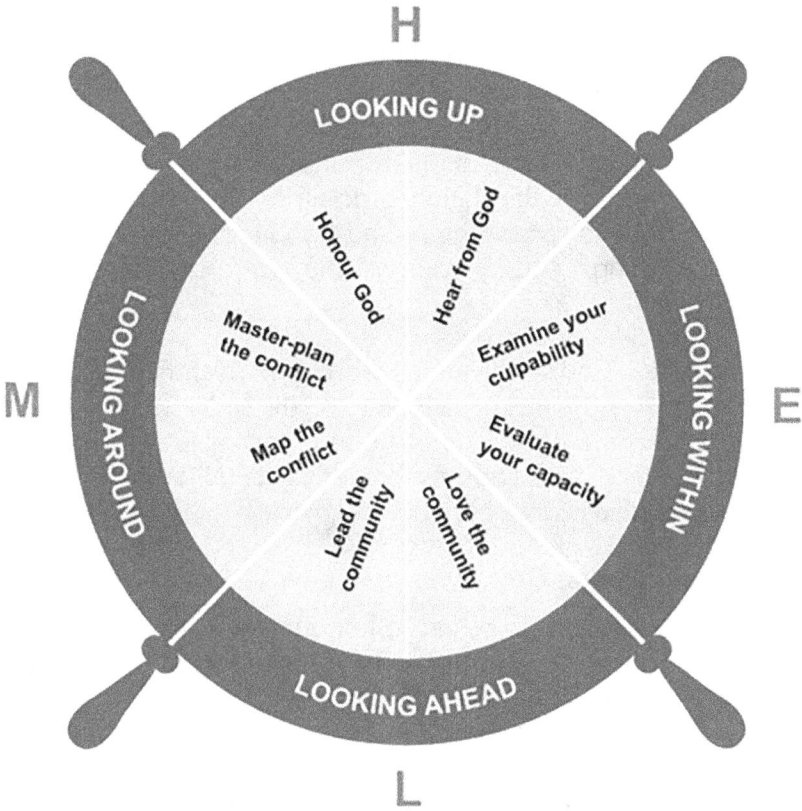

FIGURE 8: THE HELM

While this diagram seems neat and orderly, the truth is that conflict in a community is always messy. Leaders seeking to stay the course are unlikely to manage themselves and the situation according to any such 'carefully sequenced' list or framework. They are much more likely to be thinking and looking about in several directions simultaneously – up, within, around and ahead – scanning the full context in which they find themselves. They will inevitably move backwards, forwards and amongst these eight categories all at the same time as the need arises.

6.1 *Honour God* – looking up

From beginning to end scripture exhorts the people of God to uphold God's honour and give him glory above all else. He is the only fitting recipient of our honour in the whole of creation. In recognition of God as originator and sustainer of the created order, the book of Revelation proclaims: 'You are worthy, our Lord and God, to receive glory and honour and power, for you created all things, and by your will they were created and have their being' (4:11).

Furthermore, God's salvation works in history make him unquestionably the fitting recipient, worthy of our honour. As the psalmist acknowledges: 'Full of honour and majesty is his work, and his righteousness endures forever' (111:3 NRSV). Conflict not addressed, sullies God's honour.

(a) Honour God as God

God is God. There is no other. To honour God is to acknowledge this. It is to detect the urgency behind the words of the Lord God himself as he seeks to bring to the attention of humankind a cosmic reality which is so far outside our impossibly limited worldview: 'I am the Lord, that is my name! I will not yield my glory to another or my praise to idols' (Is 42:8). He alone, in all creation, is truly and completely 'honourable, impressive, worthy of respect'.[74] Even if *we* don't fully comprehend, *God* sees the cosmic, eternal reasons why it is so vital that his followers uphold his honour.

Unfortunately, conflict clouds our vision of who God is.

The psalmist records the almost despairing words of the Lord when he said: 'How long will you people turn my glory into shame? How long will you love delusions and seek false gods?' (Ps 4:2) Conflicts, as we have seen, arise from desires, even good ones, which we allow to twist away from honouring God towards honouring something or someone other than God. Deluded, we privilege their place in our lives over the place of the one true God. Our desires attain the status of idols of the heart. When this occurs, we besmirch God's name and malign his reputation and character. We turn his glory into shame; we damage our communities.

138

> **Key perspective:**
> Leaders who understand who God is, who let God be God, and commit to honouring him from the outset are well placed to navigate conflict effectively.

> **Key advantages** of honouring God as God include:
> - lifting our gaze beyond the immediate to the eternal;
> - living authentically with God and with one another;
> - seeking and telling truth;
> - unmasking the hidden idols of our hearts; and
> - providing purpose and energy for seeking holistic outcomes.

If leaders do not strive to bring honour and glory to God amidst conflict, they will ultimately allow honour and glory to pass to another – themselves, the protagonists, the spiritual forces of evil. Leaders will preserve God's honour as they know him and his word more deeply.[75]

(b) Honour God in how we live together

The importance of giving honour to God, and living for his glory, saturates all scripture, in both Old and New Testaments. Not only are we to make this our constant response individually, but whole communities are called to respond in this way. A serious consideration of what it means to honour God in how we live together is not something to engage with lightly.

The Apostle Paul was zealous to see God's name honoured. He was fully aware of the many disputes in which the fledgling Christian communities found themselves. He challenged the young Corinthian church to honour God in every aspect of their daily activities, to build up the integrity of their community and as a testimony to others:

> *So whether you eat or drink or whatever you do, do it all for the glory of God. Do not cause anyone to stumble... For I am not seeking my own good but the good of many, so that they may be saved.* (1 Cor 10:31-33)

And we also see Paul encouraging the young church in Rome to understand the fundamental link between striving to live in accord with one another and honouring God:

> *May the God who gives endurance and encouragement give you the same attitude of mind toward each other that Christ Jesus had, so that with one mind and one voice you may glorify the God and Father of our Lord Jesus Christ.* (Rom 15:5, 6)

Undoubtedly most Christians, if asked, would acknowledge they do desire to honour their Lord and bring him glory. However, they might wonder if it is even possible amidst serious conflict. There are many pointers in God's word to suggest, *yes*, this is possible. Along with those already offered above, here is a further brief sample of lifestyle attitudes and actions the Bible indicates bring glory and honour to God:

- accepting suffering for his sake (Jn 11:4; Rom 8:17; 1 Pt 4:14);
- letting his presence shine through our involvement in community life (2 Cor 4:6; Eph 3:20-21);
- living lives worthy of God (1 Thess 2:12) and the gospel (1 Cor 10:31);
- encouraging truth-telling (Jos 7:19);
- offering him our wholehearted worship (Ps 29:2; Eph 1:3-6; Rev 14:7); and
- glorying in his name (1 Chron 16:10; Ps 86:9).

> **Key perspective:**
> Leaders who honour God in how they live, who model his up-side-down kingdom values and challenge every member of their community to do the same, will be well placed to navigate conflict effectively.

> **Key advantages** *of honouring God in how we live together include:*
> - demonstrating our love for God by obedience;
> - changing our perspective on the gravity of the issues;
> - engendering commitment to lasting solutions; and
> - positioning the community to receive God's covenant of peace.

When we give God the honour due to him, we begin to realise there is far more at stake than our conflict. God's reputation may be tarnished. People may be damaged and stumble in their commitment. The organisation's reputation may be irreparably harmed.

It is also important to actively look for evidence of God's glory surfacing in the life of the community during conflict. To publicly testify to this grace as it is uncovered and experienced provides encouragement and hope.[76] It is comforting to know God does not abandon us at such perplexing times.

(c) Honour God in prayer

One foundational practice to bring honour and glory to God during conflict is the discipline of prayer. This is not to assume it is easy. If we are to be guided by the way Jesus taught his followers, talking to God during conflict calls us to difficult grace, honest self-reflection and costly forgiveness:

- 'pray for those who mistreat you' (Lk 6:28) and 'persecute you' (Mt 5:44); and
- 'when you stand praying, if you hold anything against anyone, forgive them...' (Mk 11:25).

Prayer is part of the warp and woof of ministry in the early churches, amidst all their conflicts and stresses. There are, for example, over thirty references to prayer in the book of Acts alone. Paul *models* the importance of prayer by consistently praying for the churches himself (Col 1:3) and in turn *exhorts* these communities to be 'faithful in prayer' (Rom 12:12).

> **Key perspective:**
> Leaders who model prayer and encourage protagonists and the wider community to pray along with them, will be well placed to navigate conflict effectively.

Hebrews encourages us to '...approach God's throne of grace with confidence, so that we may receive mercy and find grace to help us in our time of need' (4:16). This is not some narrow, esoteric, complicated, unattainable spiritual practice. Turning confidently to God in a time of need suggests prayer is part of the stuff of life;

sometimes pre-meditated and reflective, sometimes nimble and creative, sometimes swift and urgent.

Key advantages *of honouring God in prayer include:*
- taking a stand against the enemy of peace, the evil one;
- recognising the other party as our brother or sister in Christ;
- seeing others as broken people like us;
- opening our hearts to confession and forgiveness;
- breaking down barriers to healing and restoration; and
- lifting our gaze to the higher interests of God's kingdom perspectives.

While we may not fully understand the mystery of prayer, there is no doubt that prayer, individually and collectively, is foundational to honouring God during conflict. As we pray, we can be reassured by Jesus' profound promise given in the heat of strife between believers: 'Again, truly I tell you that if two of you on earth agree about anything you ask for, it will be done for them by my Father in heaven. For where two or three come together in my name, there am I with them' (Mt 18:19-20).

Speaking to God is one side of the equation; the other side is attuning our hearts to listen.

6.2 **H***ear from God* – looking up

The inner turbulence associated with periods of discord and heightened emotion can easily dull our sensitivity to our personal relationship with God. If we do pay attention, however, conflict 'may be "an arena of revelation", a time when we hear God's voice as we never have before'.[77]

As we have already established in section 1.4, 'God's word provides a trustworthy navigational chart for every conflict' and 'conflict provides an opportunity for everyone, leaders *and* followers to learn and experience the principles of biblical peacemaking'.

(a) Hear God's truth

God will reveal to us new insights of truth as we sit with his word, actively listening and sincerely hearing what it says. It will refresh our past understanding. It will be a precursor and catalyst for transformation. God's voice has the power to stimulate change in attitude, direction and behaviour. This potential for change is possible for leaders, protagonists and whole communities.

The leader who hears

'To lead a [community] into the character of God will require leaders who form and are formed by the life, death, and resurrection of Jesus Christ. To be the kind of community that forms people around God's character, we need a way of hearing, seeing, thinking, and acting informed by God's Spirit', Van Yperen says.[78] He is backed up by Eugene Habecker, who understands how important it is that leaders hear and reflect upon God's truth... 'leaders need to be continually involved in self-confrontation, using God's Word as their standard.'[79]

That said, leaders often discover conflict is far more likely to elicit any number of knee-jerk questions about God and his purposes:
- Why did God allow this to arise in my community?
- Why did he let this happen on my watch?
- Why now when we were poised to achieve great things?
- What is going on when we have been consistently praying about our situation?

King David, a leader with a fair share of enemies, had similar questions. In Psalm 27 he wrestles deeply with the conflict he faced. As we read, we recognise his long, anguished wait, during exceedingly troubled times, to see God act. We are grateful for his honesty.

We are privy to the moment he resolutely turns his heart towards God, and begins to reflect on his principles and promises, even as the unresolved tumult swirls around him. We listen in as, having entered God's presence, he carries on an honest dialogue. We watch David manage his anxiety by seeking out and claiming the protection he knew was available to him. We see how immersing himself in the truth of God rebuilt David's confidence in the Lord's goodness, despite all human evidence to the contrary. We are humbled to hear the great and knowledgeable King David ask God to continue to teach and lead him, because of the conflict.

And we are captivated as he grasps fresh insights into what it means to wait on the Lord: it calls for and calls out new-found strength; and it engenders a resilient heart, full of purposeful hope grounded on the goodness of God. David knows, because he has heard from God, that *...in the day of trouble he will keep me safe in his dwelling ...and set me high upon a rock* (v.5).

Therefore, to make the shift towards David's more reflective way of hearing from God, the kind of hearing encouraged by Van Yperen and Habecker, leaders may benefit from asking:

- Lord, what will you have me learn through this difficult time?
- What are some of the opportunities in this conflict to grow more like you?
- What are the principles and promises you have for me from your word in relation to this situation?

The protagonist who hears

Most of us will have been protagonists in a conflict at some point. The accompanying chaotic confusion may not be unfamiliar to us. Along with leaders, protagonists may also have many knee-jerk questions as conflict lays bare their fears, doubts or even unbelief:

- Where has God been in this situation?
- Why did he allow it to occur?
- Didn't he promise us a community of peace?
- Has God really said...?
- Can I trust Him?
- Even if the worst befalls me, is God still good?

As a protagonist, I may understand in theory my obligation to look for ways to hear from God. The overwhelming force of my instinctive responses to the conflict may, however, make it almost impossible for me to do so, at least initially. Recognising this, leaders do well to thoughtfully draw protagonists gently and sensitively into the orbit of God's word. As Paul advised Timothy, 'Opponents must be gently instructed' (2 Tim 2:25).

It doesn't take much to understand the necessity for such instruction – most of us know all too well the impulse towards retribution when we are party to a conflict, notwithstanding being people of faith.

We also fully appreciate why such 'instruction' needs to be 'gentle'. If we are teetering on the brink of fight or flight, seeing only danger, we will not take kindly to a leader's well-meaning attempts to set us straight!

Timing is everything. The right moment will, hopefully, come for protagonists to hear from God. When it does, they will discover that:

> If there is to be vengeance for human sin it is for God to mete out, for God is the only perfect judge... To take revenge and demand pound for pound is to go down a blind alley. No good ever came from it. It simply multiplies evil. It also presupposes that the one who takes revenge is morally superior to the one avenged.[80]

Along with this, the protagonist willing to hear God will discern the releasing wisdom of trusting God. Such a person will be surprised, in time, by the creative, life-giving alternative outcomes God brings about when we leave revenge and judgment in his hands.[81]

The community who hears

A critical role for leaders during conflict is to empower their community to hear from God. Clear biblical guidelines at such a time will assist people to come to grips with their many questions and anxieties. Barthel and Edling observe that in their experience:

> the church that turns first to a study of the biblical process of conflict resolution rarely finds it necessary to deal with the many collateral conflicts generally associated with the tension caused by the core issues of the conflict. Significant material issues may need to be answered, but the way these issues are

145

> *resolved changes radically once people begin to deal biblically with each other in their personal relationships.*[82]

These observations, of course, apply equally to any Christian faith-based community – this is gospel work, after all. If a group loses its sense of identity in Christ, a default position will inevitably emerge. Partially formed views, disrespectful language and practices which dishonour God, are likely to dominate. Often these will be the beliefs and ideas of the most articulate and forceful individuals or groups in the community. It is disturbing to hear God's profound disappointment, anger and call to repentance when such articulate and forceful groups and individuals almost derailed the churches at Pergamum (Rev 2:14-15) and Thyatira (Rev 2:20, 24).

> **Key perspective:**
> Leaders who openly nurture teaching and learning about biblical peacemaking principles in the midst of conflict enable their community to hear from God.

Of course, it is far preferable to be preventative rather than be reactive. It will always prove beneficial to teach the principles *before* tensions arise as a way of developing a community culture of peace. In this respect, see chapter 12, 'A better way' where we develop this concept.

> **Key advantages** *of teaching biblical peacemaking principles include:*
> - appreciating the need to address conflict promptly;
> - providing common language around conflict;
> - creating an environment conducive to God moving in people's hearts;
> - allowing breathing space for angst to settle, for people to gain clarity;
> - gaining fresh insight into distinctive biblical processes; and
> - safeguarding the community against being '...blown here and there by every wind of teaching and by the cunning and craftiness of people...' (Eph 4:14).
>
> **Note**: *cautions in regard to teaching biblical principles during conflict are addressed in section 7.2.*

The Apostle Paul fully appreciated the power of God's word to build his people up: 'For everything that was written in the past was written to teach us, so that through the endurance taught in the Scriptures, and the encouragement they provide we might have hope' (Rom 15:4).

Leaders can empower their people to endure. They can encourage them from God's word. They can foster hope. The role of the community is to hear these truths, then respond faithfully by applying what they have heard. As Jesus said: 'Anyone who loves me will obey my teaching' (Jn 14:23). Those obedient to what they hear from God will themselves become influencers, encouraging the work of God in the lives of other bystanders distressed by conflict, as well as those caught up in it.

(b) Hear God's end-goal

Given the frequency of conflicts in the early church, the importance of getting along with each other was a preoccupying theme in the apostle Paul's letters and teaching. At times, as we see below, he held up a vision for God's end-goal, his ultimate outcome for them beyond conflict:

Context	The desired end-goal
Church in Rome This was a community quarrelling and passing judgment on one another over theological issues of their day which were open to different but, in their minds, arguably valid interpretations.	*...with one mind and one voice you may glorify the God and Father of our Lord Jesus Christ. Accept one another... just as Christ accepted you...* (Rom 15:6-7).
Church in Corinth This community fell into conflict over many issues including the practice of eating meat which, in their culture, may or may not have been sacrificed to idols.	*...whether you eat or drink or whatever you do, do it all for the glory of God. Do not cause anyone to stumble* (1 Cor 10:31-32). (See also 1 Cor 1:10)

Church in Philippi Two women in this community had fallen out with each other.	...be of the same mind in the Lord (Phil 4:2).
Philemon was being challenged to reinstate his former slave Onesimus, whom he believed to be 'useless' to him.	...welcome him as you would welcome me (Phlm 17).

Paul considered it most important these conflicted communities hear and understand God's end-goal – who and how they were called to be, as they did life together. It would seem sensible to take note of this. Leaders today can also actively listen for God's end-goal for their communities and help them hear and understand it as the desired destination beyond the conflict.

Obviously, the overarching biblical themes of pursuing peace, discovering truth, acting justly and seeking reconciliation will always be in play. They are integral to both the process of conflict resolution and any God-honouring end-goal. However, what Paul does in these examples, and what leaders today would be wise to do, is ensure each community hears God's heart for a specific end-goal arising from, and related to, the nature of each conflict.

Barthel and Edling take our thinking in a similar direction: 'When church leaders embrace a conflict and recast it as God's agenda for growth, conflicts are usually shorter, less intense, and bear the fruit of positive spiritual growth'.[83]

> **Key perspective:**
> Leaders who set out to hear God's end-goal, or vision, for the outcome of a conflict will be well-placed to navigate conflict effectively and leave a God-honouring legacy.

The story is told of a team of three stonemasons labouring together on a project. Amidst harsh blows of metal upon rock, dust and grit, someone asked what they were doing. The first replied: 'I am laying bricks'. The second responded: 'I am constructing a wall'. The third answered: 'I am building a cathedral'. In anxious times leaders, protagonists and the community *all* need the vision of the third stonemason – that God's end-goal beyond their distress will bear fruit with eternal significance.

> **Key advantages** *of adopting a specific end-goal for a conflict include:*
> - lifting the community's gaze to *God's agenda* for the outcome;
> - shaping strategies to master-plan the conflict; and
> - gathering the community around a unifying vision.

(c) Hear what God values

Some of the disciples who journeyed with Jesus harboured desires for prominence and honour in God's coming kingdom. Jesus was distressed by their shallow understanding and overbearing pride. The issue came to a head when he predicted his death. Although they were distraught and filled with grief at the possibility of losing Jesus, it didn't take long for what they really wanted and valued to predominate – as an active dispute over which of them would take leadership, be 'the greatest', once he had gone.[84]

The conflict highlights both their confusion regarding the kingdom of God and how steeped they were in self-interest. Jesus seized the moment to help them hear what God truly values in an aspiring leader. His sermon, recorded in Matthew 18, provides a blueprint for mature, non-anxious leadership which promotes peace.

Verses 15-20, with their specific focus on dealing with conflict person-to-person, are well-known amongst people of faith in the context of conflict. However, it is valuable to consider the *whole* sermon as a foundation for addressing conflict. It sets out ways of being (we could say 'values', if we wanted to reference organisational jargon), which function as an antidote to destructive self-interest. If you really want to be seen as 'great' in my kingdom once I'm gone, Jesus is saying (to his disciples and through them to us today), you can do so by:
- *changing* your stand-point (v.3);
- *humbling* yourselves (v. 4);
- *welcoming* fellow believers (v. 5);

- not being a *stumbling block* (v. 6ff);
- *locating and nurturing* those who wander away (v. 10ff);
- *listening* to each other (v. 15, 16);
- initiating *resolution* (v. 15ff); and
- *forgiving* one another as a way of life (v. 21ff).

These are what God values. The one who hears and embodies them, whether leader, protagonist or community member, is the one who exhibits true leadership, true greatness in God's eyes and the eyes of others amidst conflict.

Variations on what God values resound throughout the Apostle Paul's letters.[85] The young conflicted churches in Corinth, Colossae, Philippi and Rome, heard Paul remind them how much God cherishes:

- prayerfulness;
- love;
- respect;
- humility;
- gentleness;
- patience; and
- unity.

Walter Wright observes the 'role of leaders is targeted primarily at the values level.' Values, he says, are 'the visible expressions of the organization's culture – the stated affirmations that communicate how we intend to work together and the operational assumptions that actually determine our behaviours'.[86] Further, values are 'the stated or assumed beliefs, commitments, ethos, and qualities that govern everything that the organisation does: the character of the organization, if you will – the manifestation of its soul, its faith and beliefs'.[87]

The values – whether positive or negative – from which leaders operate during conflict will directly affect the responses of protagonists and their community. The conflicted disciples mentioned above harboured self-interest and hubris, attitudes the Bible calls out as sinful. These negative values inevitably translate into destructive behaviour. Leaders, protagonists and whole communities who entertain similar negative values (it doesn't take much to think of anger, frustration, insularity, resentment and many more) will also behave in ways which reveal and reflect those values. Nurturing positive values taught by Jesus and Paul, on the other hand, will drive transformative behaviours which honour God and lead to healing.

Many organisations decide what they value as part of their strategic planning. This kind of purposeful process can equally be employed as part of dealing with conflict. Imagine what your community would be like if the values you adopted during conflict were the manifestation of God's values.

> **Key perspective:**
> Leaders who nurture and embody godly values as a visible expression of their community culture are well placed to navigate conflict effectively.

> **Key advantages** *of adopting core values for navigating conflict include:*
> - agreement about community character and culture;
> - shared commitments regarding community behaviour;
> - a yardstick for calling one another to account; and
> - a basis for strategic planning and action.

6.3 *Examine your culpability – looking within*

Whatever the circumstance of an emerging conflict, leaders are wise to examine whether they carry any culpability before jumping to conclusions too quickly.

Even Jesus assumes each person involved in conflict will have some culpability. It might be significant – a 'plank', a 'log' in the eye; it might be minimal – just a 'speck'. Jesus loathed hypocrisy. He was blunt in his criticism of leaders who did not own their culpability. 'First take the plank out of your own eye', he said to them, 'and then you will see clearly to remove the speck from [the other person's] eye' (Mt 7:5). Paul recognised our human propensity to be blind to our faults. 'If anyone thinks they are something when they are not, they deceive themselves,' he warned. 'Each one should test their own actions' (Gal 6:3-4).

The 'specks' or 'logs' in the eyes of leaders may be related to unexamined belief systems. What do we, in fact, believe about conflict? Are these beliefs valid? Halverstadt observes that conflict offers the opportunity for 'rethinking gut theologies... the updating of one's habitual unexamined inner beliefs and ideas with Christian messages'. Perhaps we are holding onto 'gut theologies ... feeling-based ideas and assumptions that have not been shaped by scripture; only caricatures of scripture'. [88]

Our beliefs, our attitudes and our actions all have practical consequences in our lives. While we may think we have been consistent in following God's Word, we are wise to remember we '...see only a reflection as in a mirror...' (1 Cor 13:12). We often only see part of the truth, or a distortion of truth. As lawyers, consultants and mediators know, there is always much more to a story. Hence, leaders need to take stock and examine their level of culpability.

Where leaders detect they do indeed carry some level of culpability, what is their leadership obligation? To ignore it by pretending innocence? To save face by shifting blame?

A God-honouring leader lives transparently, from the inside out. Scripture teaches when conflict arises, resolution begins with me, in *my* heart, not with the *other* party. Ouch! Surprisingly (or maybe not) experience shows that when people of faith, even leaders, are polarised by the perceived injustice of a conflict, it takes a while to bring God into the picture.

James encourages his readers, and through them encourages us as leaders, to do this quickly. After speaking about the causes of 'fights and quarrels' among them, he calls them to humble themselves, to think and reflect on the state of their own hearts and conduct. He urges them to consider the consequences of their behaviour: 'If they have sinned, they will be forgiven. Therefore, confess your sins to each other' (Jas 5:15-16).

Leaders who live from the inside out are role models for their communities. Their willingness to recognise and name their faults, to turn around and choose God's way shows their community what it means to live a life of repentance. As we saw in the story of the elders of Israel who sought an answer from God in Ezekiel's day, the Lord answers when we 'repent, and turn from (our) idols...'.[89] The wise leader will join the psalmist in honestly praying: 'Search me, God, and know my heart; test me and know my anxious thoughts. See if there is any offensive way in me...' (Ps 139:23-24).

Examining our culpability is as important for a leadership group as it is for an individual. Where an executive, or a ministry team, or a governing board, is a party to the conflict, or has contributed to it even slightly, it is essential the group scrutinises its responsibility.[90] Steinke quotes Daniel Goleman's observation that: 'groups begin to change only when they first have fully grasped the reality of how they function'.[91] Even if the group does not consider itself to have contributed in any way, it is still wise to take stock.

Leaders who are used to success may resist examining themselves. Highly defensive, they may blame anyone but themselves. The world suggests one should lead by one's strengths and never admit anything wrong. Thus, acknowledging failure may not come easily. For such leaders, even inviting God to search their hearts may be a challenge. There will be the temptation to protect themselves and their own reputations along with that of their organisation. If they negate their responsibility, they deny themselves the opportunity to learn and grow. Remember, God is merciful. He has clearly stated: 'Whoever conceals their sins does not prosper, but the one who confesses and renounces them finds mercy' (Prov 28:13). And again: 'If we confess our sins, he is faithful and just and will forgive us our sins and purify us from all unrighteousness' (1 Jn 1:9).

> **Key perspectives:**
> Being willing to admit that a leadership group is functioning with even a minimal level of culpability – just a 'speck' – can protect and strengthen a group's capacity to lead well in times of conflict.

> ***Key advantages*** *of examining our culpability include:*
> - giving witness to their community of God's Spirit at work;
> - reducing tension as leaders humble themselves;
> - modelling Christ-honouring confession and forgiveness;
> - empowering others to also confess;
> - being set free to address the issues by facing truth; and
> - forestalling potential regret for our actions or inactions.

There is a list of practical questions in section 7.3 designed to help leaders examine their culpability. Having done so, they may need to confess that culpability and apologise for its consequences. This is a pivotal moment. Leaders must choose between pride or humility; self-protection or release for the other person. What will you choose in that moment?

Ken Sande outlines seven elements of a sincere and holistic confession:[92]
- Address everyone involved;
- Avoid if, but, and maybe;
- Admit specifically;
- Acknowledge the hurt;
- Accept the consequences;
- Alter your behaviour; and
- Ask for forgiveness.

We have listed them as well as developing the ideas behind each of them in the resource, *Guidelines for writing a holistic confession and apology* found in Part 3, Resources, 16.3(b). Without all seven elements, its value is diminished; the other party is left still hurting, often full of doubt and questions. In my mediation experience, where an apology covers all seven elements it is usually accepted. More than that, there is often a breakthrough to transformation and renewed relationship.

Leaders who humbly and honestly examine their culpability provide compelling leadership. As they model self-reflection, confession, apology and forgiveness, the community will be impacted positively. People will be encouraged. People will change. A community will heal.

6.4 **E**valuate your capacity – looking within

The thrust of this book has been on *leading* your community throughout conflict. Here we turn our attention to your role in *resolving* the conflict itself. This is the moment to evaluate consciously whether you have, or your leadership team has, the necessary skills *and* time to become involved in the actual conflict resolution process. Making this judgment may require a level of humility. Leaders are not immune from believing they can deal with anything and everything!

We are in good company when we undertake the task of evaluation. God is himself an evaluator. He weighs things up, determines their worth, judges their value. In one of the first biblical accounts of God's self-revelation, we see him at the beginning of the ages, evaluating the result of his vast creative endeavour. He pronounces it 'very good' (Gen 1:31).

The letter of 1 Corinthians provides a glimpse of God at the end of the ages. Here he is seen evaluating his *new* creation, the church and all the work done for kingdom purposes in his name. On this final day of judgment, God will pronounce his verdict on the worth and the value of his followers' contribution to building his new community. He will 'test the quality of each person's work' (1 Cor 3:10-15).

In the time between, God evaluates how his people live their lives: 'I the Lord search the heart and examine the mind, to reward each person according to their conduct, according to what their deeds deserve' (Jer 17:10). The psalmist understands this: 'You have searched me, Lord,' he acknowledges, 'and you know me' (139:1).

Further, in this time between, God challenges us, his followers, to evaluate ourselves – our actions[93] and our priorities.[94] Paul recognises a whole world of wisdom available for the 'person with the Spirit' of God to evaluate widely, that is, to '[make] judgments about all things'. Paul points out that this wisdom, which is not open to the 'rulers of this age', is beyond normal human wisdom. Its source is 'the mind of Christ' (1 Cor 2:6-16). Think about this for a moment. The Spirit of God reframes our thinking beyond the merely human. The mind of the Lord himself, of Christ himself, instructs us as we make judgments about our capacity to address the conflict in our midst.

If this is so, it is not surprising that God reserves some of his harshest evaluation for those who set themselves up for leadership, but don't deliver. We see this in Isaiah chapter 28. The NIV headlines with the words, *Woe to the Leaders...*, foreshadowing a lengthy and caustic evaluation of those who fail to step up to their leadership obligations. In contrast, throughout, is the vision of the leader who draws on the spirit of the Lord Almighty to lead with justice and as their source of strength (Is 28 – 32; 28:5, 6). It makes sobering reading for anyone in leadership.

What is also sobering is that God calls communities to evaluate their leaders. They are encouraged to judge their leadership qualities (1 Tim 3), their performance (1 Tim 5:17-20; Acts 18:24-26) and their behaviour (Col 1:28; Phil 2:21-22).

> **Key perspective:**
> Leaders who evaluate their capacity to intervene and resolve a conflict honestly, show respect for the community and open the possibility for both immediate and lasting solutions. Leaders who neglect to honestly evaluate their capacity to address a conflict do not demonstrate love to themselves, the protagonists or the community.

> **Key advantages** *of evaluating your capacity include:*
> - modelling God's character;
> - providing a reality check on the group's resources;
> - maximising the potential for the resolution process to begin well;
> - reducing the potential for surprises down the track;
> - freedom to prioritise core leadership obligations;
> - allowing the group to organise for optimal effectiveness; and
> - building community trust.

Leaders are therefore called to exercise wisdom to sensibly evaluate their capacity to deal with a conflict before them. At lower levels of conflict, leaders may be in a position to address the dispute themselves. When conflict becomes more complex, however, it will be far wiser for leaders to humbly seek assistance beyond themselves.

6.5 *Love the community* – looking ahead

We have noted the wealth of biblical teaching on characteristics which define Christ-honouring leadership. While all these characteristics are equally relevant during conflict, there is one which stands out. It is, of course, love. As Jesus told his disciples, it is the representative feature which marks out people as belonging to him:

> *A new command I give you: Love one another. As I have loved you, so you must love one another. By this everyone will know that you are my disciples, if you love one another.* (Jn 13:34)

Paul identifies love as a 'fruit of the Spirit' (Gal 5:22). John claims those who do not love one another are not God's children (1 Jn 3:10) and challenges those who say they love God to also love one another (1 Jn 3:10, 4:21).

In her book on 1 Corinthians, Margaret Mitchell explores chapter 13's classic 'love' passage, under the title: 'Love as the Antidote to Factionalism'.[95] Mitchell's academic research shows that, in the ancient world of the Corinthians, love had multiple meanings including brotherly or neighbourly love. She also observed a strong connection between love (in its various meanings) and peace in the ancient world. Love was understood to play a foundational role in addressing discord.[96]

Paul draws on this latter understanding to emphasise love as a fundamental way of restoring cohesion in the fractured Corinthian church. Love is the counterpoint to their divisions. Only love will reunite them. Mitchell says those behaviours which the Corinthians display which are the opposite of love (that is, being envious, boastful, proud, self-seeking) 'bear a one-to-one precise correspondence with Paul's description of factional tumult...' in the everyday culture of the city of Corinth. In other words, behaviours which are antithetical to love, breed conflict.

The general population was known for being fractious, for arguing offensively, for being envious, boastful, proud and self-seeking. Paul challenges the people of God in Corinth to be different, to rethink their cultural factionalism and abandon their propensity for conflict. Love, says Paul, is the antidote to all this, *'the most excellent way'* (1 Cor 13:1, italics added). It is the glue which holds the community together. Paul sums up his challenge succinctly: 'Do *everything* in love' (1 Cor 16.13, italics added).

Love was a constant theme in Paul's teaching. He brings it up again in his letter to those in the church in Galatia. Their behaviour, it seems, was not characterised by this 'most excellent way'. In fact, quite the opposite. They too were so fractious and conflicted that Paul described them as 'biting and devouring each other'. He warned they should 'watch out or you will be destroyed by each other' (Gal 5:15). He once more emphasised the imperative to love, reminding them that 'the entire law is fulfilled in keeping this one command: 'Love your neighbour as yourself' (5:14).

He did the same in his letter to the Colossians:

> *Bear with each other and forgive one another if any of you has a grievance against someone. Forgive as the Lord forgave you. And over all these virtues put on love, which binds them all together in perfect unity.* (Col 3:13, 14)

Love is thus a central theme in Paul's teaching. He applies it just as much to brothers and sisters in conflict as to their ethics in normal Christian life. As the book of Proverbs tells us, it opens the way to achieving goals and developing positive relationships:

> *Let love and faithfulness never leave you; bind them around your neck; write them on the tablet of your heart. Then you will win favour and a good name in the sight of God and humankind.* (3:3, 4)

Martin Luther King Jr concluded: *Mankind must evolve for all human conflict a method which rejects revenge, aggression, and retaliation. The foundation of such a method is love.*[97]

> **Key perspective:**
> Wise and genuine love is a key antidote to conflict.

Love is equally as central to our Christian communities and organisations today. Leaders who love their communities will provide appropriate care. In the words of Walter Wright: 'leadership is a relationship of love... Only people who care about people will be effective leaders today'.[98] Barthel and Edling conclude that: 'the most common hurt leaders inflict on followers [that is, all connected to the community who are not leaders] is neglect – leaders fail to give followers the proactive attention and care they long for'.[99]

Jesus' parable of a *wandering* sheep in his sermon on greatness in God's kingdom illustrates the depth of God's love and concern for people at risk of being lost to the faith and to their community (Mt 18:12-14).[100] This sheep is wandering, but not yet completely lost. The shepherd is responsible to go after the sheep and bring it back to the fold. Where conflict causes people to wander away, leaders are responsible to watch out for them and where possible, reunite them with the community.[101]

Steinke warns against counterfeit love which misunderstands the nature and purpose of love:

> *One of the nagging questions facing leaders is how long can the mess be endured before it becomes a major infection. Love, after all, is long-suffering. Indeed it is. But love is not long-suffering and foolish. Love is not overindulgent. Love is not a failure of nerve. Love suffers long so that something new can be erected out of the old. Yet love does not suffer long because it is anxious about naming and confronting violation... Long-suffering love is about doing away with suffering that issues from the harm of others, not being an accomplice to the harmful invasion.*[102]

> **Key advantages** *of loving a community amidst conflict include:*
> - noticing people, hearing their story, recognising their needs;
> - creating a safe place;
> - sharing the conflict burden;
> - understanding people with sufficient insight to know when to refer them out for professional assistance; and
> - leaders are seen to be acting as leaders.

Love is the mark of the person who belongs to God. Without love, no leader can effectively navigate conflict. Without love, conflict will sink the ship.

6.6 *L ead the community* – looking ahead

Leading during conflict involves providing leadership for every individual in the whole community. It is 'a relationship of shalom', says Walter Wright: 'In a world of conflict, leaders bring calm. In a world of brokenness, leaders offer healing... It is a relationship that works actively for the total well-being of the person being led.'[103] Leaders cannot differentiate between categories of people for whom they are responsible. They cannot play favourites. They lead for each party involved in a dispute. They lead for each person impacted by a conflict. They lead for the whole community.

> **Key perspective:**
> Providing leadership is never optional when conflict erupts.

Conflict is family business. It implicates everyone – the paid staff, the governance group, the members, and the volunteers. Jesus uses the familial language of child, children, brother, father, household, community ('church') in the context of conflict in Matthew 18. Paul uses similar language in 1 Corinthians ('brothers', 'sisters', 'household') when addressing significant conflict in that community (1 Cor 1:11, 8:11f). Elsewhere he encourages the kind of mutual care a family would give each other, urging everyone to:

warn those who are... disruptive, encourage the disheartened, help the weak, be patient with everyone. Make sure no one pays back wrong for wrong, but always strive to do what is good for each other and for everyone else. Rejoice always, pray continually... (1 Thess 5:14-17)

Poirier confirms this point: '...Jesus sets our conflicts in the framework of family relationships – relationships with our brothers and sisters'. They are the ones who sin against us, the ones to whom we are to go, the ones who we 'seek to win [back] and restore...' And of course, there is the parent, because '...all these peacemaking efforts fall under the blessing, wisdom, strength, and imitation of our Heavenly Father'.[104]

There is no point being a leader and failing to lead. Leadership defines an organisation. Research has shown there is a direct relationship between the effectiveness of the leadership of not-for-profit boards, and the overall effectiveness of their organisations. In this research, community members perceived their board's effectiveness as the most critical determinant of their perceptions of broader organisational success. Thus, in the context of community conflict, organisations were perceived to be effective when, amongst other initiatives, their leaders became directly involved in ensuring disputes were addressed.[105]

A real or perceived vacuum in leadership allows conflict to escalate. The environment can quickly become toxic. Secrecy fuels further conflict. When the truth is not communicated, nor well-considered action taken, rumours, confusion and disillusionment reign. People take sides, split into factions; relationships disintegrate. Because leaders operate at the heart of their community, they are best placed to change the conflict environment.

Effective communication goes a long way to alleviating these significant downsides of conflict. It mirrors God's commitment to timeless, relational, relevant and ongoing communication with his people. It is a significant factor in enabling a community to remain healthy.

Leaders, therefore, have no choice but to use their God-given gifts and responsibility to lead for the whole community in times of conflict. There is no exemption.

Key advantages *of leading, staying steady at the helm, throughout conflict include:*
- fulfilling the leader's biblical mandate to lead the community;
- engendering community trust, respect, and a healthy morale;
- building hope for the future;
- protecting the health and viability of the community; and
- empowering the ministries of the community to continue with confidence.

6.7 $\boxed{M}$*ap the conflict* – looking around

To map a conflict is defined here as the process of uncovering the various aspects of a conflict event, namely, the story, the contributing facts, conflicting interests, underlying values and needs, the parties, the fractured relationships, the issues (including structural), and the timeline of events.

Read any of the Old Testament prophetic books and it becomes clear their writers, people with enormous insight, undertook this kind of process. In doing so they displayed three characteristics relevant to our discussion:
- a laser-sharp observation of what was happening in their communities, and who was involved;
- clarity as to the spiritual and communal significance of this; and
- courage to deliberately name and document what was happening, and campaign for the changes needed to restore love and justice.

They were also jealous that God's name be honoured. Understanding that the Lord detests those who stir up conflict in the community (Prov 6:16-19), they identified those who were disrupting the nation's peace, destroying its security, and bringing down devastation upon them all. These writers noted the salient facts and extent of the problems. They scoped their impact. They brought sin and injustice into the light. They were passionate advocates for the powerless amongst the people, seeking loving justice for their legitimate concerns and needs.

To map a conflict in your community is to lead like this. It still calls for those same three characteristics today. Put slightly differently, mapping a conflict requires:

- an astute helicopter view of what is happening and who is involved;
- spiritual insight into possible individual and group idols of the heart (*What do people fear? What do people crave? What are people judging?*) – their impact on God's reputation and the well-being of the community; and
- deliberate, courageous action to map out the conflict as per the definition above.

> **Key perspective:**
> To map conflict in your community is a profoundly prophetic act.

Those who undertake this task need to be people of sensitivity, wisdom, tact, preparation and prayer. They also need to be self-aware. As they map the conflict, the questions they will ask of the parties to the conflict, they also need to ask of themselves. We might also ask: How did the writers of the Old Testament prophetic books, and the apostles of the New, come by their insights into what was happening and who was involved? How did they pick up the spiritual and communal implications? How did they identify the issues and conflicts to map them out so as to know what was needed for healing?

Apart from anything else, they must have *listened* to people's stories and reports about what was happening (given either in person or via letter) to discern the facts, emotions and heart issues.

Listening is a discipline with spiritual roots and implications. Its importance is reiterated throughout scripture:

- it is valuable – *Like an earring of gold... is the rebuke of a wise judge to a listening ear* (Prov 25:12);
- it is patient – *Everyone should be quick to listen, slow to speak and slow to become angry* (Jas 1:19); and
- it is wise – *To answer before listening – that is folly and shame* (Prov 18:13).

Listening takes resolve, attentiveness and grace to let go one's personal judgments. It is a discipline to listen for the emotions and the heart issues behind the facts; for the Spirit's still, small voice amongst the clamour.

Proverbs says: 'The purposes of the human heart are deep waters, but those who have insight draw them out' (20:5). Listening includes being able to draw people out. Everyone involved will have their own story. It is a discipline to slow down sufficiently to listen carefully, and gently ask the questions which will elicit the stories.

Susan Nienaber studied twelve congregations which had come out well on the other side of substantial conflict. She observed one of the most significant keys to their recovery was leaders with good listening skills. She reported that: 'Within the congregation, these leaders maintained this same nonreactive stance. They listened well. They didn't respond defensively, curtly, or disrespectfully. They took time to listen and practiced good empathy.'[106]

> **Key perspective:**
> The art of listening well is a foundational leadership discipline to map conflict effectively.

> **Key advantages** of mapping conflict include:
> - proactively establishing facts in place of conjecture and assumptions;
> - basing response strategies on accurate information;
> - minimising the risk of conflict escalating;
> - building trust and mutual respect;
> - demonstrating care; and
> - providing a secure foundation from which to move forward.

Listening is an essential discipline for leaders who set out to map conflict. It opens the chance to weigh up and if need be to acknowledge the validity of the concerns raised. Refusing to listen closes this opportunity and places people at odds with their community.

6.8 *Master-plan the conflict – looking around*

Master-planning a conflict is the highest strategic level of responsibility leaders carry to lead their community through a conflict. It is about taking a step back from the fracas of the conflict itself to plan what to do overall. This type of planning follows in the footsteps of the New Testament apostles such as when they successfully navigated the deep theological divide between different groups at the Jerusalem Council (Acts 15:1-35).

This eighth stay-at-the-HELM principle for navigating conflict in Christian communities focuses leaders' attention on their mandate to:
- lead strategically in regard to the conflict;
- decide how the conflict will be managed on a practical basis, that is, will leaders:
  - manage the conflict themselves;
  - engage skilled people from within their community; or
  - engage outside assistance?
- develop a comprehensive master-plan setting out a suite of practical measures; and, having done so,
- act decisively and confidently without losing overall leadership focus or organisational purpose.

> **Key perspective:**
> The HELM principles outlined in this chapter are designed to serve as a basis, a framework, to master-plan a conflict.

Key advantages of master-planning the conflict based on the steady-at-the-HELM principles include:
- a strategic leadership focus that holds firm for the whole community;
- decisive and confident action to stem the conflict;
- protection of organisational purposes; and
- a process for the community to begin to heal.

6.9 *Summary*

The eight stay-at-the-HELM principles provided here will assist leaders chart a course through conflict. It is a resource to engender stable, strategic leadership. It can guide biblical thinking, decision-making and action. It will allow leaders *to stay steady at the helm* as the title of this book indicates.

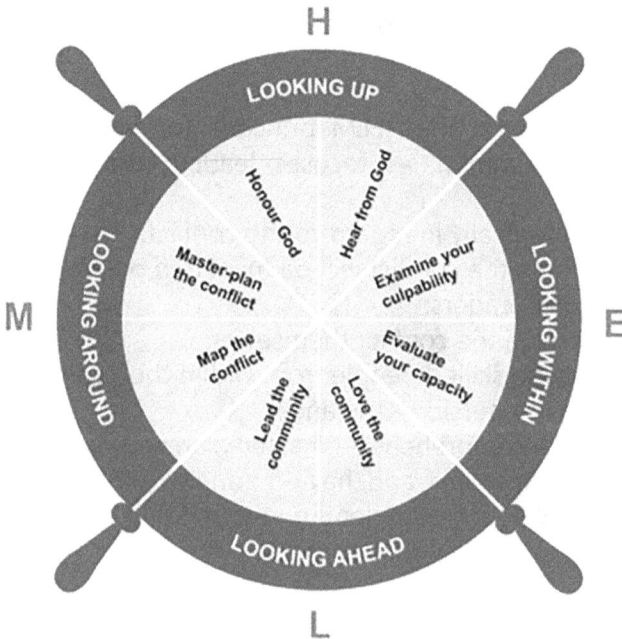

FIGURE 8: THE HELM

Questions for reflection and discussion

1) Which elements of the stay-at-the-HELM framework resonate with you?
2) Which elements do you resist?
3) How would this framework help Steve and Lyall's board in responding to the sample questions at the beginning of this chapter?
4) How comfortable are you with how your leadership honours God?
5) What impact does conflict have on your group's purpose, vision and unity?
6) What are the likely implications of not addressing the conflict in a biblically faithful manner?
7) Discuss some 'Key perspectives' from this chapter.

In Part 1 of this book we explored perspectives and principles around conflict and the questions: *Who will I be? Who will we be?*

We now turn to Part 2 to give these principles legs. Here you will find the practical strategies (anticipated throughout Part 1) to help you answer the questions: *What will I do? What will we do?*

They are unpacked under the eight elements of the HELM framework to help leaders stay steady at the helm as they navigate community conflict to the glory of God.

74 Harris, R. Laird, Archer, Gleeson L. Jr., Waltke, Bruce K., Editors, *Theological Wordbook of the Old Testament*, Moody Press, Chicago, 1980, Volume 1, p. 427.

75 As the early believers did in Psidian, Antioch; after hearing from Paul and Barnabas they 'honoured the word of the Lord' (Acts 13:48).

76 As Paul and Barnabas in the conflict recounted by Luke in Acts 15:3ff.

77 Brubaker, *Promise and Peril*, quoting Kraybill, founding director of Mennonite Conciliation Service, p. 109.

78 Van Yperen, *Making Peace*, p. 80.

79 Goertzen, *Understanding*, quoting Eugene B. Habecker, *The Other Side of Leadership* (Wheaton, IL: Victor Books, 1987, p. 99) p. 46.

80 Rev Ray Galvin in a sermon Auckland, New Zealand District Law Society Annual Church Service, 1 February 1991.

81 Rom 12:19-20; Heb 10:30; Jas 5:7-9.

82 Barthel, Tara Klena & Edling, David V., *Redeeming Church Conflicts: Turning Crisis into Compassion and Care*, Baker Books, 2012, p. 44.

83 Ibid, p. 223.

84 Mt 18; Mk 9:33ff; Lk 22:24ff.

85 See Rom 12:9, 10, 12, 16; 1 Cor 13; Gal 6: 1; Eph 4:2-3; Phil 2:3-5; Col 3:12, 14.

86 Wright, *Relational Leadership*, p. 154.

87 Ibid p. 102.

88 Goertzen, *Understanding*, (quoting Eugene B. Habecker), p. 36.

89 See section 2.4 above, Ez 14:1ff.

90 See 1 Cor 5, 6:1-8; Gal 6:1.

91 Steinke, *Congregational Leadership*, quoting Daniel Goleman (*Primal Leadership: Realize the Power of Emotional Intelligence* (Boston: Harvard Business School Press, 2002), p. 172) p. 73.

92 Sande, *The Peacemaker*, p. 126ff.

93 See Prov 4:23; Mt 7:1-5; Lk 12:56-58; Rom 7:14-25; 1 Cor 11:28; Gal 6:1-4.

94 See Rom 12:2; Gal 6:7-10; Eph 5:10; Phil 1:10; 2 Tim 2:22-24.

95 Mitchell, *Paul*, p. 165.

96 Ibid p. 168.

97 Martin Luther King's Acceptance Speech, on the occasion of the award of the Nobel Peace Prize in Oslo, December 10, 1964. https://www.nobelprize.org/prizes/peace/1964/king/26142-martin-luther-king-jr-acceptance-speech-1964/

98 Wright, *Relational Leadership*, p. 18.

99 Barthel and Edling, *Redeeming*, p. 151.

100 Cf. the parable of the lost sheep in Luke 15:1-7.

101 Interestingly, Matthew positions this teaching immediately before the section on the *procedure* to specifically address conflict between Christ's followers.

102 Steinke, *Congregational Leadership*, p. 94. (Copyright 2006 © by the Alban Institute. Reproduced with permission of the Licensor through PLSclear.)

103 Wright, *Relational Leadership*, p. 18f.

104 Poirier, *Peacemaking Pastor*, p. 108.

105 Ostrower, Francie & Stone, Melissa M., *Governance: Research Trends, Gaps, and Future Prospects* in W.W. Powell & Steinberg (Eds.), *The Non-profit Sector: A Research Handbook* – 2nd edition, New Haven: Yale University Press, 2006, p.621.

106 Nienaber, Susan, *Leading into the Promised Land: Lessons Learned From Resilient Congregations*, posted on July 13, 2006 by Alban Institute p. 3 https://alban.org/archive/leading-into-the-promised-land-lessons-learned-from-resilient-congregations/ NB: Nienaber provides a disclaimer to her findings, *Although the sample of churches is too small to determine statistical significance, we believe*

the information is important enough to warrant sharing at this time. Additional follow-up studies will be necessary. p. 6.

PART 2

STRATEGIES

Part 2 will equip you with practical strategies for:

- navigating a community-wide conflict (chapter 7);
- navigating other types of conflict (chapters 8 – 11); and
- navigating towards ongoing biblical peacemaking in your community (chapter 12).

Billabong Before & After School Care (affectionately known as Billabong Care) had a long and proud history of community service providing care for children out of regular school hours. Under its congregational governance model, the Billabong Community Church members had voted to establish this as a ministry to connect with young families.

At the outset, the church council doubled as the governing committee for Billabong Care. However, with the need to secure government funding and comply with ever-increasing regulatory requirements (and not to mention the extra workload), the church leaders recommended that Billabong Care be restructured as a separate legal entity with its own board.

The church membership agreed on the condition Billabong Care's constitution stipulated it was a 'ministry of Billabong Community Church'. Further, that members of its board must include the senior minister of the church, persons who were full members of the church community, and one representative from the district who was a Christian.

Additionally, the constitution provided for the minister of Billabong Church to act as a part-time chaplain to Billabong Care. There was also to be a group known as the 'Friends of Billabong Care,' a fund-raising committee comprising interested church members and parents who used the service. Although not explicitly stated, the church community understood that the Team Leader employed to carry out Billabong Care's ministry must always be a Christian.

For a minimal rent, the church entered into a ten-year lease with Billabong Care with options to renew. This lease was granted, once again, to comply with regulatory requirements and demonstrate separation of the governance arrangements between the church and Billabong Care.

With the outreach potential of this ministry in mind, over the years, the church embarked on many strategies to connect with parents and children from the community who used Billabong Care. However, there had been a minimal response, and most of the strategies had been discontinued.

Eventually, this led to much soul-searching among the church people. To their dismay, two distinct groups emerged. For some, 'ministry of the church' continued to be understood in purely evangelistic terms – to connect with parents and children to influence them with the gospel and draw them into the church.

For others, however, including those who comprised the preschool board, 'ministry of the church' now meant an unconditional service to the local community – a well-run, low-fee enterprise with Christian beliefs and values. The 'Friends of Billabong Care' group also understood this as the purpose – a highly valued community asset with the minister of the church as the part-time chaplain.

The tensions generated by these different perspectives came to a head when the board of Billabong Care appointed a Team Leader who, although sympathetic, did not share the church's beliefs. The Billabong Care board argued they had not been able to secure the services of a suitably qualified Christian person for the role. Some church members supported the appointment. Others trenchantly opposed it, fearing they had lost control of their vital ministry. There were many comments like:

> How are we going to reach the community now? What is the board thinking? We are not interested in just providing a service to the community. There are other groups around who will do that. So, if there is nothing more to it, perhaps we should close it down.

Several also noted the church had all but given up valuable facilities for minimal rent. They also observed that under the lease, the church had to maintain, at its own cost, the buildings in which Billabong Care operated. This was the case even though the childcare service was enjoying a healthy financial surplus.

The church council, itself divided, wrestled with the implications. What should it do with this division? Should it appoint some of its members to respond, or let the matter lie? Should it work to replace the board of Billabong Care? If so, how might this be done? Moreover, what about the childcare service's strong following in the district? How would the parents respond? Perhaps the church could engage consultants or mediators. What might happen if the local press became involved? Should the council seek legal advice?

Storm clouds gathered. A member of the church gave formal notice to move a motion at the next quarterly church business meeting:

> *That Billabong Care shall remain a vital evangelistic ministry of the church and that the Team Leader shall always be a Christian. If the board of Billabong Care does not replace the Team Leader with a Christian person within six months of this meeting, Billabong Care will be obliged to pay market rent for the church property they are occupying.*

All the different elements of Billabong Church and Billabong Care:

- the entire community
- individuals and small groups
- top-tier governance leaders
- senior executive leaders

were in the grip of a grave confrontation driven mainly by differences in:

- beliefs and doctrine

with the uncomfortable possibility of involving:

- outside professionals
- the media, and
- lawyers.

----------oo0Ooo----------

Leaders trying to navigate a conflict like the one above will have their talents and patience sorely tested. They will need to utilise all their God-given gifts of insight, discernment and courage. Moreover, as Part 1 indicates, they will be well placed to safely navigate the situation confronting them if they have a sound understanding of conflict and a good grasp of the relevant biblical principles.

Think for a moment of the person at the helm of an ocean-going vessel. They will always be:

- *looking up* at the weather and listening to the forecasts;
- *looking over* the charts and the performance of the crew and ship;
- *looking ahead* to the immediate concerns, the course, other ships; and
- *looking around* the vessel's environment to ensure the intended passage keeps all onboard safe and adequately cared for.

So also, in deciding on strategies to navigate a community conflict well, leaders will always be thinking and looking about in several directions at any point in time.

> **Key perspectives:**
> The practical strategies here in Part 2, which arise directly from the eight HELM principles developed in chapter 6, are not necessarily designed to be followed sequentially. They are a guide only, not a definitive checklist or statement of 'do's-and-don'ts' which will guarantee success. That said, leaders are encouraged to aim for a holistic approach covering all eight areas over time.[107]
>
> The strategies are designed to provide areas of primary focus to kick-start dependable, immediate, high-level leadership action in the face of conflict. They can also inform discussions about further steps needed in the context. They have been devised as an organised, relevant 'ready-reference' to embolden and equip leaders to:
> - remain *steady at the helm* without faltering or losing precious time;
> - be seen by their community to be doing so; and
> - appreciate the scope of the leadership context where actions are needed.

Undoubtedly, other actions, apart from those included here, will also be relevant from time to time. As each community conflict is unique, leaders need to determine their priorities and exercise their judgment.

How to use chapters 7 to 11

Chapters 7 to 11 give legs to the eight HELM principles outlined in chapter 6. Therefore, chapter 6 is foundational reading for chapters 7 to 11.

To recap: the eight HELM principles are:

- Honour God
- Hear from God
- Examine your culpability
- Evaluate your capacity
- Love your community
- Lead your community
- Map the conflict
- Master-plan the conflict

Chapter 7 focuses on conflict affecting an entire community. The strategies provided in this chapter are then *summarised* in table form in Part 3, Resources, 16.8(a) for quick reference. This resource also prioritises the strategies into those which are potentially *high priority* and those which may have a *medium priority.*

Many of the strategies outlined in chapter 7 will also be relevant to the other types of conflict considered in chapters 8 to 11.

Therefore, chapter 7 is foundational reading for chapters 8 to 11.

Chapter 8 addresses conflict between individuals and small groups.
Chapter 9 addresses conflict between top-tier governance leaders.
Chapter 10 addresses conflict involving the senior executive.
Chapter 11 addresses conflict involving beliefs or doctrine.

---

[107] The practical strategies outlined here in Part 2 are informed by my own experience as a leader, trained church consultant and mediator; the expertise and insights of other leaders and practitioners with whom I have worked and who have been discussion companions on the journey; my investigation into the practice of leaders internationally; and, the dependable, counter-cultural logic and leadership wisdom offered in scripture.

THE ENTIRE COMMUNITY 7

In this chapter, we look at practical strategies for leaders:
- **to remain steady at the helm when conflict impacts the *entire* community; and**
- **to give legs to the eight HELM principles when responding to this type of conflict.**

Note: this chapter assumes the reader will have read chapter 6.

The story of Billabong Community Church and Billabong Care (which opens Part 2) has all the hallmarks of a conflict impacting an entire community, including:
- an unsettled membership;[108]
- governance issues;
- senior executive leadership tensions;
- differences in core beliefs and values;
- reputational risks within the district; and
- actions aimed to threaten.

Encouragingly, the seeds of health always lie somewhere within a community. Renewal may often germinate in unexpected quarters. It will inevitably arise amongst those who seek to follow

Christ wholeheartedly, be they leaders, followers, the young, the elderly, volunteers, the newly connected or long-time members. Wherever people live humble and obedient lives, there is an opportunity for resilience and health. This is the case even in dire circumstances, such as those of Billabong Community Church and Billabong Care.

As we have mentioned, in 2005 Susan Nienaber studied twelve congregations who had experienced substantial conflict in their communities and emerged well. All had seen high levels of adverse impact – 'loss of staff, a sense of betrayal, erosion of trust, loss of focus on the... mission and purpose, burnout, exhaustion, and feelings of demoralization...'. Nienaber concluded her study by observing that transformation was not achieved by the 'problem-focused, deficit-based language and theories' so often seen in situations rocked by conflict. Rather:

> At the core of [resilient churches'] success in bouncing back from their conflict... lies a simple yet profound decision: They chose to heal. They made an intentional decision to get healthy and focused their efforts toward that goal. They saw an opportunity in their crisis, and they acted upon it... What this tells me is that any congregation has the capacity to be resilient.[109]

God continually calls his communities to that place of healing.

To this end, here are suggested strategies under each of the eight HELM principles for leading well in the context of *substantial conflict involving the entire community.*

7.1 **H**onour God – looking up

> **Note – see section 6.1 for:**
> - the *theory* lying behind the strategies in this section; and
> - the *advantages* of adopting them.

Leadership goals:
- lift our gaze from the tensions to God as our source of strength and hope; and
- purposefully and communally commit to letting God be God during conflict.

Focus question:

How can you honour and please God in your leadership throughout this conflict?

(a) *Agree that honouring God will undergird all you do in leading this conflict*

Each of us as leaders will likely, at some deep level and as our best selves, desire to honour God when responding to conflict. However, there is a danger in leaving this as an assumed private reality. How easy it is to default to our instinctive norms (as outlined in chapters 4 and 5) and, in doing so, lose sight of honouring God. So, at the outset, find ways relevant to your context to highlight and reinforce this shared desire. These might include:
- developing and signing an agreed statement;
- physically standing together as an act of commitment; or
- passing a formal resolution such as *'We agree that we will seek to honour and please God in all we do to address this conflict'.*

(b) *Practise honouring God in your meetings*

With the emotions conflict generates, even for leaders, meetings can become tense, focussed and overly formal – or completely chaotic. It can be wise, therefore, to practise spiritual disciplines within leadership meetings. So consider taking a proactive

approach to incorporate spiritual disciplines. Options could include:
- planned and spontaneous times of praise and worship;
- seeking guidance from God's word; or
- other practices designed to honour God that reflect your community traditions, such as communion, laying on of hands, fasting.

(c) *Pray throughout*

As we have seen, scripture exhorts God's people to pray in times of conflict. So:
- plan and carry through an ongoing prayer strategy, for the leadership group and for the community, which will remain in place while leading through conflict; and
- create safe prayer spaces, based on agreed covenants of attitudes and behaviours, for those on opposite sides of the conflict to hear each other's hearts (safety ensures these do not disintegrate into occasions for point scoring, judging or emotional outbursts).

Prayer strategies might include:
- incorporating prayer into meetings;
- gathering specifically to pray; or
- taking creative approaches, e.g. '...arrow prayers, meditative prayer on scripture, prayers of confession, intercession, lament, imaginary prayer, contemplative prayer, and so on'.[110]

(d) *Review*

Throughout the conflict, check-in with each other to ask if God has been and is being honoured during your meetings and by your actions. Also, reiterate that you desire to continue to honour God through your decisions and activities.

7.2 **H**ear from God – looking up

> **Note – see section 6.2 for:**
> - the *theory* lying behind the strategies in this section; and
> - the *advantages* of adopting them.

Leadership goals:
- ensure, at the outset, you take time to allow God, not your instinctive responses to conflict, to shape your leadership; and
- hear and put into practice God's principles for healthy leadership throughout the conflict.

Focus question:

What does God want to teach us and our community about responding to conflict at this time?

A note of caution

- Due to divergent theological understandings, history and culture, different groups may process how they hear from God differently.
- Individuals may also approach the question of how to 'hear from God' in different ways.
- Even within a theologically homogenous Christian community, differences of approach will, in all probability, exist among leaders.
- In times of heightened emotions, the capacity to think clearly can be clouded so that 'hearing from God' can become problematic, with the potential we can even tend to read into our 'hearing' what we want to hear.
- Further, no one individual, and indeed no group, will ever be fully aware of *all* the facts of a situation at any given point, nor be able to hear from God perfectly.
- God's adversary, the evil one, may seek to confuse, to take advantage of a group's theological vulnerability, or may tempt them to claim personal, inside knowledge of God's voice.
- Conflict may become a battleground where beliefs expressed and heart responses do not reflect God's truth.

So, in light of these realities:

- Avoid being dogmatic.
- Remain humble and teachable, prepared to change perspective where needed.
- Test everything; check the validity of a single individual's conclusions against the wisdom of the group.
- Revisit initial conclusions about what you or others claim to have heard from God against biblical understandings and any additional information.

(a) *Decide you will use the principles of the Bible as your primary foundation for addressing this conflict*

In most Christian communities, the constitution, or some other foundational document, such as a statement of beliefs, will contain a declaration affirming the place of scripture in the community's life. It is imperative you take the opportunity to consider what this statement means for the current conflict. Historically, your community's leaders may not have addressed conflict using biblical principles as their modus operandi. If this has been the case, the current conflict provides an opportunity to understand the requirements of God's word in this area afresh.

It would not be surprising to assume that everyone wants to respond to the conflict in obedience to God's word. However, experience shows that in a high-level conflict, people are often not ready to respond biblically. Given this and the power of instinctive responses to conflict (covered in chapters 4 and 5), it may not be wise to simply assume your community will want to be obedient to scripture.

So, at the outset, find ways relevant to your context to highlight and cement your commitment to scripture through this time. These might include:
- developing and signing an agreed statement;
- physically standing together as an act of commitment; or
- passing formal resolutions, for example...

We affirm the place of the Bible in the life of our community as set out in our community's [include here the name of your community's foundational document(s).]

We agree that in all we do to address this conflict, we will use the principles of the Bible as our primary foundation and guide. All strategies and resources we decide to use in addressing this conflict will also be consistent with biblical principles.

As we learn more about what God requires of us as leaders in responding to conflict in our community, we will review our strategies and decisions in light of our further understanding of what the Bible requires.

(b) *Hold a leaders' retreat*

Collective discernment is essential in times of conflict. Rarely does one individual alone have access to the whole counsel of God. Leaders are therefore wise to seek God's guidance as a group for the way forward. A retreat provides you with the opportunity to slow down, listen to God's voice together and gain perspective.

In planning a leaders' retreat, consider the following questions:

1) *Should we invite an outside facilitator, familiar with biblical principles on leading well through conflict, to lead the retreat?*
2) *What might the programme include to help us hear from God?* Suggestions could be:
    - worship and teaching from scripture;
    - guided individual reflection;
    - group reflection;
    - time to repent; and
    - discussion on selected matters from this chapter
    - other...
3) *Does each person need to prepare individually in advance, and if so, how?* What are relevant reading materials available on leading through and resolving conflict according to scripture?

A note of caution

- If the conflict is of a high level and the leaders are involved somehow, holding a leaders' retreat is likely to be counter-productive.
- In such circumstances, only hold a retreat under the recommendation and supervision of an external consultant.

(Note: Section 7.4(a) lists the different categories of conflict tension. The detailed *characteristics* of each category are provided in *Tool for assessing the category of conflict tension* to be found in Part 3, Resources, 16.4(a). Experience shows that leaders will more than likely be parties to the conflict at category 3 or above.)

(c) *Teach the principles of biblical peacemaking to leaders, the conflicted parties and the community*

A time of dedicated teaching provides an opportunity for everyone to slow down, hear from God and reflect on what is occurring. It allows people to reframe the situation as a holistic opportunity to grow and move away from the competitive, win-at-all-costs mentality.

In designing the teaching, consider the following questions:

1) *Should we utilise the services of a trainer not connected to the community?*
   The advantage of this is that it ensures impartiality. An impartial trainer can head off any perception of agenda-setting. Such a person will reduce the possibility of people imagining they can 'read-between-the-lines' about the present conflict or believe the leaders are targeting anyone specifically.
2) *What might be covered in this training?* Options include:
   For Leaders
   Theory:
   - An overview of foundational biblical principles on resolving conflict.
   - The origins and nature of conflict in Christian organisations.

- The eight biblical HELM principles for navigating community conflict.
- The influences affecting the responses of leaders to community conflict, both individually and as a group.

Practice:
- Organisational structure and processes for addressing conflict already in place within the policies and procedures of the community.
- Potential strategies arising from the eight HELM principles.
- Processes that may be used to address conflict.
- Options for the ongoing study of biblical principles for navigating conflict which the leadership group could undertake individually and together.

Resources:
- An outline of the kinds of resources available (such as online, books, the relevant peak body, counselling, mediation, consultancy – examples are listed in the bibliography).

For protagonists and the community
- Understanding the origins and nature of conflict.
- Understanding our typical responses to conflict.
- Foundational principles for biblical peacemaking.
- The role and responsibility of leaders during times of conflict.
- The role and responsibility of parties to a conflict as well as the role and responsibilities of the members of the community.
- The biblical norms of behaviour to which the community is called to adhere to in the situation.
- Processes that may be used to address conflict.
- Responding to questions found at the end of the various chapters in Ken Sande's book *The Peacemaker: A Biblical Guide to Resolving Personal Conflict.*
- Some available relevant resources (online, books, peak body, counselling, mediation, consultancy) are listed in the bibliography and in Part 3, Resources, 16.9(f).

3) *How do we respond if people react negatively to the idea of training?*
   - *'We don't need the teaching.'*
   - *'We are already aware of what the Bible teaches.'*
   - *'We have done Matthew 18 to death.'*
   - *'We have to get moving on this.'*

This is not surprising. People don't know what they don't know. In responding to these objections, leaders could highlight that training provides a key opportunity to hear from God. Additionally, training gives people the opportunity to receive new biblical peacemaking insights. Further, leaders may emphasise that training gives people a depth of understanding and a common language around conflict. Training also creates time and space for emotions to settle and God to move in people's hearts as they hear him.

A note of caution

- Leaders have been known to undertake a teaching event believing that this *alone* will solve the mounting problems in their community. At other times, the training event has been conducted to divert attention from the issues or even to mask the conflict.
- Leaders, therefore, need to honestly examine and discuss their motivation when scheduling conflict resolution training. Training alone rarely solves the presenting issues, but it can help restore community health when undertaken with other strategies.
- If the person chosen to lead the training is involved in the conflict or is perceived as taking a particular side, the training won't achieve its purposes. People will either avoid or ignore the teaching if they believe the teacher is not neutral. Additionally, if someone else attempts to teach similar things at a later stage, people are likely to criticise it and declare it ineffective because of the previous experience.

(d) *Settle on a God-honouring vision or end-goal for the outcome*

As we have seen, agreeing on a God-honouring vision for the outcome of the conflict can lift people's horizons and give them a picture of hope for the future.[111]

The questions you might ask in this context include:
- *How do we hear from God and determine this vision or end goal?*
- *Why would such a vision be worthwhile?*
- *What will our community look like at the end of this conflict?*
- *What do we want our children to observe in the way we handle this conflict?*
- *How do we want this time of conflict, and our role in it, to be remembered in the future?*

(e) *Encourage leaders to engage in a time of private spiritual retreat*

The questions *leaders* might ask here include:
- *Why would a private retreat be worthwhile?*
  It would be a time to:
  - draw near to God through a time of reading, reflection and prayer;
  - gain perspective by slowing down;
  - come to grips with some of the concepts developed in this book; and
  - recognise and settle internal tensions, destructive attitudes and unhelpful emotions, especially concerning fellow leaders and any protagonists in the conflict.
- *What could be included in a private retreat?*
  It could include times of:
  - *Honouring God* through worship, reading his word, remembering the birth, death and resurrection of his Son, thanking him for all his benefits.
  - *Examining one's self* by:
    - identifying the influences which shape the meaning an individual leader attributes to a conflict;
    - naming the emotions which result (see the *Tool for identifying your feelings* in Part 3, Resources, 16.3(a) for a list of feeling words);
    - asking the tough questions listed at the end of various chapters in this book especially chapter 2 for this context;
    - repenting of any sin, (e.g. Have I lost confidence in God's power? Have I become bitter? Am I

entertaining hostile thoughts? Am I engaging in vengeful behaviour?); and

- identifying one's conflict resolution style (see chapter 4.1(b) and *Tools for assessing your conflict resolution style* found in Part 3, Resources, 16.2(b)).

- *Affirming your relationship* with the Lord by acknowledging him as your helper and the one in whom your security lies in times of trouble.

- *Affirming your love for God's people* by resolving to exercise healthy leadership throughout this conflict.

- *Will we hold one another to account for the outcomes of a personal spiritual retreat?*
Being willing to be accountable is a hallmark of maturity. Accountability:

  - keeps us on track as we bring things into the light;
  - strengthens the confidence others have in us; and
  - allows for the learning each has gleaned through the personal retreat to enrich the broader discussion with the whole group.

A personal and group challenge:
It may be beneficial during the stress and discouragement of a conflict to be a little creative. Attempt some spiritual practices which have either been neglected or not generally practised as part of your tradition. The spiritual disciplines of meditating, fasting, extended time spent alone with God, silence, and retreats are well developed in the literature of many Christian traditions. Now may be a great time to explore these, extend your boundaries, and open new spaces that can lead to fresh perspectives.

(f) *Identify the preferred conflict resolution style of each leader, your leadership group and your community*

As we have observed, taking time to explore the preferred conflict resolution style of both the individual leaders in your group and the group as a whole can enliven their relationship with our Lord, allowing him to show us where we are most vulnerable. It can foster insight and wisdom to help us understand ourselves and others more deeply. It can strengthen our leadership capacity and expand our contribution to leadership discussions.

A useful tension-releasing exercise is to have leaders identify their conflict resolution style. There are *Tools for assessing your conflict resolution style* to assist you in Part 3, Resources, 16.2(b). Having done that, discuss how the group you are part of, and then your community, naturally respond to conflict events (their instinctive norm). (See section 5.1(a) and (c).)

7.3 **E**xamine your culpability – looking within

> **Note – see section 6.3 for:**
> - **the *theory* lying behind the strategies in this section; and**
> - **the *advantages* of adopting them.**

Leadership goals:
- gain self-awareness;
- face truth; and
- model a healthy leadership culture.

Focus question:

How might we, as leaders, both individually and collectively, have contributed to this conflict?

(a) *Undertake an 'attitude and culpability check' as individuals and as a leadership group*

As we have seen, leaders bring a variety of backgrounds and responses to any situation of conflict, both individually and collectively. Therefore, healthy leaders need to evaluate whether they hold any level of culpability, large or small, for this conflict. This is the time to take stock and look in the mirror, as individuals and as a leadership group.

Undertaking this work provides excellent potential for a God-honouring outcome. In addition, we may be surprised by what we discover about our mindset and the effect of our behaviours and decisions on others.

So, we might ask of *ourselves and others* in our leadership group the questions listed at the end of chapters 2 and 4 and other questions like these:

- *What actions do we regret taking or not taking in this situation?*
- *What might we be denying, not disclosing, not bringing into the light?*
- *What do we need to hang on to at any cost?*
- *If we put ourselves in the position of any of the parties to the conflict, how would we respond to this leadership group's actions or inactions?*
- *Could others perceive us as being heavy-handed, quick to lay blame, or overly legalistic?*
- *What destructive heart issues do we exhibit as a group? (In answering this question, revisit section 2.6, 'Desires and idols in the hearts of leaders' and section 5.1(f), 'Group idols of the heart'.)*
- *Are we making demands of any individual or group; judging any individual or group; punishing any individual or group?*
- *Are we viewing the parties to this conflict as enemies or as brothers and sisters in Christ?*
- *What language have we been using to describe the parties? That is, have we honoured God in what we have said?*
- *Do we fear losing control? If so, what does this imply?*
- *What other fears might we have as leaders?*
- *What feelings debilitate us: fear; frustration; resentment; anger; concerns; disappointments; anxiety...? (See the Tool for identifying your feelings in Part 3, Resources, 16.3(a) for a list of feeling words.)*
- *What might be our response to the statement: if only we could..., then we would be able to move ahead? What does our response say about us as a group of leaders?*
- *Where are we overreacting, underreacting or reacting wisely to this situation?*[112]

While everything is spiritual, self-awareness of our specific *spiritual* responsibilities *as a group* of leaders might also lead us to ask:

- *How or where do we see God in this situation?*
- *Is sin involved either as a result of actions taken or not taken?*

- *What does God wish to do in me, in us, as we lead through this conflict?*
- *Do we expect God will work to his glory?*
- *Are we still able to offer praise and thanks and mean it?*
- *Have we, as a group, been praying about the situation? What have been the specific requests?*
- *Are we as leaders able to say we trust God and will continue to trust until the parties have resolved their conflict?*
- *Alternatively, do we see this conflict as frustrating and inconvenient?*
- *What other attitudes might we be exhibiting?*
- *What effect are the issues in this conflict, and the way we are leading through it, having on the organisation's reputation?*
- *How is this conflict affecting our mission?*

A note of caution

- Self-examination is a vital step in maintaining leadership health. That said, we need not become unduly introspective and self-obsessed. It may be wise to begin the 'attitude and culpability check' and then agree to come back to it to avoid the danger of losing confidence.
- If you rate the conflict you are addressing at category 3 or higher, you may not be ready to undertake this 'attitude and culpability check'. So, be guided here by your consultant.

(b) *Admit (confess) and apologise for any identified individual and group failings*

Leaders who admit their culpability in a conflict, and openly apologise, provide a compelling model of mature Christian leadership in their community and beyond. Such a response is a tangible demonstration of humility, vulnerability and trust. It immediately reduces emotion in the community and builds goodwill toward the leaders.

Thus, given your answers to the questions immediately above (in 7.3(a)), how would you respond to the following:
- *What do I, as an individual leader, need to admit to?*

- *What do we, as a group of leaders, need to admit to?*
- *What do we need to apologise for to the protagonists?*
- *What do we need to apologise for to our community?*
- *What do we need to apologise for to one another?*

When leaders confess their failings, their sin, and apologise, they are both confessing to God and their brothers and sisters in Christ whom they have wronged.[113] The process of offering, receiving and pronouncing forgiveness in this context is also vital.[114]

To assist you in dealing with your culpability, see 16.3(b) for *Guidelines for writing a holistic confession and apology* and Part 3, Resources, 16.3(c) for *Guidelines for a confession and apology by leaders.*

(c) *Identify the influences which shape the meaning your leadership group attributes to a conflict event and the emotions which result*

One practical strategy here is to review chapter 5, which addresses this area in detail, then reflect on the questions at the end. This exercise will not only help you understand the influences at work within your leadership groups but could also provide insight into the ways your community has traditionally responded to conflicts.

7.4 **E**valuate your capacity – looking within

> **Note – see section 6.4 for:**
> - **the *theory* lying behind the strategies in this section; and**
> - **the *advantages* of adopting them.**

Leadership goals:
- check whether you are equipped to handle the situation; and
- ensure you are sufficiently well organised to lead the strategy.

Focus question:

What time, skills and resources do we, as leaders, possess to lead our community in resolving this conflict effectively?

(a) *Analyse the strengths, weaknesses, opportunities and risks within your leadership group for resolving this conflict within yourselves*

Many leaders assume they will be the ones to resolve a community conflict. However, that might not be as apparent as you first think. The reason is that beyond a certain point, leaders may quickly find they are out of their depth.

How will you assess this? Many practitioners working in the conflict resolution space classify conflicts according to the following categories:[115]

Category 1: Problem to solve – there is an issue that needs to be addressed

Category 2: Disagreement – there is a mixing of personalities and issues

Category 3: Contest – there are power and win/lose dynamics emerging

Category 4: Fight/Flight – there is intent on getting rid of or punishing others

Category 5: Intractable – there is intent on destroying others; self-righteousness reigns; issues are irrelevant

For a detailed outline of the features of each category, along with pertinent leadership skills and strategies for navigating each category, see Part 3, Resources 16.4(a) *Tool for assessing the category of conflict tension.*

In assessing whether or not you should be navigating a particular conflict, consider at the outset the category of conflict complexity you are dealing with. If you assess the conflict at category 3 or higher, experience demonstrates inevitable failure whenever leaders attempt to manage a conflict themselves. Therefore, for conflict at these categories, you must seek relevant assistance from outside your community.

A note of caution

- Experience shows that:

  If you do not recognise the conflict [category] then it is likely that whatever you do will at best be ineffective and at worst counter-productive. Misjudging the conflict [category] can do more harm than good.[116]

- A staunch refusal to agree to external assistance, or even to assess whether external aid could be helpful, is a red flag in and of itself. Moreover, it is a warning you are probably not well equipped to handle the situation from within yourselves. Remember the adage: *a doctor who treats himself for an ailment has a fool for a physician.*

If you assess the conflict at category 1 or 2, you may consider handling the resolution process yourselves. In making that decision, think about the following:

Consider your leadership group's strengths:
- *Do you have people in your leadership group, or community, who are trained in resolving conflict biblically?*
- *Do the leaders who will manage this conflict have the experience, track record, time and resources to do this well?*

Consider your leadership group's weaknesses:
- *Is your group, or a member of your group, a party in the dispute?*
- *What has been your track record in resolving community conflict by yourselves in the past?*

Consider the opportunities:
- *Who within your wider community may have the skills to help you handle the conflict resolution process?*
- *Could this situation be an opportunity to model healthy conflict resolution strategies that honour God, grow relationship with Jesus, and build community?*

Consider the risks beyond yourselves:

- *What general risks do you see if you decide to address the issues yourselves?*
- *Will the time you need to handle the resolution process yourselves distract you from your community purposes?*

(b) *Assess whether to seek assistance from experts outside the community (sooner rather than later)*

In her research into the factors which led twelve congregations to recover from substantial conflict, Susan Nienaber concluded that a critical factor was leaders who readily sought help. 'They weren't committed to going it alone. They knew that they didn't need to solely trust in their own abilities and willingly took advantage of outside resources...'[117]

Sadly, however, leaders do sometimes miscalculate their own ability to handle the resolution process in-house. An experienced church consultant in Australia estimates that eighty per cent (80%) of the many Christian communities, with whom he had worked, put up their hand for help too late when responding to conflict.[118]

Seeking assistance is never an indication of weakness or failure. On the contrary, it demonstrates a leadership group's maturity. Skilled people are available. Their knowledge and experience provide objective and productive pathways which may never occur to leaders. By drawing on external expertise, leaders can confidently focus on their primary role to lead their community holistically.

The following are examples of the kinds of circumstances when it would be wise to call in external expertise:
- When, as discussed above, the conflict is assessed as level 3 or higher.
- When conflicts emerge that are characterised by such a high level of inherent complexity, leaders find themselves out of their depth or utterly distracted from their primary leadership responsibilities. These situations include those types of conflict addressed separately in chapters 9 (conflict which involves yourselves, the leaders), chapter 10 (conflict which

involves the senior executive leader) and chapter 11 (conflict which involves core beliefs or doctrine).

- When leaders are divided about what they should do.
- When there is suspected ethical or moral misconduct on the part of a senior executive or other significant leaders.

(c) *Clarify who should hold the role of chair of your leadership group during a conflict*

The person who typically chairs a leadership group may or may not be the person to chair the group during a conflict event. He or she may, for example:

- have a conflict of interest;
- be unable to ask the hard questions; or
- lack the experience, gifts or confidence to chair volatile meetings.

The regular chair may be excellent under normal circumstances, but since the role of chair, convenor or recognised contact person of a group of leaders is vital when conflict erupts, consider who is best placed to lead strategically throughout the conflict. Suppose a chair refuses, or is reluctant, to allow a discussion on this issue. In that case, that refusal or reluctance in itself may indicate the person is not the right chair while navigating a conflict in the community. Further, there have been instances where a chair leaves or has left a community whilst retaining the position of chair. Such a person would rarely be the right person to continue leading during a conflict.

The role of chair of a leadership group is vital at all times but especially in periods of conflict. The role includes:

- sensitively keeping meetings on track;
- gently challenging group members about unfitting attitudes and behaviours;
- initiating private sessions to care pastorally or to support leaders who may be struggling;
- holding the group on task to the agreed vision, values, ground rules, strategies and processes, including the eight HELM principles;
- asking the necessary hard questions;

- negotiating difficult community meetings; and
- responding well to difficult people.

It is always beneficial to define the role of the chair in writing.

Conflict of interest

- A conflict of interest occurs when a leader has a divided loyalty, or owes a duty to two different causes or people at the same time due to a relationship the leader has with each of them. This undeclared interest has the potential to adversely affect the decision-making process by the group concerned and may lead to the leader gaining an actual or perceived benefit for themselves or someone close to them (such as a relative). As part of developing healthy governance practices, many organisations cover the situation by formally adopting a conflict of interest policy.
- It is always wise to ask the question, at the beginning of a dispute, whether any of the leaders dealing with the matter have a conflict of interest they should disclose.
- Legal obligations may also require disclosure of conflicts of interest.

(d) *Identify any additional roles which could support the leadership group*

Experience shows that during conflict, it may be helpful to consider additional support for a leadership group. Such support roles might include:
- *a chaplain;*
- *a group researcher;*
- *an accountability person outside the group; or*
- *an expert in the subject area of the conflict.*

The role of a *chaplain* can be beneficial in a situation of high tension. Such a person can offer pastoral care to the leaders and any who find the going particularly perplexing.

As seen in Part 1, there is much to learn about biblical peacemaking. So it can be wise to consider appointing a *researcher* from among your group to continue searching for new insights relevant to managing the dispute. Then, have that person report back on their discoveries and discuss how that might help in the context.

An *accountability* person outside your leadership group can support your resolve to implement your conflict master-plan, and any behavioural standards to which your group has covenanted. (See for example Part 3, Resources, 16.6(b) *Sample community covenant of behaviour.*)

Depending on the nature of the conflict, an external *expert* might be someone who can provide objective commentary based on facts not hitherto understood relating to the issues. Examples of such people might include a human resources consultant, a builder, an accountant, an engineer.

It would also be wise to ensure each role has its own written outline of the group's expectations, including a clause regarding confidentiality.

(e) *Discuss how you as leaders will manage yourselves individually while addressing this conflict*

Navigating conflict as a leader will always be costly. Conflict will take something away from your spirit and your normal *joy-de-vivre*. There are likely to be:

- extra meetings;
- decisions that need to be made which are personally challenging and may affect people you know;
- people who try to triangle you[119] or manipulate you by other similar human psychological responses to keep an upper hand;
- people who criticise you unjustly and trenchantly;
- those who sabotage your strategy when they do not get what they want or feel they are losing control of the situation; and
- times when you cannot publicly provide all the facts you are aware of, and so on.

So, resolve as a group:

As far as we are able, we intend to keep ourselves healthy (spiritually, physically, emotionally and socially) and maintain a sense of humour during the management of this conflict. However, if this conflict develops to a category 3 or above, we may not care for ourselves well. So we will each seek outside professional assistance (for example, a counsellor, mentor, conflict coach) to remain healthy.

7.5 *L*ove the community – looking ahead

> Note – see section 6.5 for:
> - the *theory* lying behind the strategies in this section; and
> - the *advantages* of adopting them.

Leadership goals:
- address whole-of-community needs along with the pastoral needs of individuals, couples, families and other groups within the community; and
- develop strategies to put love into action purposefully throughout the conflict.

Focus question:

How will we model and practise love in our community as a hallmark of our leadership throughout this conflict?

(a) *Resolve to give whole-of-community needs high priority*

It goes without saying, healthy leaders love people as individuals within their community. Nevertheless, in their haste to move the matter forward, leaders can inadvertently overlook their obligation to love the community as a whole. In all substantial conflict involving the whole community, everyone deserves, at the very least, generous and authentic access to:
- timely information (see section 7.6(c) on developing a communication strategy);
- avenues to feel included;
- pathways to seek God-honouring justice;[120] and

- some level of communal ownership of the outcomes.

One of the characteristics of the twelve congregations researched by Susan Nienaber, who recovered from substantial conflict, was the conscious practice of 'putting the congregation first'. The leaders did not view the situation 'as being about their own personal or political agenda. They were not out to be heroes or to gain public recognition...' On the contrary, the community's 'well-being, purpose, and call were most important to them'. This approach led to 'enhanced credibility and trustworthiness' in those leaders. [121]

So, resolve:

We will assess whole-of-community needs as a matter of priority and develop strategies to purposefully address these on an ongoing basis throughout the conflict.

Key perspective:
If people feel excluded or marginalised, they may withhold their consent to the actions they are being requested to take. They may even actively undermine leadership decisions. Thus, leaders must hold the community's needs forefront and centre throughout any conflict.

(b) *Attend to pastoral care*

Pastoral care is of paramount importance because the impact of substantial community-wide conflict rolls outward in an ever-broadening wave through:
- *the primary parties* – the individuals or groups directly involved;
- *the secondary parties* – those individuals or groups indirectly involved who have some alignment or affinity with the primary parties and who are stressed by what has unfolded;
- *the impacted parties* – those who are not aligned but who have been hurt by what has occurred and are confused and uncertain;

- *the third parties* – those who maintain neutrality and retain the capacity to ask the hard questions and influence the initiatives toward health in the community once again;[122]
- *the avoiders* – those who decide not to engage with the problems but still belong to the community; and
- *the newcomers* – those who have recently joined the community and have no connection to the conflict events.

Consider, therefore, the need for pastoral care, especially by those who are the primary, secondary and impacted parties. Questions that will need to be addressed include:

- *What kind of pastoral care is required?*
- *Who will provide the pastoral care?*
- *How will the pastoral care be arranged?*
- *What will be the criteria and the process to enable people to access pastoral care?*
- *What accountabilities will be in place for those who carry out the pastoral care?*
- *What debriefing will be needed for the pastoral carers?*

Reassuring people that the leaders intend pastoral care to be available both during and after the dispute is resolved may prove comforting to many and build trust in the leadership.

> **Key perspective:**
> When Christian communities are in conflict, pastoral care for leaders and members is often lacking. Leaders need, therefore, to commit to being proactive in providing such care.

Surprisingly, it has not always been recognised that spouses of the parties in a conflict are often significantly impacted by what has occurred. Even spouses of the leaders may feel the hurt and weight of the situation.

Invariably, spouses have nowhere to go with their vicarious pain and worrisome feelings. They can find themselves just as anguished, and sometimes more so, than their spouse, who is involved in the process of addressing the conflict. At least the spouse involved has a forum to express their thoughts on the situation and perhaps influence the way forward. However, the spouse on the sidelines has no such platform and is powerless.

Wise leaders will take action to monitor the needs of spouses and offer appropriate care. Teenage and adult children of pastors and other senior leaders involved in community conflict invariably feel the pain of their parents deeply. Wise leaders will also consider their care needs.

In a few cases, one of the parties to the conflict may have a mental illness, psychological issues, be addicted to substances (drugs or alcohol), or be suffering from physical ailments such as dementia or chronic pain. It is beyond the scope of this book to provide detailed suggestions on the ways forward in these cases. There are, however, several basic actions that could assist:

- consult a suitably qualified practitioner to gain insight on an appropriate response;[123]
- engage a support person for such an individual to be present at any conversation relating to the conflict; and
- provide pastoral care.

It is also worth noting that even though someone may suffer in these ways, they will still benefit from hearing God's Word. Never underestimate the power of the gospel message, the comfort of knowing God's love and the relief of being forgiven by Jesus.

(c) *Offer professional counselling*

The hurts from the situation can go so deep that people may benefit from being referred out to professional counselling. Such referral could be for an individual, or for a group that finds itself on the same side of the conflict. It is important to determine upfront whether the organisation will pay for professional counselling. As with pastoral care, providing access to professional counselling, both during the conflict and following its resolution, will not only go a long way to reassuring and healing those affected but also to building confidence in your leadership.

(d) *Visit any who have become detached, drifted away or left as a statement of grievance*

In most conflicts of a substantial nature, there will be some who:

- decide to move on;
- resign their membership;
- stay away until things 'blow over'; or
- become detached and irregular in their connection, just watching from the sidelines.

It is vital to determine a strategy here. People left to drift can be lost, not only to the community but, more importantly, to their faith. Their ongoing connection is as essential for the well-being of the whole community as it is for their wellbeing. Leaders must hold the community together during times of conflict rather than allowing it to devolve into an unloving and disillusioned collection of disconnected individuals.

Meeting with such people to provide both care and information as appropriate could be a make-or-break moment for their spiritual and emotional welfare. The tone leaders set in this context will be vital to the outcome. Love calls for reaching out, respect and openness. People who are drifting need to be loved and feel loved, as much as those in the thick of the conflict.

Generally, it is best to conduct this type of conversation in pairs, as a matter of probity and as a check and balance for information given and received. The information gained from such visits may also provide clues to help leaders protect others who are also drifting. (See Part 3, Resources, 16.5(a), for a *Sample outline of a conversation with a community member* who is beginning to drift due to a community conflict.)

(e) *Agree on what to say to new people who arrive*

New people may arrive and wish to join a community in the middle of a conflict. The person might be the latest staff member or director, or someone exploring membership in a Christian community. Such people bring with them all the hopes and dreams of a fresh beginning and new relationships. They could well be leaving a previous community having experienced some difficulty, or perhaps even conflict. How do you want them to hear about the conflict in your organisation? Via the grapevine or directly from you, the leaders?

It is wise for your leadership group to be prepared for this eventuality and have a settled form of words to explain what is happening. Having a clear strategy, a vision, a set of values in place to communicate to newcomers has positive benefits. It will reassure them that the leaders have a plan and build confidence as they observe the leadership acting with honesty and not trying to hide the truth.

7.6 *Lead the community* – looking ahead

> **Note – see section 6.6 for:**
> - **the *theory* lying behind the strategies in this section; and**
> - **the *advantages* of adopting them.**

Leadership goals:
- preserve community foundational purposes;
- maintain community safety and health;
- sustain community hope for a positive outcome; and
- consolidate and strengthen community trust.

Focus question:

What are the strategies which will maximise the potential for our community to remain organisationally safe, hopeful, healthy and trustful throughout this challenging time?

Conflict in a community involves more than just the parties themselves. It ripples out to affect a great many people not directly involved. While leaders are certainly responsible to both ensure the conflict is addressed, and the parties are cared for, nevertheless the primary leadership responsibility is broader. It is always to look out for the strategic organisational interests and purposes of the whole community. That's what it means to navigate throughout a conflict, to stay steady at the helm.

(a) *Identify relevant organisational documents*

Identifying the group's foundational documents is a crucial step to see if they relate in any way to how you need to lead the community through the conflict at hand.

The Bible, of course, should be one of these, first and foremost. Other foundational documents may include:

- Constitution or similar, such as by-laws: what are the community's core purposes that need to be steadfastly preserved during this conflict? Are there clauses that guide how a conflict is to be addressed? What constitutional objects can we not afford to lose?
- Strategic plan: which elements need to be maintained throughout this time and which can be put on hold until the conflict is resolved?
- Conflict resolution policy: if there is one in place, how can you use it for the current situation?
- Leadership covenant: does one exist, and if so, does it guide you in responding to conflict?
- Statement of beliefs, code of conduct, statement of values, philosophy of ministry, vision or purpose statement, membership pledge: how might these be used?
- Workplace policies: are any of these relevant to the context?

(b) *Confirm community expectations*

In times of significant conflict, it is vital to bring implicit community expectations into the open and consider what is realistic. Of course, many more elements than can be addressed here comprise community expectations. Three obvious examples are the prevailing culture, the organisational context and community values.

If the prevailing culture has been for directors to update community members regularly, and in some detail, the community will naturally expect to be informed about any significant community conflict. Similarly, suppose your organisational context includes membership of a wider group (such as a peak body or denomination). In that case, your community may expect their representatives to be advised or even invited to assist. Finally, how do the stated values of the organisation, if any, determine communal expectations?

Whatever shapes your community's expectations, failing to understand and respond to them can create tension and confusion. Therefore, take the initiative to:
- identify community expectations as carefully as possible;
- accept it is impossible to satisfy all individual and collective expectations;
- consider which expectations you can meet realistically;
- decide what you, as leaders, must, can and will provide to the community; then
- confirm publicly what the community can expect.

Tabling expectations like this will lessen the likelihood of unrest. Moreover, it will clarify what the community can legitimately expect as you navigate the conflict.

(c) *Develop a holistic community communication strategy*

Conflict poisons healthy communication. People may stop or shrink from communicating, or worse, convey selective information supportive of their position and critical of others. Often what is said is poorly worded, incomplete, incorrect, emotive, even provocative. Additionally, the emotional condition of many in the community can inhibit effective communication as people block out what they don't want to hear or misconstrue, or minimise what they do hear.

Consultants observe that when around twenty per cent (20%) of people connected to a community are aware something is amiss, such as a conflict, it is not long before everyone knows.[124]

Leaders in conflicted communities struggle with both extremes in communication. Either:
- they don't communicate (assuming that everything needs to be confidential, or people need to be protected); or
- they disclose too much information or make hasty public judgments (especially when accusations have not yet been proven).

Both approaches only serve to escalate the conflict (not to mention the potential for legal liability). So what are some broad communication guidelines? Consider the following:

- Keep people informed about the issues in general terms, being careful to avoid hasty judgments or revealing confidential information prematurely.
- Outline your strategy to address the conflict.
- Draw people's attention to any relevant foundational documents which will deepen their understanding of what is being done and why.
- Advise how people can appropriately participate.
- Anticipate questions and clarify as much as you can.
- Indicate where they can go for personal help (counsellor, pastor, elder).
- Weigh up the potential legal implications of what you share with the community's need to know.
- Invite people to adhere to any standards of behaviour found in any foundational document.

It is vital for you, as leaders, to take the initiative to communicate early in a conflict.[125] Decide how often you will connect and by what means. Then simply keep on keeping on communicating throughout. It has been well said that 'he who communicates leads.'[126]

> **Key perspective:**
> If the leadership does not communicate, the protagonists in the conflict will do so. Human nature being what it is, the rumour mill will fill any gap in useful and timely information.

Develop a communications plan

The nature of your communications plan will depend on the size and volatility of your context. It will be shaped by the conflict's depth, breadth, and seriousness and the skills available to you. If your community is large and complex, with multiple stakeholders, you may already employ a communications manager. If not, you might consider engaging a professional communications consultant. If you are a small organisation without the resources to hire someone to assist, Part 3, Resources, 16.6(c), provides *Guidelines for developing a holistic communications strategy.*

Involve your consultants/mediators

If you have engaged external consultants or mediators, you will be wise to involve them in crafting communication content and process. Involving them ensures a transparent, 'no surprises' environment where nobody is (even unwittingly) acting at cross purposes or caught off guard.

Tell the positive stories

The account of actions taken by the leaders in the conflict recorded in Acts 15 provides us with a noteworthy insight into their practice. Even as they addressed the conflict, they also told stories of what God had done in and beyond their community (v.12). No doubt this would have greatly encouraged the believers, and provided hope. Telling positive stories can also be a powerful strategy in managing your conflict. Publicising such stories can lift people from grief and despondency to the hope that 'it's not *all* bad around here'! Of course, communicating such stories needs to be done with the right motives in a timely and sensitive manner. It is crucial to avoid being construed as minimising the difficulties or trying to divert attention from them.

(d) Consider appointing a community contact person

When conflicts arise, people in the community may not know who to turn to for information. While parties to a dispute may be communicating with leaders and vice versa, those not directly involved may not be. Instead, they can perceive a vacuum in information, especially if the leadership is slow to communicate publicly.

Therefore, it is helpful to appoint someone who is highly respected to act as a community contact person. There are several benefits to this:
- the community will receive clear information;
- the community will have a safe person with whom to raise concerns and suggestions;

- a contact person can monitor the well-being and prevailing attitudes of the community;
- a contact person can help dispel misunderstanding, especially when leaders intend one thing, but the community hears something else entirely; and
- the contact person can identify uplifting stories and testimonies of what God is currently doing in the community.

A note of caution

- Usually, this contact person would not be part of the leadership group, especially during a high-level conflict (category 3 and above). The reason for this is that leaders will often be involved in the conflict. Therefore their attempts to communicate may not be trusted.
- If you have engaged a consultant who has put in place a trusted 'oversight team', this group will generally take the place of a community contact person.

(e) *Secure communal commitment to a covenant of behaviour*

Section 6.2(c), which dealt with what God values, posed the question: *imagine what your community would be like if the values you adopted during conflict were the manifestation of God's values.*

As noted in Part 1, conflict can elicit behaviours that do not honour God, others or ourselves – what the Bible calls sin. This is not only true for those directly involved in a dispute; it is also likely to occur across a whole community when it is under stress. Sinful behaviour can occur in meetings, in casual conversations, and via social media.

Section 6.2(c) also noted that committing to agreed values during conflict can create an environment conducive to a positive outcome. In a more settled time in the organisation's life, the community may well have developed a values' statement. As values translate into actions, this statement may also have set out agreed behavioural standards generally. If so, this will be immediately useful in the current conflict context.

However, if no statement exists or what you have does not immediately help you, you may be assisted by the *Sample community covenant of behaviour* provided in Part 3, Resources, 16.6(b). Such a covenant may be useful across the whole community or for subgroups of the community most impacted by the conflict. It aims to not only reflect the values of your community but, quintessentially, to reflect the fruit of the Spirit. An agreement can be secured by:

- developing and signing an agreed written Covenant of Behaviour;
- having people physically stand in solidarity at a community meeting as an act of commitment to uphold the behaviours identified; or
- passing a formal resolution such as:
  We agree that we will abide by the following Covenant of Behaviour in all we do to address this conflict.

(f) *Decide what to do when people breach agreed community standards of behaviour*

Naturally, adopting a *Covenant of Behaviour* will not guarantee good behaviour, nor will it necessarily change people's hearts. However, it will remind them of their obligations to one another in a community under God, and provide a benchmark against which they may be called to account when they breach its terms.

Acting in these contexts takes courage and decisiveness. Leaders will need to ask themselves what calling people to account looks like. Will it, for example, be as simple as a gentle conversation or as intense as disciplinary action? As difficult as it is to hold people to account, it is worth considering that whatever you tolerate, you will get more of – failing to act usually results in people repeating behaviours that reinforce an unhealthy culture.

Wise and responsible community leaders will be attuned to breaches of community values and initiate relevant responses, including calling people to repentance, confession and forgiveness, to maintain trust and interpersonal respect.

7.7 **M**ap the conflict – looking around

> *Note – see section 6.7 for:*
> - the *theory* lying behind the strategies in this section; and
> - a list of the *advantages* of adopting them.

Leadership goals:
- triage the conflict – gather data as swiftly as possible;
- identify those involved and the state of their relationships;
- discern the issues in dispute as far as possible;
- make a preliminary assessment of the category and magnitude of the conflict; and
- assess whether this is a reportable issue.[127]

Focus question:

How do we gauge the gravity and extent of this conflict, the 'who', the 'when', the 'what' and the 'why'?

In the world of medicine, 'triage' is a term used to indicate 'the assignment of degrees of urgency to wounds or illnesses to decide the order of treatment of a large number of patients or casualties'.[128] It is a practice common in hospital emergency departments. Staff categorise people on a scale of 1 to 5 based on whether they have an immediately life-threatening condition (which should be addressed within the next 2 minutes) to a less critical condition (which should be treated within the next 2 hours).[129]

The term comes from the French verb 'trier', meaning 'to separate, sift or select'. This process unfolds typically according to recognised steps. Similarly, leaders of Christian communities need to undertake an initial *triage* when a conflict emerges.

This section, 7.7, will explore the following three steps in a *conflict* triage process:
- gathering the facts;

- investigating the condition; and
- assessing the need by allocating a 'triage' conflict category.

The following section, 7.8, will explore the remaining steps in a *conflict* triage process, namely:
- deciding on the 'treatment' needed;
- delivering the required 'treatment'; and
- providing ongoing re-assessment of the 'triage' conflict category.[130]

Key perspective:
Speed Leas observes: '...the way a board faces a problem in its earliest stages may profoundly affect its outcome. The way information is gathered (and from whom), as well as how it is analysed, may also affect the outcome.'[131]

(a) *Meet asap to set up the triage process*

The meeting agenda will involve agreeing on:
- what needs to be done;
- who will do what (for interviews, it is wise to do this in pairs);
- when will it be done by; and
- when will the group meet again to review the information collected.

Those who are assigned to gather data should be:
- perceived to be neutral in the eyes of those from whom information is sought;
- held in high regard in or by the community;
- appointed by a group of leaders – they should not self-select;
- represent different viewpoints;
- sufficiently skilled to undertake interviews or conduct small group community meetings;
- prepared to work in pairs at all stages of the gathering data process; and
- given a written statement of what is expected of them.

Once these decisions have been agreed upon, the serious triage work can begin.

(b) *Identify the most significant strained relationships – the 'who'*

There will always be a small group at the heart of any community conflict, even if the conflict has developed to involve the whole community. The initial thrust of your response will mean identifying these people.

Some people will openly acknowledge they are in conflict. Others, however, may deny it. Still others may genuinely not recognise their contribution. Therefore:

- note anyone who *resists* your leadership;
- identify *factions* forming around the small group at the heart of the conflict;
- look for *patterns* in how people associate and the language they use; and
- watch for anyone whose *performance* is deteriorating in a given role.

(c) *Hold face-to-face or video-based meetings with those identified*

Holding face-to-face or video-based meetings is crucial to create legitimate and safe spaces where parties to a conflict can tell their story. Doing this as quickly as possible can minimise the potential for conflict to gain further traction. Such meetings allow people to table the emotions conflict often generates – fear, anxiety, disappointment, disgust, distrust, anger. Meetings also potentially build trust as people feel heard. They provide leaders with insight into what has occurred.

Dealing with strong emotions and unsettling stories is challenging. Remember the adage: 'you won't rise to the occasion, you'll sink to your level of preparation'.[132] It is, therefore, imperative to be well prepared for these meetings, as suggested below.

(i) Prepare a draft meeting outline: interviewers and known parties

A *Sample outline for a meeting between leaders and known parties to a conflict* is provided in Part 3, Resources, 16.7(a). It may be modified as needed.

(ii) Prepare the best questions

Taking time to prepare effective questions is essential for:
- building trust;
- creating a safe environment to bring issues into the light;
- avoiding thoughtless or knee-jerk interrogation, which is intrusive, legalistic or judgmental;
- gathering useful information to understand what is happening;
- developing mutually respectful relationships; and
- establishing an open and communicative culture.

You will find:
- *Guidelines for developing the best questions to gather information to map a conflict* in Part 3, Resources, 16.7(b); and
- a *Pro forma questionnaire to gather information to map a conflict* in Part 3, Resources, 16.7(c).

(iii) Refresh or develop your active listening skills

The biblical mandate for listening well was developed in chapter 6.7. Actively listening to people elicits a fuller understanding of the circumstances while building trust and respect. Failing to listen actively does the opposite.

A resource, *Sample process to facilitate active listening*, for leaders and interviewers to use in a face-to-face or video-based meetings with parties to a conflict, is located in Part 3, Resources, 16.8(c).

(iv) Schedule the meetings

Each person or group involved needs to be allowed to tell their story, know they have been heard, and table what they think should happen. These early meetings are held separately with those on different sides of the conflict.

Often people will feel safer and more comfortable if they bring a support person to the meeting. Also, experience shows there is wisdom in having two interviewers present at all meetings as a check and balance on each other and as a witness to proceedings.

(d) *Establish the broad issues, interests, needs*
and values – the 'what' and the 'why'

Susan Nienaber quotes one lay leader as wisely observing: 'Don't ever be afraid of openness. Determine the issues early on and create vehicles to talk about them. Don't allow strong feelings to go underground and fester.'[133]

Face-to-face, or video-based meetings provide the vehicle to ask parties to identify their issues, name them as precisely as possible and prioritise them. Keep a record of these as you go by whatever means best suits your context. Don't leave this record-keeping until later as experience shows important details will inevitably be forgotten! At some point in the meeting or afterwards, separate the issues, identifying them into:

- relational, that is, personal (these are issues about broken relationships, the person-to-person stressors, destructive sinful behaviours and words used against each other); and
- material, that is, substantive (these are differences over things such as money, property, services, beliefs and rights).

> **Key perspective:**
> Relational and material issues are invariably intertwined. It can take quite some skill and patience to separate them. Nevertheless, this is an essential step as relational issues are addressed through repentance, confession, apology and forgiveness, while material issues are mostly negotiated.

One way to confirm if you have accurately identified an issue is to reflect it back to the protagonist as a question. Unfortunately, it is harder to craft questions around relational matters than it is for material ones, given the former are usually subjective and abstract, while the latter are mostly objective and tangible.

An example of questions to confirm a relational issue might be:

> *I hear you say you were deeply hurt by Heidi's email to the congregation, which accused you and the committee of being incompetent. Have we heard that right? What could be some God-honouring ways you believe would address this issue?*

An example of questions to confirm a material issue might be:

> *Have we heard correctly that you ended up paying much more than you had been led to believe due to the changes in the school's fee structure? What would be some of the options you think could be taken to address this?*

It is imperative to keep to the broad issues here and resist the temptation to drill into the detail. Remember, your responsibility right now is to lead, to gather information for master-planning how and by whom the conflict needs to be addressed. It is *not* to solve the matter for and with the party.

(e) *Identify and name any secrets, hidden agendas, private loyalties and conflicts of interest*

Decoys and unknown loyalties can hide the real issues. This step may prove difficult. It needs to be done carefully and sensitively whilst remaining alert to the following:

- personal and work connections people have within the community and beyond;
- revealing (maybe unexpected) body language;
- conflicts of interest;
- the same names surfacing on several occasions; and
- people whom you might expect to have been mentioned but were not.

> **Key perspective:**
> Leaders should assume that conflicts have multiple causes. 'Usually, there is not just one person or one incident that has brought all the troubles to the fore.'[134]

This process of accurately identifying and naming issues calls for all the tact, humility and tentativeness of a skilled interviewer. In addition, one needs to keep an open mind and be careful not to judge the person being interviewed.

(f) *Consider how well the individuals or group(s) are organised*

As you gather the information and triage the conflict, be alert to whether smaller groupings or factions, have formed, or are forming, within the community. Are these gathering around a particular person? Are people taking action to consolidate their position? The development of smaller groups like this may be a possible indicator of the level and magnitude of the conflict. Research suggests that 'the more organized are the movement and countermovement within a given ...congregation the more likely will be high-intensity conflict or even division'.[135]

(g) *Observe any who appear to be neutral and potential peacemakers*

In most Christian communities, there will be former governance or executive leaders, people with other significant life experiences and skills, and those who exhibit spiritual maturity and insight. Such people can be invaluable to assist leaders in navigating community conflict. They could potentially fill roles such as interviewing, acting as a community contact person, being a member of an oversight team.

So, be on the lookout for people of this calibre who don't align themselves with the protagonists and are respected in the community.

(h) *Prepare a timeline of significant events – the 'when'*

After completing the face-to-face meetings, develop a detailed timeline of what you have identified that led to this conflict. This will help you understand more concretely what has transpired. It will also provide an invaluable reference tool as the stages in the master-plan, and the ultimate resolution process unfold.

> **Key Perspective**
> As you gather information, keep your conclusions tentative. You will need to re-assess as further information comes to hand.

(i) *Compile a conflict map*

Having taken the above steps, you are now able to collate the information and compile a conflict map. To assist you in this step, a *Tool to compile a conflict map – pulling it all together*, may be found in Part 3, Resources, 16.7(d).

(j) *Allocate a 'triage' conflict category*

Once you have gathered the facts and investigated the nature of what has happened, your next step is to allocate a 'triage' conflict category, that is, the category of conflict tension in your community.

The five primary categories of conflict at increasing levels of intensity and complexity were explained in section 7.4(a). You may have made a preliminary assessment of the category you are working with in the current conflict. If so, it would be wise to review that conclusion now in light of the information collated within your conflict map. If not, now is the time to do so. The relevant resource to do this is called *Tool for assessing the category of conflict tension* and may be found in Part 3, Resources, 16.4(a).

When Speed Leas developed these categories (or 'levels' as he called them), he indicated they were based on the following assumptions:
- 'Not all conflict is the same';
- 'One's "gut reaction" is not a reliable indicator of the actual level of difficulty'; and
- 'Responses to conflict should be adjusted to the level of difficulty'.[136]

Since the original development of the categories of conflict tension, other practitioners have expanded the list to include a 'Category 0: There is nothing wrong!'. This is the 'head-in-the-sand' category where the conflict is neither acknowledged nor addressed. The fact you are reading this book probably indicates you are not trapped in this category!

We also noted in section 7.4(a) that this triage step is vital because it will help you understand whether to handle the conflict from within yourselves or outsource it to conflict resolution experts.

The importance of triaging the category of conflict tension, and acting promptly, cannot be overstated. This is underscored when you realise, for example, that unless there is a satisfactory outcome for a category 3 conflict, experience shows you risk losing more than twenty per cent (20%) of the people associated with your community.[137]

A note of caution

- Even after assessing the triage or category of conflict tension, leaders may be reluctant to intervene. They may believe the risk of bringing things into the open is too high.
- Therefore, leaders may decide to suppress or ignore the problems. Be careful of this, however, as 'the burden of proof that the risk in allowing a problem to be acknowledged is too great must lie with those who want to suppress it. The risks of suppression far outweigh those of working it through.'[138]

Having mapped and assessed the situation, you are now ready to follow the remaining steps in the conflict triage process, namely, to master-plan the conflict.

7.8 *Master-plan the conflict – looking around*

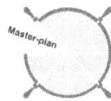

Note – see section 6.8 for:
- *the **theory** lying behind the strategies in this section; and*
- *a list of the **advantages** of adopting them.*

This is the final step in the triage process. This is where you pull together all the strategic elements that go into navigating community conflict while still preserving the community's constitutional objects and purposes. This is what will empower you to stay steady at the helm.

Leadership goals:

- pull it all together – create a co-ordinated master-plan to address the conflict, incorporating all eight HELM elements; and
- maintain trust with the parties and the community.

Focus question:

What are the essential elements which need to be put in place to resolve this conflict and bring healing to all parties and the community?

The diagram below sets out all the strategic elements to master-plan the conflict. Each part will be considered in turn.

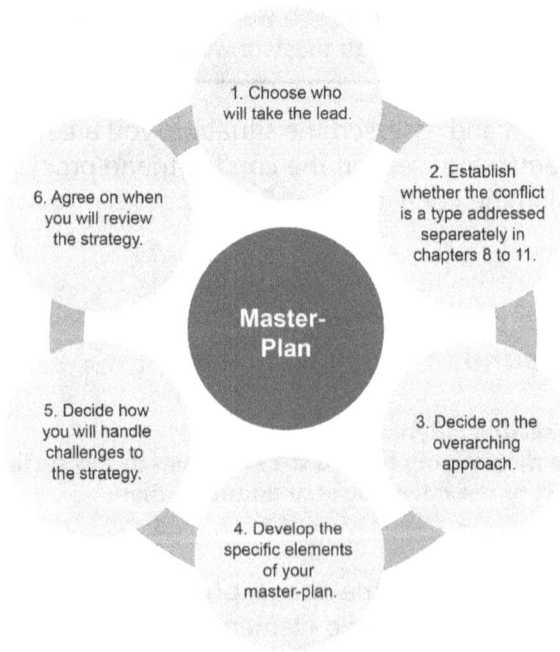

FIGURE 9: DEVELOPING A MASTER-PLAN

(1) *Choose who will take the lead*

Who will take the lead during a conflict event is an important question worth asking.

- Will it be the governing group, the senior executive leader (CEO, senior minister, school principal), a group leader, or someone else?
- Is the person who would typically take the lead the right person in this situation?

The governing group of the community is ultimately always the group responsible for ensuring there is a master-plan in place, and action is being taken to address all known conflict in their community. The governing group may choose to delegate the master-planning process, and the practical strategies to others, such as to the leader of the section in the community where the conflict arose. However, it cannot avoid its obligation to ensure all steps are taken to bring its community back to health. Therefore, the governing group needs to monitor progress closely.

There are likely to be relevant accountabilities in place already for executive staff delegated to take decisive action. However, it is wise not to make assumptions and to revisit accountabilities where the stakes are too high not to do so.

Sometimes it may be better to engage someone who is not part of the senior executive. This is because, as Leas and Kittlaus caution, an executive leader may:

- 'have invariably already taken a position on the issue in question';
- 'have already been implicated by one or both of the parties as being part of the problem'; and
- 'wrongly perceive reconciliation as the absence of conflict'.[139]

Thus, at the outset, the governing group needs to ask searching questions to determine whether leaders have compromised themselves in any of these ways. Suppose the governing group finds leaders are compromised. In that case the healthiest path forward will be to delegate responsibility for leading the conflict to some other appropriately gifted and godly person, either from within the community or beyond. Remember, 'sailing in big waves is a test of seamanship and steering, which is why you should put your best steerer on the helm'.[140] Of course, when someone not already delegated to lead is asked to step up during a conflict, specific accountabilities will need to be established.

(2) *Establish whether the conflict is a type*
   addressed separately in chapters 8 to 11

Due to their prevalence and unique characteristics, several types of conflict are dealt with separately in chapters 8, 9, 10 and 11. The information you gathered as you mapped the conflict should help you establish whether you are dealing with one of these.

If this is the case, read the relevant chapter to most effectively master-plan the conflict. For disputes concerning:
- individuals or a group – see chapter 8;
- those in top-tier governance leadership – see chapter 9;
- those in senior executive leadership, such as a minister, rector, pastor, CEO or school principal – see chapter 10;
- beliefs or doctrine – see chapter 11.

The targeted strategies offered within each chapter will help you as you develop your master-plan.

(3) *Decide on the overarching approach*

Generally, leaders have four overarching master-planning options available to them:
- handle it exclusively themselves;
- delegate aspects of it to a special purpose group from within the community;[141];
- outsource aspects of it to their denomination or peak body; or;
- outsource aspects of it to outside experts, such as counsellors, mediators, consultants, investigators, conflict coaches. (If you decide to do this, you will find guidelines to assist you in choosing the right person in bonus chapter 13 on the book's website, *Working with Outside Professionals*.)

(4) *Develop the specific elements of your master-plan*

The specific elements that go into your master-plan will comprise leadership strategies you decide to adopt from those outlined:

- in chapters 8-11 (if applicable);
- under each of the HELM principles in sections 7.1 to 7.7; and
- under each of the categories found in the *Tool for assessing the category of conflict tension* located in the Part 3, Resources, 16.4(a).

Once you have decided who will lead the master-plan, the overarching approach, and the specific elements you intend to adopt, it is important to scaffold the plan with nuts and bolts questions like the following:

- Who else will assist?
- When will we begin?
- When do we hope to have it completed?
- What are the cost implications?
- How will we know we have achieved the outcomes?
- Who will be held accountable?
- When will we review the master-plan? (See section (6) below.)

As a check and a balance on your approach, and to contribute to its success, reflect on these questions:

- Is the process fair and legal?
- Do the parties have sufficient opportunity to influence the outcome?
- Will participants view the environment as safe?
- Have clear ground rules been established for all discussion about the conflict?
- Does the community understand the process ahead of time and know how it will unfold?[142]

> **Key perspective:**
> In master-planning an approach to addressing conflict, you may need to act contrary to your feelings. However, recognise that this is a time to act courageously and continue to trust God and trust your process, whatever one's emotions.

If your master plan involves scheduling a community meeting, to assist you in running such a meeting, a resource, *Guidelines for a community meeting,* may be found at Part 3, Resources, 16.8(d). A resource at 16.8(e) also contains a list of suggested meeting ground rules.

A summary of the strategies provided in this chapter may be found in table form in Part 3, Resources, 16.8(a). The table also prioritises the strategies into those which potentially require immediate action and those which might wait a little longer to be implemented.

(5) *Decide how you will handle challenges to the strategy*

Steinke comments that 'the sabotage of a process to deal with conflict should be expected. The usual saboteurs will be those who are losing control or not getting what they want from the process.'[143]

So, don't be surprised if you encounter criticism from various sources. There is a list of pervasive one-liners, under various themes, along with brief suggestions on possible correctives in Part 3, Resources, 16.8(f), *Suggestions for countering common objections and obstacles.*

Your task at this point is to be prepared for when challenges to your master-plan arise so that you can *stay steady at the helm.*

(6) *Agree on when you will review the strategy*

Nothing is set in concrete when it comes to conflict. Leaders will need to adjust to changing circumstances such as new information coming to light or unexpected critical incidents (such as violations of the agreed *Community Covenant of Behaviour*) and review their approach accordingly. Also, leaders' initial assessment of the situation may be incomplete or ill-informed.

Nienaber observed that leaders in communities that recovered well from substantial conflict were able to adjust 'to what was needed... They were willing to try new things and to be creative.'[144]

Leaders must avoid becoming fixed in their view about the situation and dogmatic about the way forward.

So, build into the master-plan both a flexible willingness to review along the way and an intentional review date that provides time to consciously reflect on the situation, the attitudes and the responses experienced thus far.

7.9 *Conclusion*

Just as navigating an ocean-going vessel in a storm is a complicated business, so charting a course in times of conflict and holding to that course is complicated. It takes time, energy and commitment. Recognising this at the outset can avoid drift, ambiguity and unhelpful surprises which you might otherwise experience along the way.

Thus, having completed your triage assessment and master-planned a principled and strategic response, you will have done your best to set your community up for the conflict to be resolved to the glory of God.

---

108 'If around twenty-five per cent (25%) of a community's members are involved in a conflict then it should be treated as a community-wide conflict'. Rev Les Scarborough, John Mark Ministries, conversation October 2019.

109 Nienaber, *Leading,* p. 2.

110 Boyd-Macmillan, Eolene & Savage, Sara, *Transforming Conflict, Conflict transformation amongst senior church leaders with different theological stances,* The Foundation for Church Leadership, York, p. 107f.

111 In a conflict in which I was involved, the vision of one of the parties was for all of us to resolve the tensions and conclude by 'having a bar-be-que'. Sadly, while there was some resolution to the conflict, it was never finally settled, and the bar-be-que never held. However, the vision for all the conflicted parties getting to the point where we could gather together for a bar-be-que was often referred to and provided some hope amidst the trauma.

112 These questions are mainly taken from Sande, *The Peacemaker*, chapter 7, p 143ff.

113 See *Guidelines for writing a holistic confession and apology*, Part 3, Resources, 16.3(b).

114 For a full exploration of this process, see Ted Kober, *Confession & Forgiveness: Professing Faith as Ambassadors of Reconciliation,* Concordia Publishing House, St Louis, MO, 2002.

115 In his book, *Moving*, p. 19ff, Speed Leas was the practitioner who first articulated a scale for conflict tensions in a community. Leas describes the categories as 'levels'.

This can imply a potential rise or fall in the tensions. Using the term 'category' implies the state or condition which actually exists and recognises that there is often a gap between the various categories.

116 Boyd-Macmillan and Savage, *Transforming Conflict*, p. 76.

117 Nienaber, *Leading*, p. 4.

118 Observation by Rev Les Scarborough, church consultant, supervisor and trainer, John Mark Ministries, Church Consultancy Training, Sydney, Australia, circa 2002.

119 To 'triangle' someone is 'a manipulation tactic where one person will not communicate directly with another person, instead using a third person to relay communication to the second, thus forming a triangle'. www.en.m.wikipedia.org under the word 'Triangulation (psychology)'.

120 In the writer's experience, one value which leaders can overlook when addressing conflict is the matter of justice. This omission can especially be the case where the leadership is keen to restore harmony in the community quickly. Courageous leadership requires that any issue of justice not be avoided or minimised so as to ensure a lasting and settled resolution of the conflict.

121 Nienaber, *Leading*, p. 4.

122 Tim Dyer, consultancy training handout entitled: *Assessing a Congregational Conflict.*

123 Boyd-Macmillan and Savage, S. *Transforming Conflict* p. 84ff provide a list of the most prevalent personality disorders. They also offer several strategies on how to constructively engage with such people.

124 Tim Dyer, an observation made during consultancy training in circa 2008.

125 In her research on the factors which cause twelve churches which had experienced substantial conflict to heal, Suisan Nienaber concluded that one of the traits which distinguished these congregations was that they communicated well. *The lay leaders in our study emphasized the need to keep the congregation informed and to be as transparent as possible. The leaders communicated to the congregation through various modes of communication – newsletters, e-mail, announcements in worship, congregational gatherings, and staff meetings.* Ms Nienaber noted that even letting the congregation know when there was no new information to report was significant. Such a strategy demonstrates respect for the members, builds trust in the leaders, and leads to the community receiving the news as a sign of the leaders care for them. Nienaber, *Leading*, p. 4.

126 David M Martin, *The company directors' desktop guide*, 3rd edition, 2006, Thorogood Publishing Ltd, London quoting Jack Jones, p. 225.

127 Remember this book does not provide advice on, or assistance to, leaders facing conflict arising from sexual misconduct and abuse cases, incidents involving children, criminal conduct, or necessary intervention by an outside body or group. In such situations seek outside professional assistance immediately.

128 See www.bhi.nsw.gov.au for the basis of this information.

129 Ibid.

130 Ibid.

131 Leas, *Moving*, p. 23.

132 Navy Seal principle – see *Prepare...Prepare...Prepare* http://www.tipnational.org/pdf/prepare.pdf

133 Nienaber, *Leading*, p. 2.

134 Leas, *Moving*, p. 29.

135 Brubaker, *Promise and Peril*, p. 16 referencing research by Fred Kniss, *Disquiet in the Land: Cultural Conflict in American Mennonite Communities* (New Brunswick, NJ: Rutgers University Press, 1997).

136 Leas, *Moving*, p. 17.
137 Rev. Les Scarborough, John Mark Ministries, observation made during consultancy training, 2002.
138 Leas, *Moving*, p. 26.
139 Leas, Speed B., and Kittlaus, Paul, *Church Fights: Managing Conflict in the Local Church*, Philadelphia: Westminster Press, 1973, p. 74.
140 https://www.northsails.com/sailing/en/2016/09/how-to-sail-safely-through-a-storm
141 David Brubaker has outlined a helpful process entitled 'Forming a Reference Committee in Congregational Change or Conflict'. Brubaker, *Promise and Peril*, p.147ff.
142 Lott, David B., Editor, *Conflict Management in Congregations*, The Alban Institute, 2001, an interview with Speed B. Leas, p. 17.
143 Steinke, *Congregational Leadership*, p. 115. (Copyright 2006 © the Alban Institute. Reproduced with permission of the Licensor through PLSclear.)
144 Nienaber, *Leading*, p. 4.

INDIVIDUALS AND SMALL GROUPS 8

In this chapter, we look at:
- addressing conflict between individuals and small groups in churches and other Christian communities;
- strategies to stay steady at the helm through such conflict; and
- a suggested process to resolve issues and reconcile relationships when leaders decide to *manage* a category 1 or 2 conflict themselves.

The primary aim of this chapter is to equip the governing leadership group to provide stable ongoing biblical leadership to a community throughout the duration of a conflict involving individuals or small groups, or both.

If you are connected with a Christian community of any sort, you will have no doubt experienced conflicts between individuals, between individuals and small groups or between several groups. These conflicts often surprise, even bewilder us when they emerge. However, emerge they do.

How to use this chapter

This chapter has been written on the assumption that, having assessed you are dealing with a conflict involving individuals or small groups, you have:

- read chapter 6, which develops the eight stay-at-the-HELM principles; and
- read chapter 7, so you can select which of the high-level strategies outlined there are relevant in this context.

Familiarity with these chapters will position you to now consider conflict involving individuals and small groups.

8.1 *The context*

It goes without saying that any leader must address conflicts between individuals or groups within a community that directly impact communal life and purposes. But what about disputes between individuals or groups connected to the same community, which occur in a context outside that community, where the impact on communal life and purposes is only tangential or indirect? What obligations do leaders have in such a situation? And are there different obligations for church leaders compared to leaders of other Christian communities?

(a) *In the church*

Reflect on the obligations of church leaders in each of the following scenarios.

- The governing council of a church becomes concerned about a reduction in weekly offerings. Eventually, they discover the treasurer regularly takes money and uses it for his daughter's university education. He admits to misappropriating around $20,000 and pleads he cannot repay because he is a pensioner. The council, however, know they could sue him as he owns his home.[145]
- Two neighbours, Adrian and Colton, attend the same church. Adrian wants to replace their sagging boundary fence. However, they disagree about the type and cost. They argue

about it so loudly in the street that several other neighbours overhear them. Eventually, Adrian takes matters into his own hands, removing the existing structure. Colton is enraged. Exasperated, both men vent their frustrations in their respective church home groups.

In the first scenario, we find a group and an individual in a church where the conflict *directly* relates to and affects the church's life and purposes. In the second scenario, we find two individuals attending the same church involved in a conflict unrelated to the church but which *indirectly* affects its reputation, life and purposes.

So, what might be the biblical principles relevant to these scenarios?

When conflict occurs within the context of the church, there is no ambiguity. (See Acts 6 and 15; Phil 4:2, 3; Mt 5:24 and 18:15.) If conflict *directly* relates to and affects the church's life and purposes, leaders are duty-bound to take the initiative to address it. This is because conflict, left unattended, poisons relationships, tarnishes God's name and sullies the church's reputation. It is no wonder Jesus used the imperative of the verb 'to go' to urge his disciples to 'go and be reconciled' when conflict arose between them. If church leaders fail to address conflict, it can directly ruin the reputation of God's people, compromise the church's life and purposes and endanger the faith of many.

However, what about conflict which is more tangential, conflict which may only *indirectly* affect the church's life and purpose? Surprisingly, scripture calls on church leaders to address this type of conflict as well. We see this principle at work in the intriguing scenario outlined by Paul in 1 Corinthians 6:1-11. Two Christian brothers aired their grievances in the secular court held in the public square of downtown Corinth. The apostle's reaction, his arguments and confronting language show how seriously he took the obligation of church leaders to intervene. He declares, *If any of you have a dispute with another, do you dare to take it before the ungodly for judgment instead of before the Lord's people?* (6:1)

While this dispute may not necessarily have related *directly* to the life and purpose of the church, Paul argued it nevertheless impacted the church's reputation and, ultimately, that of Christ. He was bitterly disappointed by the church leaders' reluctance to intervene or mediate.

Experience shows that today, church leaders are still just as reluctant to address external disputes between people who belong to their community. Many leaders will not believe such conflicts to be their responsibility as they are considered only tangential to the life and purposes of the church.

Of course, the flip side to this reluctance is that the conflicted parties may themselves also be reluctant to accept assistance from leaders. There could be numerous reasons for this:
- a belief in the right to privacy;
- embarrassment or anxiety;
- lack of confidence in the church's leaders;
- one party will accept leadership involvement while the other will not;
- one party may be connected to the community and the other not; or
- one may be a Christian and the other not.

Overcoming this resistance, either within the leadership or amongst the protagonists, needs to be a matter of prayer and discussion. The truth is that all conflict between church members, whether directly or indirectly connected to the community's life and purposes, will impact the community they belong to in some way.

This book, therefore, seeks to take this obligation seriously by inviting *church leaders* of today to:

(1) apply the relevant biblical HELM principles whenever anyone connected to their community finds themselves in conflict; and
(2) ensure the issues are thoroughly dealt with – either by themselves or with outside assistance.

(b) *In Christian communities other than the church*

So, what then about the obligation of Christian leaders in contexts other than the church? Does the responsibility extend to conflict that is both directly or indirectly connected to the community's life and purposes just as it does for the church? Consider the following scenarios:

- Teachers in a department of a Christian school vote to ignore a new policy restricting student excursions. The department head sends a vitriolic email to the school's executive venting the frustrations of her staff and indicates they will not adhere to the policy. The executive reacts with frustration and annoyance. The staff denigrate the executive amongst themselves and other staff.

- The wife of a long-standing board member of a para-church organisation asks her husband for a divorce and property settlement. An amicable resolution cannot be reached, so the matter goes to court. The board member fails to attend board meetings. He does not provide an apology nor apply for leave of absence. When the chairperson calls to discuss the situation, the board member becomes angry, argumentative and resentful. While the board member has a long-standing connection with the organisation, his wife has never had a connection

In the first scenario, we find two groups in a Christian community where the conflict *directly* relates to and affects its life and purposes. The second involves two individuals, one certainly directly connected to this non-church community and the other not. Their marriage breakdown only *indirectly* affects the life of this organisation. However, the board member's membership does *directly* affect the organisation's reputation and work.

What should leaders of Christian organisations do in contexts such as these? Are their responsibilities the same for each conflict as it is for church leaders?

The Bible does not provide specific teaching concerning Christian organisations as we understand them today. That said, such organisations typically espouse Christian beliefs, values and ethos. Many are independent of but associated with church denominations. Others have no denominational alignment. Nevertheless, these organisations may hold biblical approaches toward many aspects of their business, including healthy relationships. Their conflict resolution and other policies and procedures may reflect this.

For the leaders of Christian organisations such as these, their obligations toward conflicted individuals and groups connected to their community are more complicated than in the church. The test of whether the conflict relates 'directly' or 'indirectly' to the life and purposes of their organisation discussed above is probably a good place to start in considering this issue.

Where it does relate *directly*, leaders must become involved. (Strategies for leaders in this context are provided in section 8.2 below.[146]) If the conflict *indirectly* impacts the organisation, there is more choice. Leaders have several options should they decide to become involved. Examples are outlined at the end of section 8.2 below under the heading 'Where the conflict *indirectly* involves a Christian organisation'.

8.2 *Additional strategies to stay steady at the helm*

Where the conflict:

- *directly* and *indirectly* involves a *church* community; or
- *directly* affects a Christian organisation *other* than the church.

The following comprise *additional* strategies under the *stay-steady-at-the-HELM framework* for leaders to consider when navigating conflict involving individuals and small groups.

(A) *Hear from God*

- Encourage those involved to read a book on biblical peacemaking principles such as *The Peacemaker: A Biblical Guide to Resolving Personal Conflict* by Ken Sande or *Resolving*

Everyday Conflict by Ken Sande and Kevin Johnson (for details, see the Bibliography).
- Urge the parties to become familiar with the process outlined in *Tool to manage low-level conflict: the PAUSE to HEAL process* in Part 3, Resources, 16.8(b).

(B) *Examine your culpability*

- The focus question under 'Examine your culpability' in chapter 7 is: *How might we, as leaders, individually and collectively, have contributed to this situation?* If your answer identifies any contribution, then accept one hundred per cent responsibility for your culpability. Even if it is small, acknowledge your contribution and deal with it, including apologising sooner rather than later.

To assist you in dealing with your culpability, see 16.3(b) for *Guidelines for writing a holistic confession and apology* and Part 3, Resources, 16.3(c) for *Guidelines for a confession and apology by leaders.*

(C) *Map the conflict*

- Analyse the implications of clauses within the relevant organisational documents which relate to how conflict should be addressed.
- Clarify whether the conflict is being fuelled by systemic organisational issues such as inadequate role descriptions, unclear expectations, dual accountabilities, conflicts of interest. (There could be several different conflicts here.)

(D) *Master-plan the conflict*

- Resolve to address the issues either within yourselves or by engaging outside professional assistance.

A note of caution

- Speed Leas observes that leaders, especially of high-level conflict involving individuals or small groups, can be tempted to avoid dealing with the issues by saying to the protagonists: *'If you don't like it here, you can always leave'.*[147] Avoidance, however, is never a biblical response. It does not honour God.
- Of course there may be a place for someone, or a group, to leave a community. However, this would only be after the issues have been thoroughly addressed and always open to the possibility of the persons returning where there is a change of heart and a willingness to abide by the outcomes of the conflict resolution process.[148]

- If you assess the conflict at category 3 or higher, engage and be guided by expert outside assistance.
- If you decide the conflict is at category 1 or 2 and you choose to manage it in-house, consider section 8.3 below.

Where the conflict:

- *indirectly* involves a Christian organisation other than the church

In these circumstances, if you decided to assist, you could consider exploring one or more of the following approaches:
- offer to help the parties by locating Christian mediators;
- offer to hold parties accountable as they move toward resolution externally;
- bring the dispute to the attention of the parties' church with a view to church leaders taking action;
- offer to locate a suitable conflict coach; and/or
- provide pastoral care support.

8.3 *Strategies to manage the conflict in-house*

The potential strategies here include:

- Invite the parties to overlook the offence. (For a discussion on when this is applicable, see Sande, *The Peacemaker*, pp. 79-83).
- Engage the parties in the process outlined in the *Tool to manage low-level conflict: the PAUSE to HEAL process* in Part 3, Resources, 16.8(b).
- Alternatively, consider utilising the *Sample process to facilitate active listening* outlined in Part 3, Resources, 16.8(c).

8.4 *Conclusion*

Perhaps the most testing aspect of addressing individuals and groups in conflict in a Christian community will be your reticence and that of your fellow leaders to render assistance and secure accountability from those involved.

In societies that express individual rights and maintain personal privacy, acting in biblical obedience will be challenging. However, this is the role to which Christ calls leaders. So, surround all your decisions and actions with prayer and a gentle, non-judgmental strategy, trusting God for an approach that honours him.

---

145 In a situation where a crime is committed, there are two overlapping God-ordained authorities: the civil authority (Rom 13:1-7) and the church's authority (e.g., Mt 18:15-17; 1 Cor 5). Just because there may be a crime that needs to be addressed by the government, the Christian community is not relieved of its obligations to deal with issues related to faith. After all, the Christian community is responsible for addressing sin and proclaiming forgiveness.

146 Note: processes around performance appraisals and industrial relations frameworks, which are also likely to come into play, are not addressed here.

147 Leas, *Moving*, p. 35.

148 See ibid, p.35f for a discussion on circumstances where it is appropriate, as a last resort, for individuals or a small group to be asked to leave a church.

TOP-TIER GOVERNANCE LEADERS 9

In this chapter, we look at:
- **conflict between leaders within a Christian community;**
- **additional strategies stemming from the eight HELM principles for leaders to consider in this context; and**
- **a process to resolve issues and reconcile relationships when leaders decide to manage a category 1 or 2 conflict themselves.**

A recent change to the constitution of a well-established peak body allowed the board to co-opt two additional people. The intention was to enable the board to access skills not otherwise available among the existing members.

Rex was due to retire when his term expired in two years. He had been good friends with Katrina and her family for longer than anyone could remember. They were also distantly related by marriage. Katrina had worked for the organisation for several years as head of its human resources department. In that role, she advised the organisation's CEO on matters relating to staff entitlements and terminations.

Additionally, she also advised in these areas to the organisation's 150 affiliated members. Rex had also contributed to the board in these areas. He believed that with his pending retirement, the board could benefit by harnessing Katrina's extensive experience. So he nominated her to fill one of the co-opted positions.

The chairperson tabled the nomination at the next board meeting, and the matter was open for discussion. Rex was first to speak. He highlighted Katrina's longevity and knowledge. Then, the chair invited more discussion. After a pause, Sam spoke. She affirmed Katrina's contribution to the organisation and her experience. However, she cautioned, there were several glaring problems.

> I cannot understand how Katrina could continue to be accountable to the CEO when the CEO is accountable to her at the board level. I have never heard of an employee becoming a board member and remaining an employee. All this troubles me. She has been a great employee. However, will she make a good board member when you have to look out for the organisation's interests in a whole range of areas? Then there is the personal connection between Katrina and Rex. I don't know what to think about that. Also, so far, we as a board have not assessed our needs. I thought this was a prerequisite for co-opting an additional member.

Rex reacted immediately. The chair interrupted him. 'Rex, you have made your contribution. We need to hear from others.' However, Rex ignored him and pushed on:

> What Sam just said belittles Katrina and taints her reputation. She has been a most honourable employee over many years. She has always acted in the best interests of the organisation. So how could there possibly be a problem? I move we appoint her immediately.

The chair called on others to speak. Howard and Magnus spoke in favour of the appointment. They had worked closely with Rex on the board and its committees over the years. Several others, however, agreed with Sam and spoke persuasively against the nomination. Rex got up and left, slamming the door behind him.

There was a long silence. Then, finally, a younger director commented on how he thought directors should be responding. Indignant, Howard and Magnus told him to grow up before they left the room as well.

----------ooO0oo----------

Of course, there was nothing in the strategic plan which gave space for these tensions. The organisation had never developed a conflict resolution procedure. No one ever thought that would be necessary. So how would they address this polarising conflict between their leaders?

How to use this chapter

This chapter has been written on the assumption that having assessed you are dealing with a conflict involving the leaders themselves, you have:

- read chapter 6, which develops the eight stay-at-the-HELM principles; and
- read chapter 7, so you can select which of the high-level strategies outlined there are relevant in this context.

Familiarity with these chapters will position you to now consider conflict involving top-tier governance leaders.

9.1 *The context*

As Part 1 has shown, leaders can experience internal stressors from any number of sources. Section 2.6 explored the power of desire in a leader's heart. Section 4.1(d) noted how the influence of your colleagues and the lens through which you interpret them could negatively impact your capacity to respond well. Section 5.1(f) addressed heart idols that can emerge within a group of leaders. Any one of these may lead to anxiety and polarising conflicts with fellow leaders.

Conflict, where individual leaders are protagonists, can significantly destabilise a leadership group and noticeably distract it from leading effectively. What then are the leadership obligations of the whole group in the face of such a dispute?

While today's leadership structures are not directly paralleled in biblical times, there are nevertheless examples of conflict between leaders which can assist us in our thinking:

- Jesus' disciples argued over who would be acknowledged as the greatest, the most honoured leader in the kingdom of heaven. Jesus intervened by:
  - naming their heart issues and attitudes;
  - outlining the consequences of their behaviour;
  - indicating the values which they need to adopt for resolving the problems; and
  - exhorting them to specific action. (Mt 18; Lk 9:46ff)
- The Corinthian church split into factions, with each group having a pseudo-leader. In this factional dysfunction and their many other disputes, no one stepped up to lead holistically. Paul viewed this lack of leadership as a matter of shame. He believed they needed to embrace their identity in Christ by addressing the issues. (1 Cor 4:14-17, 6:5, 15:34)

In each of these situations, there is a challenge to the church to take strategic action. It is to this we now turn.

9.2 *Additional strategies to stay steady at the helm*

The following comprise *additional* strategies under the *stay-steady-at-the-HELM framework* for leaders to consider when navigating conflict involving top-tier governance leaders.

(A) *Hear from God*

- Encourage those involved to read a book on biblical peacemaking principles, such as *The Peacemaker: A Biblical Guide to Resolving Personal Conflict* by Ken Sande or *Resolving Everyday Conflict* by Ken Sande and Kevin Johnson (for details, see the Bibliography).

- Hold a retreat. However, if the level of emotion is high, engage an outside facilitator. Establish basic ground rules to provide a safe environment for discussion.
- Encourage each leader to become familiar with the *Tool to manage low-level conflict: the PAUSE to HEAL process* provided in Part 3, Resources, 16.8(b).

(B) *Examine your culpability*

- The focus question under 'Examine your culpability' in chapter 7 is: *How might we, as leaders, individually and collectively, have contributed to this situation?* If you can identify any level of contribution, then accept one hundred per cent responsibility for it. Even if the contribution is small, acknowledge it and deal with it, including apologising sooner rather than later.

  To assist you in dealing with your culpability, see 16.3(b) for *Guidelines for writing a holistic confession and apology* and Part 3, Resources, 16.3(c) for *Guidelines for a confession and apology by leaders.*

- In addition to the questions listed in section 7.3(a), undertake an attitude check-up by asking questions such as:
  - Am I, and are we, willing to see God in our fellow leader?
  - How am I, or are we, viewing our fellow leader as the enemy?
  - Am I, and are we, willing to hear and understand the pain and hurt my or our fellow leader has experienced?
  - Am I, or are we, willing to name my, or our, pain in this situation?
  - What am I, or what as a leadership group, are we:
    - craving to see happen;
    - fearing most; and/or
    - judging in this situation?
  - What areas might you need to confess to God, your fellow leader and anyone else involved?

A note of caution

- Be aware of the issues peculiar to conflict involving governing leaders, as the story at the beginning of this chapter illustrates.
- The role of governance leadership carries a fiduciary duty to act in the best interests of the community. This is a legal obligation and an expression of love to ensure that the members of the community achieve and maintain their highest potential in realising the purposes for which they gather.
- If governance leaders are compromised by conflict to the point where they cannot fulfil their role, they must consider their position. They may need to resign or step aside until the dispute is resolved.
- Failing to do so undermines confidence in leaders and escalates the conflict. In a worst-case scenario, this could see the situation spiral out of control to the point where the organisation's viability is put at risk.

(C) *Evaluate your capacity*

- After noting the needs of the parties, mapping the nature of the conflict and deciding on the strategies to address it (see below), discuss as a leadership:
  What skills and resources do we as leaders possess to assist our conflicted colleagues in resolving their conflict effectively?

- The chair of the leadership group will be instrumental in this context to steer a healthy way forward. Consider:
  - If the chairperson is one of those involved in the conflict, should the person continue in the role? (A change in the chair may be imperative sooner rather than later.)
  - Does the chair have a good understanding of healthy group process to address the matter productively?
  - Do we need to appoint a chair from outside the community to avoid exacerbating the conflict and any perceptions of bias?

(D) *Love the community*

- Consider:
  How might we model and develop love in our community and to those involved in this conflict as a hallmark of the process we will use to address this conflict?

(E) *Lead the community*

- Consider whether the conflict relates primarily to issues between the parties or does it have community-wide implications or connections?

(F) *Map the conflict*

- An initial question here may be:

  Do we have actual conflict here or a healthy disagreement?

  The following questions may help identify the difference:

  - Are discussions on the differences threatening either individual or group desires or both?
  - Are the discussions arousing adverse emotional reactions?
  - Are the discussions prompting antagonistic behaviours?

  From our definition of conflict (section 2.1), if these characteristics are present, then conflict exists.

- Consider whether the leader(s) involved may be 'toxic' in light of the discussion 'Unique considerations when faced with a 'toxic leader' in section 10.4.
- If there are several leaders involved, how well organised do they seem to be?
- Ask: *Do, or is it likely that, more than 20% of the people in our community know about this conflict?* (If so, this may indicate that the conflict has risen to category 3 in which case see chapter 7 again.)

(G) *Master-plan the conflict*

> ***Key perspective:***
> In master-planning your response to conflict between leaders, note the following two principles:
>
> - *Principle 1: respect and fairness for leaders*
>   Because leaders can be open to vexatious accusations, it is crucial to heed Paul's advice to Timothy:[149]
>
>   *Do not entertain an accusation against an elder unless it is brought by two or three witnesses. But those elders who are sinning you are to reprove before everyone, so that the others may take warning* (I Tim. 5:19, 20).
>
> - *Principle 2: keep leadership strong*
>   Hebrews 13:17 points out that those working with leaders in conflict have an obligation to ensure the leader's office engenders confidence and provides a mutually beneficial environment for leaders to work in ways that are a 'joy, not a burden'.[150]

- If you assess the dispute at category 3 or higher, engage and be guided by expert outside assistance immediately.
- Consider section 9.3 below if you decide the conflict is at category 1 or 2 and choose to manage it in-house.
- If your organisation has developed a document such as a *Leadership Covenant, Code of Conduct, Statement of Team, or Leadership Values,* consider whether its terms have been breached in this current situation.
- Consider if one or more of the leaders should step down from their role or take leave of absence while you are addressing the conflict. (In practice, the actual implementation of such an idea can become a significant point of conflict itself. Leaders often fail to acknowledge that such action is necessary, and if they resist, conflict escalates. This reality should be noted so that leaders do not hold any unrealistic expectations in this regard.)
- In light of Matthew 5:23, 24, does the group, or any members of it, need to consider abstaining from formally worshipping

Christ in his church until a further effort is made to resolve the dispute?

- Ask: *What accountabilities might be helpful if you put them in place?*
- If you are a leader not involved in the conflict, test your understanding of what is happening by talking to:
  - your fellow leaders who are also not involved; and
  - where appropriate, the protagonists, to help gain perspective.
    (It is wise to be transparent in any such conversations by keeping the chairperson informed of what is happening.[151] It should be noted, however, the specific discussions between the parties are best kept confidential. Otherwise, if that confidence is broken, it will lead to even worse conflict.)
- Consider whether you could allocate a specific role to members of the governing group *not* involved in the conflict. Someone could be asked to:
  - undertake further biblical research on the principles of God-honouring conflict resolution;
  - identify a chaplain for the group;
  - reflect on alternatives to address the dispute; or
  - act as the leader's liaison with the parties in the context.

  Table the group's expectations of any person who is given a specific role.

- Consider the role, if any, of the senior executive officer (minister, rector, principal or CEO) in the situation where they are not a party to the conflict? Table the obligation for them to remain neutral and agree on any other expectations, such as their interaction with the chair.
- Support the chair in all of their appropriate actions and attitudes. Show respect and honour to the chair by confronting sinful behaviours in private as much as possible.
- If the struggle continues, try to agree on the *process* to be followed to gain a solution. This may well be to engage an outside facilitator or mediator.

9.3 *Strategies to manage the conflict in-house*

- Engage the parties in the process outlined in the *Tool to manage low-level conflict: the PAUSE to HEAL process* in Part 3, Resources, 16.8(b).
- Alternatively, consider utilising the tool outlined in Part 3, Resources, 16.8(c), *Sample process to facilitate active listening.*
- If you have assessed the conflict at category 1 or 2, and you consider managing it internally, it still could be helpful to appoint someone outside the organisation to take on specific responsibilities such as chairing important meetings.

9.4 *Conclusion*

Leaders who carry on leading unreconciled are open to the charge of hypocrisy. Jesus, of course, had much to say about the issue of hypocrisy. (See Mt 23.)

Therefore, in the difficult circumstances of conflict between leaders, to stay steady at the helm, be prepared to promptly navigate a course which:
- proactively addresses the broken relationships and the issues;
- engages protagonists in a process to humbly examine their contribution and admit their faults;
- acts to protect the health and reputation of the community; and
- maintains hope that the relationships can be reconciled and the matters resolved.

---

149 Based on wide experience, retired consultant, Rev Les Scarborough will only receive a complaint against a leader if it is brought by either three individuals or two couples. (Conversation, 9 September 2019.)

150 *Have confidence in your leaders, and submit to their authority, because they keep watch over you as those who must give an account. Do this so that their work will be a joy, not a burden, for that would be of no benefit to you.* (Heb 13: 17)

151 Board Matters: A Newsletter for Non-profit Boards, Volume 12, Number 4, April 2013 p. 5.

SENIOR EXECUTIVES 10

In this chapter, we look at:
- **conflict involving the senior executive leader – a rector, senior pastor, school principal, CEO;**
- **additional strategies stemming from the eight HELM principles when governance groups need to address conflict of this nature; and**
- **a process to resolve issues and reconcile relationships when leaders decide to manage a category 1 or 2 conflict themselves.**

Under Alex's leadership, Split Rock Christian School had grown significantly. Universally, staff, parents and the wider community had come to respect this young, energetic leader. However, the school was struggling to gain a full complement of board members, comprised mostly of parents.

One reason was that the Split Rock farming and mining region was burgeoning from a community culture of being progressive and innovative. Parents claimed they were too busy managing work and family to commit to the board.

There was another, less apparent reason. Over time, those parents who did join the board were taken aback to see another side of Alex in the board room. Coming as they did with a sincere appreciation of the obvious gifts their talented principal exhibited, they found Alex often disparaged their ideas and treated board members with subtle condescension. This contrast between Alex's positive public persona and attitude towards directors behind the scenes, put the board in a dilemma as it considered renewing their principal's employment contract for a further five years.

Keen to see the school grow further, Alex pushed the board to draft a new strategic plan to reflect more closely the community ethos of being progressive and innovative. Alex also wanted to dismantle the long-standing philosophical resistance to achievement certificates and establish an awards program.

While an initial draft seemed to gain consensus, it was short on detail. Nobody had time to wrestle with the various dilemmas to develop the plan further. When the board eventually put the strategic plan in the 'too hard' basket, Alex was furious.

At the next Annual General Meeting, Alex decided to grasp the initiative. After giving the usual principal's report, Alex presented another paper, *Moving Forward Together*, complete with a revised school fees structure to pay for future growth and an awards program. While still standing, Alex moved a motion, 'that the school adopt *Moving Forward Together* as its strategic plan'.

This presentation and motion took the board entirely by surprise. Although the plan roughly followed the draft which had been discussed, it had never been adequately debated, let alone ratified by the board. Members of the board were livid.

Nonetheless, the parent body was interested in the plan. As questions flooded in, board members felt marginalised, steamrolled, and thrown onto the back foot. They knew their dilemma about renewing Alex's contract had just sharpened.

----------ooO0Ooo----------

How to use this chapter

This chapter has been written on the assumption that, having assessed you are dealing with a conflict involving the senior executive leader, you have:

- read chapter 6 which develops the eight stay-at-the-HELM principles; and
- read chapter 7 so you can select which of the high-level strategies outlined there are relevant in this context.

Familiarity with these chapters will position you to consider conflict involving a senior executive leader.

10.1 *The context*

The senior executive leader of any community, whether a pastor, rector, principal, team leader or chief executive officer holds a unique position. Usually, she or he is:

- a career professional who is well qualified, skilled and experienced;
- responsible to manage or direct other employees;
- highly visible as the face of the organisation to stakeholders and beyond;
- assigned to oversee decision-making to achieve the organisation's purposes;
- the first port of call to discuss member concerns and issues;
- the person who develops and embodies the organisation's culture;
- tasked to remain until the job is done, however long it takes; and
- the lightning rod for the good, the bad and the ugly in their organisation.

Tensions can arise in a Christian community centring on the senior executive leader from a variety of sources such as:

- a rocky start in the position;
- a lack of fit for the role, the culture and history of the community;
- illness, burnout, poor personal discipline or boundaries;

- weak organisational systems and processes;
- mismanaged expectations, both stated and unstated;
- inadequate management and administrative support;
- personal beliefs incompatible with the organisation's foundational beliefs;
- loss of respect for the governing group;
- breakdown in the relationship with the chairperson and/or the governing group;
- becoming the symbol for success or failure in the community;[152]
- unresolved issues from an unsatisfactory ending in a previous leadership role;
- an unhealthy need to always be in control; or
- the governing group fails to fulfil its role in its relationship with the executive.

This final point is important. As Tim Dyer explains:

> The governing group can become either overprotective of the person in this role (resulting in criticism being deflected and accountability avoided) or under-protective (such that the person's faults are allowed to be publicised and the leader not protected).[153]

This, and any unhealthy relationship between the governing body and the executive leader leaves the person in the executive position particularly vulnerable during conflict. When was the last time you heard of a governing group dismissing itself for poor performance under such circumstances? Instead, as Brubaker observes: 'organizations in difficulty or decline often resort to removing the head [executive] person in hopes of improving performance'.[154]

It is also worth noting that conflict is more likely to occur, or to be exacerbated, when the executive leader's personal capacity to handle conflict is poor. McKay notes, concerning pastors, that there is 'often a lack of maturity and personal self-awareness among some of those serving in ordained ministry, which affects their leadership and how they handle conflict'.[155]

Further, a study by Speed Leas that looked at pastors who were 'involuntarily terminated' concluded that '46 percent of conflict involved the pastor's interpersonal competence. And this 46 percent divided equally into two situations. In one (23 percent of the total), the clergy were withdrawn, apathetic, not taking initiative, not providing any kind of leadership. And the other 23 percent involved pastors who were contentious and authoritarian.'[156]

To complicate matters even further, dissenting cliques can develop around an executive leader embroiled in conflict. This is especially likely where people have bonded closely with the leader. The larger-than-life expectations which accompany this kind of bonding may be naïve and unrealistic. When their 'hero' is under threat, such groups can experience strong emotions. These emotions can drive people to dissent and actively undermine considered approaches to addressing conflict.

What then, are the leadership obligations of the governing group when dealing with conflict involving their executive leader? The context of these (and, of course, many other) complex factors demands that when conflict does arise, the matter be handled sensitively and well. Addressing the issue this way is first a matter of *fairness* for the embattled leader. As the Apostle Paul encourages us: 'Do not entertain an accusation against an elder unless it is brought by two or three witnesses'. (I Tim 5:19) We are well advised, therefore, to do our due diligence to ensure any accusations relating to the conflict are valid.

Managing the situation well is also a matter of *respect* for all involved, taking into consideration the perspectives of each of the parties and the needs of the community. Hebrews 13:17 provides principles of respect for working with leaders which are equally applicable when dealing with leaders in conflict. There is an obligation to ensure the office of the leader continues to engender confidence within the community. There is also an obligation to establish an environment for executive leaders to work in ways that are a 'joy, not a burden'.[157] All this requires much prayer, wisdom, tact, pastoral care and strategic action on the part of those dealing with executive leaders in conflict.

It is to this strategic action we now turn.

10.2 *Additional strategies to stay steady at the helm*

The following comprise *additional* strategies under the *stay-steady-at-the-HELM framework* for leaders to consider when navigating conflict involving senior executives.

(A) *Hear from God*

- Encourage those involved to each read a book on the principles of biblical peacemaking such as *The Peacemaker* by Ken Sande, or *Resolving Everyday Conflict* by Ken Sande and Kevin Johnson (for details see the Bibliography).
- Encourage parties to become familiar with the *Tool to manage low level conflict: the PAUSE to HEAL process* as outlined in Part 3, Resources, 16.8(b).

(B) *Examine your culpability as the governing group*

A note of caution

Speed Leas concludes: 'remember, the [senior executive] is rarely the sole generator of difficulties in the [community]. Others usually have played a significant part in creating and sustaining these difficulties'.[158]

- The focus question under 'Examine your culpability' in chapter 7, is: *How might we, as leaders, individually and collectively, have contributed to this situation?* If you as the governing group can identify any contribution you have made, then accept one hundred per cent responsibility for your culpability. Even if it is only small, acknowledge your contribution and deal with it, including apologising sooner rather than later.

To assist you in dealing with your culpability, see 16.3(b) for *Guidelines for writing a holistic confession and apology* and Part 3, Resources, 16.3(c) for *Guidelines for a confession and apology by leaders.*

- Other questions for the governing group include:

  - Thinking about our current conflict, how effectively have we individually and collectively honoured God in all that I, or we, have done?
  - What has been the quality of our love, as a group, toward our executive leader in the past several months?
  - What has been the quality of our love, as a group, toward our executive leader's *family* in the past several months?
  - What has been the quality of our communication with our executive leader?
  - How clearly have we set out and communicated the expectations of our relationship with our executive leader?
  - How transparent have we been?
  - Does our governing group have a history of having contributed to conflict involving the executive leader?
  - Have we, as a group, been over-protective, or under-protective, of our executive leader? (See section 10.1 above.)

You may find the following exercise useful to ensure the responses to these questions reflect the thinking of the whole group. Rate the group's responses to each of the above questions on a scale of 1- 10, where '1' is poor and '10' is excellent. Calculate the group's average and use the outcome to assist you in examining your culpability.

(C) *Evaluate your capacity as the governing group*

- After noting the needs of the parties, mapping the nature of the conflict and deciding on the strategy to manage it (see below), discuss as a governance group:

  What skills and resources do we possess to assist these parties to resolve this conflict effectively?

- Consider in particular reviewing the role of the chair (especially, if the chair is involved in the conflict).
- After noting the personalities and other dynamics of and between the parties, mapping the conflict and deciding on the strategy to address it (see below), discuss as a leadership group: *Who is best qualified to act as our liaison person with the senior executive officer in this context?* Appoint the person and set out your expectations for the role. If there is no one, this in itself indicates the need to seek outside assistance.

(D) *Love the community*

- Ask: *How might we model and develop love throughout our community and to the senior executive at this time, as a hallmark of the process we use to address this conflict?*
- Remember the senior executive will more than likely have a family. The role the leader occupies could be the family's only source of income. Consider their needs carefully.
- Consider also the response of the community to the situation. Gauge the level of emotion and unrest. Watch for any behaviours which do not honour God and are likely to undermine the values and reputation of your community. How might you lead to ensure a safe and God-honouring outcome for all affected?

(E) *Lead the community*

- Consider whether the conflict relates primarily to issues between the parties, or whether it has community implications or connections? If the latter, of course, see chapter 7.6.

(F) *Map the conflict*

- The focus question to consider here is: *How do we assess the gravity and extent of this conflict, the 'who', the 'when', the 'what' and the 'why'?*

> **Key perspective:**
> Conflict with a senior executive is easier to address if the leader:
> - has a sense of call and excitement about their ongoing role;
> - exhibits humility and willingness to learn from the situation; and
> - the community is functioning well.[159]

- Objectively evaluate the character and conduct of the executive leader with honesty, grace, generosity and care. Remember, there will always be more information available which has not yet come to light. Be aware, your role does not extend to assuming the motives behind someone's actions. It is only God who can see into another's heart.

In this context, Tim Dyer helpfully suggests you ask questions such as:

- *Does the person in the senior executive role fit the community?* Is there 'a shared identity, direction, theology and a creative tension in the shared vision?'
- *Was the relationship established well at the outset?* That is, was there a bonding between the executive and the community when he or she arrived? (Bonding can take time. In the church context, this can be anywhere between nine and eighteen months.)
- *Have there been any events which have led to a lack of trust?* Are any of the circumstances outlined at the beginning of section 10.1 above, evident?
- *Is the community functional in regards to its systems, power dynamics, vision and relationships?*[160]

We could also add:

- *Does the executive leader have a realistic view of the power they hold in the community?*[161]
- *Is the executive leader:*
  - *self-aware of their impact on others in the community?*
  - *a person who has a biblical understanding of his or her authority as a Christian leader?*
  - *willing to accept feed-back without recrimination, even if he or she holds a different view?*

- *a person who can communicate their preferences, values and future desires well?*
- *someone who understands and can operate within the governance structure of the whole organisation?*
- *knowledgeable of the broader context in which the community exists?*[162]

- To gain a fuller picture, ensure as much relevant information as possible is gathered. This may mean speaking with leaders beyond your governing group such as elders, team leaders, managers, staff, peak body representatives.

- Assess the gravity of the conflict you are dealing with by using the *Tool for assessing the category of conflict tension* provided in Part 3, Resources, 16.4(a). As you do so, consider the following additional indicators to assess the conflict category.[163]

- Additional symptoms of a category 2 to 4 conflict might include:
  - the issues revolve around executive's leadership style, competence, bonding, role clarity and their fit within the community.

- Additional symptoms of a category 4 or 5 conflict might include:
  - community disquiet, offensive public statements and behaviour;
  - executive leader all but burnt out, depressed or under significant stress;
  - community comments that the executive leader should leave.

- Reflect on whether opposing factions have formed and if so, how well organised they are. (Research has found that 'the more organized are the movement and countermovement within a given ...congregation the more likely will be high-intensity conflict or even division'.[164])
  - Is it likely that more than twenty per cent (20%) of the community knows about the conflict?[165] If so, it is likely the conflict has escalated to a category 3.

(G) *Master-plan the conflict*

- As per section 7.8, the focus question for leaders at this step is: *What are the essential elements which need to be put into place to resolve this conflict and bring healing to all parties and the community?* When addressing conflict involving the senior executive, a supplementary focus question is:

  > *How do we ensure our master-plan is fair and respectful when addressing this conflict involving our senior executive leader?*

- Ensure that the executive leader is supported by an effective mentor or conflict coach (preferably, someone well acquainted with biblical conflict resolution principles), paid for by the organisation.
- Encourage the executive leader to:
  - read this book, including this chapter;
  - undertake a personal retreat; and
  - maintain a journal to reflect on his or her situation.
- If there is any suspected illegal or immoral conduct on the part of the executive leader, seek outside assistance immediately.
- Do you have any concerns the executive leader could be considered a 'toxic' leader? If so, see section 10.4 below.
- Does the conflict involve two or more executive leaders? If so, see section 10.5 below.
- If you assess the conflict at category 3 or above, seek immediate outside assistance.
- If you decide the conflict is at category 1 or 2 and choose to manage it in-house, see section 10.3 below.
- Discern whether any leader should step down while you are addressing the conflict.
- Provide a conflict coach for any other parties involved.

Key perspective:
At the end of the day, a *fair and respectful* process in addressing conflict involving the senior executive leader should include:

- affirmation of your Christian love, support and respect for the individual;
- asking what the executive leader believes is going well;
- asking what the executive leader believes could be improved;
- identifying what the governing group believes the executive is doing well;
- providing clear, specific feedback to the executive leader about problems contributing to the conflict – avoid vague, and anonymous (in reality, malicious) generalisations;
- setting out clear statements of future expectations; and
- an opportunity for the senior executive to change or improve his or her performance over a reasonable length of time (say six months).[166a]

- If the executive leader's continued employment would not be healthy for either themselves or the organisation:
  - Negotiate (or mediate with outside help) bringing his or her service to a close as soon as possible.
  - Seek appropriate employment and legal advice.
  - Ensure the time the executive remains in the employ of the organisation continues to be as healthy as possible.
  - Look for ways to generously bless the outgoing executive; consider a celebration of the person's service, especially if it has been for a long time or many accomplishments were realised.

10.3 *Strategies to manage the conflict in-house*

The following is a process to manage conflict yourselves if you assess it at either category 1 or 2:

- **Management group**:
  establish a neutral group of, say, three highly regarded people from within the community, whom you are confident will be objective, fair and respectful

- **Endorsement**:
  ensure this group is agreed upon by both the executive

leader who is the protagonist, the governing group and any other stakeholders

- **Tasks**:
  provide the management group with a written role description setting out tasks including listening to the stories of each person involved, identifying the concerns in regard to both the issues and the broken relationships, making reasonable recommendations, communicating where appropriate, maintaining confidentiality

- **Accountability**:
  ensure oversight accountability for the management group, perhaps by outside consultants or persons from a peak body.[166b]

10.4 *Unique considerations when faced with a 'toxic leader'*

Unfortunately, the Christian community is not immune from the presence and complex effects of leaders who might be considered 'toxic'.

Such a person may rise to hold a senior executive role in an organisation. Indeed, the person may even advance to become the chair or senior member of the community's governing group. Addressing toxic behaviour is an essential leadership role. Since whatever you tolerate proliferates, avoiding this difficult task may well perpetuate the conduct, destabilising, or even completely shipwrecking, an organisation.

The toxic leader is not merely someone who proves difficult or frustrating. No, as Jean Lipman-Blumen defines, toxic leaders are:

> *individuals who, by virtue of their destructive behaviours and their dysfunctional personal qualities or characteristics, inflict serious and enduring harm on the individuals, groups, organizations, communities and even the nations that they lead.*[167]

Or, as Ted Kober describes in biblical terms, the toxic leader is:

> ...one who has a pattern of sinful behaviour that harms individuals and/or the organisation and refuses to repent. Unrepentance reflects an attitude of unbelief in the forgiveness of sins, and such a self-righteous attitude from a leader can infect the entire organisation. Many people are hurt by a toxic leader including staff, supporters, and those benefiting from the organisation's mission. Such a sinful, unrepentant leader must not be allowed to remain in authority.[168]

Jean Lipman-Blumen provides helpful insight for those needing to deal with toxic leaders: 'personal options all require *keeping your cool* as you navigate the choppy seas one invariably encounters in an effort to confront or capsize a toxic leader'. [169]

The following are some steps leaders can take, while keeping their cool, to address toxic leaders biblically:[170]

- The authentic Christian organisation will always seek to be consistent with its foundational documents, including its biblical basis, as well as its community standards, across all aspects of its operation. This encompasses how leaders will be called to account and how disciplinary action may be taken.
- Therefore, when calling toxic leaders to account, define their offensive behaviour according to your foundational documents, biblical basis and community standards. Explain to them specifically what aspects of these they have breached and sinned against. Include a description of the idols of their heart which many others have observed. The more you locate your response within your documented organisational frameworks, the more just will be the outcome.
- Formalise charges in writing and be ready to give specific examples where toxic behaviour has been documented and witnessed. Remember both scripture and natural justice principles require that more than one witness is necessary to support a charge. (See 1 Tim 5:19-21).
- Maintain records of how often these issues have been addressed according to your foundational documents,

biblical basis and community standards. Include in your record keeping any continuing breaches observed following the confrontation.

- Keep a record of the impact of the negative influences of the offending behaviours on the community; consult with trusted colleagues and organisational leaders. [171]
- Whenever confronting sin, even with a toxic leader, always be ready to proclaim the promises of God's forgiveness in response to repentance.
- Never meet with a toxic leader alone; always have a witness to your conversation. Don't act as a lone ranger but work with others; strategise together on the way forward.[172]
- Where there is progress such that the leader continues to work in the organisation, ensure clear benchmarks and timelines are in place.[173]

If the situation does not resolve itself and more drastic measures are called for, the wise governing group would be well advised to seek outside assistance.

Protections to mitigate against organisations falling prey to toxic leaders:
- Ensure all your foundational documents including grievance and conflict resolution policies and procedures are in place, legally robust and up-to-date.
- Ensure the initial employment process is healthy, open, transparent with appropriate due diligence undertaken.
- Include a time limit in the initial offer of employment.
- Undertake regular performance reviews of the executive leader; explore the person's attitudes toward the governance group and the organisation.
- Hold regular accountability meetings with the board and with the community, which require the executive leader to publicly outline his or her plans and the process to reach them.
- If toxic behaviours become evident, educate the community to deal with their anxieties and fears; help them understand the potential seduction of toxic behaviour.
- If the toxic behaviour becomes untenable, follow the strategic actions listed above and consider respectful departure options sequenced over an agreed period.[174]

NAVIGATING COMMUNITY CONFLICT: STRATEGIES

10.5 *Unique considerations when the conflict is between two executive officers*

All conflict is sad. Conflicts between pastors, or between executive officers of Christian communities, is one of the most disturbing. Fuelled perhaps by trenchant criticism, persistent jealousy, lack of appreciation and basic respect, conflicts of this nature leave the community bewildered, angry and polarised.

Ironically, such conflict often arises between people with significant God-given gifts. Rather than allowing their different gifts to complement each other, people can become competitive and envious. They may manoeuvre to operate in the area of the other person's gifting, perceiving it to be superior to their own. Instead of working harmoniously for the 'common good' (1 Cor 12:7), appreciating how their own unique gifts contribute to the whole (cf. 1 Cor 14:12ff), they jostle for position and polarise relationships.

Governance boards faced with a conflict of this nature are well advised to immediately engage independent skilled mediators and facilitators. The consequences for the community of this type of destructive behaviour are too far-reaching to procrastinate or try to resolve in-house.

10.6 *The aftermath of a forced termination*

Conflict involving senior executive leaders will always be painful. This is especially the case where there is a forced termination.

The following table illustrates what can occur in the aftermath:[175]

CHARACTERISTICS:	
1. ENVIRONMENT	Fluctuating emotional winds and storms of disbelief; community damage highly likely.
2. EMOTIONS	Oscillating levels of depression, frustration, confusion, disappointment, grief.
4. ORIENTATION	The organisation resists anyone who challenges the decision to terminate.
5. SPIRITUAL ISSUES	Questions abound: Where was God in this situation? Why hasn't he protected us? Can I, and our community, trust him? Will God be with us into the future?
6. INFORMATION	As in category 4 conflict (see also *Tool for assessing the category of conflict tension* section 16.4(a)) information is limited to the cause being advocated; will not accept/listen to contrary information.
7. LANGUAGE	Sometimes akin to category 4 conflict.
8. OBJECTIVE	Grief management. Grief usually last 6-24 months with the average 16-24 months.
9. OUTCOME	An interim leader who is competent may be able to ease the grief by working with the community toward healing. NB: after a forced termination, where the aftermath is poorly handled, communities, and especially churches, often call an authoritarian leader.

10.7 *Conclusion*

The senior executive leader holds a unique position in an organisation. When the person in such a role is involved in conflict, a well-considered process is imperative. A poorly handled process can destroy the community. Handled competently, conflict involving the senior executive is an opportunity to clarify objectives, table misunderstandings, increase self-and-other-awareness and, with humility and goodwill, set a new course together.

152 This may be evident in pastoral size churches (that is, those between 70 – 150/175 adults). Here the pastor is more than likely the centre of the community's life. Hence '... conflict is likely to be defined in relation to the pastor...' Leas, *Moving*, p. 76.

153 Tim Dyer, church consultancy training materials.

154 Brubaker, *Promise and Peril*, p.71. (Copyright 2009 © the Alban Institute. Reproduced with permission of the Licensor through PLSclear.)

155 McKay, *How does the church*, p. 5.

156 "Inside Church Fights: An Interview with Speed Leas," by Marshall Shelley https://www.christianitytoday.com/pastors/1989/winter/89l1012.html

157 *Have confidence in your leaders, and submit to their authority, because they keep watch over you as those who must give an account. Do this so that their work will be a joy, not a burden, for that would be of no benefit to you* (Heb 13: 17).

158 Leas, *Moving*, p. 78.

159 Tim Dyer, church consultancy training materials.

160 Tim Dyer, *Conflict Management: Conflict with the Pastor*, church consultancy training materials.

161 Brubaker, *Promise and Peril*, p. 50, observes that 'congregational leaders appear less likely than other organizational leaders to acknowledge their own power and the power of their organizations.' (Copyright 2009 © the Alban Institute. Reproduced with permission of the Licensor through PLSclear.)

162 Ibid. pp. 86, 87.

163 Tim Dyer, *Conflict Management* materials.

164 Brubaker, *Promise and Peril*, p. 16 referencing research by Fred Kniss in *Disquiet in the Land: Cultural Conflict in American Mennonite Communities* (New Brunswick, NJ: Rutgers University Press, 1997).

165 Tim Dyer, consultancy training circa 2008.

166 (a) Leas, *Moving*, p. 78.
(b) Tim Dyer, *Conflict Management* training materials.

167 Jean Lipman-Blumen, *The Allure of Toxic Leaders: Why Followers Rarely Escape Their Clutches*, Ivey Business Journal January/February 2005 Reprint #9B05TA03 p. 2.

168 Discussion with Ted Kober, Senior Ambassador, Ambassadors of Reconciliation, Billings, Montana.

169 Jean Lipman-Blumen, *The Allure of Toxic Leaders*, p. 5f.

170 Discussion with Ted Kober except for those dot points specifically noted in footnotes.

171 Lipman-Blumen article, *The Allure of Toxic Leaders*, p. 6.

172 Ibid.

173 Ibid.

174 Ibid. p. 7f.

175 This table has been produced by Rev Dr. Geoff Cramb, Director of INTERCARE (a ministry of the Baptist Union of Queensland, Australia) and is used with permission. The resource has been modified for the purposes of this book.

BELIEFS OR DOCTRINE 11

In this chapter, we look at:
- **conflict arising from differences in beliefs or doctrine;**
- **additional strategies stemming from the eight HELM principles for leaders to consider when addressing conflict of this nature; and**
- **a process to resolve issues and reconcile relationships when leaders decide to manage a category 1 or 2 conflict themselves.**

You will recall from the Billabong Church and Preschool story at the beginning of Part 2 that a different understanding of the meaning of 'ministry of the church' was at the heart of their conflict.

Some believed the phrase should be understood only in evangelistic terms – Billabong Care Preschool existed solely to reach non-Christians and tell them of the good news of Jesus. Others believed that 'ministry of the church' meant an unconditional service to the local community – a well-run, low fee enterprise with Christian values and ethos.

How to use this chapter

This chapter has been written on the assumption that, having assessed you are dealing with a conflict involving differences over beliefs or doctrine, you have:

- read chapter 6, which develops the eight stay-at-the-HELM principles; and
- read chapter 7, in preparation for assessing which of the high-level strategies outlined there, may be relevant in this context.

Having done so, you are now in a position to consider this chapter and the *additional* strategies specific to a conflict involving differences over beliefs or doctrine.

11.1 *The context*

Conflicts involving differences in beliefs or doctrine are as old as the Christian faith itself. From Old Testament characters, Jesus' disciples and early church leaders in the New Testament, and throughout Christian history, these types of conflicts have always existed.

What we believe goes to the foundation of our identity (who we think we are). What we believe gives us purpose, motivating us to work with like-minded communities (why we do what we do). When our beliefs are challenged, it is therefore not surprising that we react. What is disappointing, however, is that when our Christian beliefs are contested, how we react does not always reflect those beliefs. Instead, we often respond in ways that dishonour God. The genuine danger here is that people who have co-laboured in the gospel together in a community over many years can quickly break fellowship. Hurtful things can be said. Unexpected emotions can be aroused.

In the heat of the moment, it is easy to forget a few obvious facts which can help protect us from destructive responses:

- There have always been and will always be differences in belief. Diversity is a reality in the Christian community. The depth of mystery inherent in our Christian faith means we must allow for other points of view to exist.

- Coupled with mystery is the truth that, in our humanity, we only see partially (1 Cor 13:12). No one can claim to ever be one hundred percent right on any given position. So, be mindful of your limitations and remain open to the possibility of more facts and perspectives than you think exist or are relevant at any given moment.
- Differences in belief and purported 'guidance' may be valid, or they may arise from decidedly subjective and self-interested motives. This can be the case for even the wisest person. So, maintain a generous spirit even as you listen with discernment for the reasons behind other perspectives.
- Arising from experience and ongoing teaching, we, and others with whom we differ, do change perspective over time. So, be patient with one another and allow for the work of God to take effect amongst you.
- Sitting behind the differences, there may be a divergence in fundamental core beliefs and worldview.[176] So, don't be unduly shocked if such deeply held differences sometimes result in a parting of the ways.
- Conflicts involving beliefs or doctrine are just as much an opportunity to grow in knowledge and faith and serve our brothers and sisters in Christ as any other conflict.

Recognising the above will help leaders remain objective, open to alternative perspectives, humble and steady at the helm.

A note of caution

Experienced consultant Rev Les Scarborough observes that if differences over beliefs or doctrine cannot be resolved within a period of twelve to eighteen months, people often leave the community and give up on their relationships.

271

11.2 *Additional strategies to stay steady at the helm*

The following comprise *additional* strategies under the *stay-steady-at-the-HELM framework* for leaders to consider when navigating conflict involving differences over beliefs or doctrine.

(A) *Hear from God*

- Encourage those involved to read a book on biblical peacemaking principles such as *The Peacemaker* by Ken Sande or *Resolving Everyday Conflict* by Ken Sande and Kevin Johnson (for details, see the bibliography).

(B) *Examine your culpability*

- The focus question under 'Examine your culpability' in chapter 7 is: *How might we, as leaders, individually and collectively, have contributed to this situation?* If your answer identifies any contribution, then accept one hundred per cent responsibility for your culpability. Even if it is small, acknowledge your contribution and deal with it, including apologising sooner rather than later.

  To assist you in dealing with your culpability, see 16.3(b) for *Guidelines for writing a holistic confession and apology* and Part 3, Resources, 16.3(c) for *Guidelines for a confession and apology by leaders.*

- Other searching questions to ask yourselves as you examine your culpability include:
  - *Have we been able to 'discern' what is happening without falling into the trap of becoming judgmental?*[177]
  - *Which facts outlined in section 11.1 are we forgetting in the heat of the moment?*
  - *Are we using this conflict over beliefs or doctrine as an opportunity to justify some long-held prejudices?*
  - *What family of origin or other deep-seated cultural (and perhaps theological) norms are influencing our responses to this conflict over beliefs or doctrine?*

- Undertake an attitude check-up by asking questions such as:
  - *Are we willing to see evidence of God's Spirit at work in those who hold a different perspective to us?*
  - *In what ways are we viewing these people as the enemy?*
  - *Are we willing to hear and understand the pain and hurt which our fellow community members are experiencing?*
  - *Are we willing to acknowledge our pain?*
  - *What do we most crave to see occur? What do we most fear might happen? How might this skew our objectivity and limit our discernment?*

(C) *Love the community*

- Whether the conflict is resolved satisfactorily or not, some may see themselves as the theological 'victors' and feel smug. In contrast, others may see themselves as the theological 'vanquished' and feel defeated. To counteract such possible triumphalism or despondency, identify and visit those holding such attitudes to:
  - listen to their story and why they hold to their position;
  - provide a reality check where needed; and
  - provide pastoral support.
- If once the conflict is resolved, changes need to be made to statements of belief and foundational documents, invest as much time and resources as necessary to show unconditional love to all stakeholders. One way of doing this is to invite people to join you on the journey by explaining and communicating the changes well across the community.

(D) *Map the conflict*

- As we have said in chapter 7, mapping a conflict involves determining both the substantive and the relational issues.
- To map the *substantive* issue in this context, identify whether this is, in fact, a conflict about beliefs or doctrine or something else entirely. Questions you might ask here include:
  - *Is the conflict based on a difference in practice rather than belief?*
  - *Is it a simple misunderstanding?*
  - *Is it masking the real issue behind the issue? As Brubaker notes, 'leadership and theology are visible and thus easy*

> *to focus on. Power and ritual are less so. The "Battle for the Bible" may be a less significant causal factor for [community] conflict than more human battles – struggles for power and disputes over ritual expressions.*[178]

- If you determine that it is a conflict over beliefs or doctrine, then ask these questions:
    - *Is the issue about 'sincere diversity' (honestly held different opinions or practices) or 'divisive pluralism' (differences in opinions or practices which mask factional power plays)?*[179]
    - *How do the various positions taken on the issue detract from or add to the gospel message such that it will not be possible to compromise?*
    - *Is the matter of secondary (peripheral) or primary importance to the central gospel message? Has it long been a matter of dispute in the Christian faith community? Is it of such importance that the community may need to divide?*

- To map the *relational* issues, see section 7.7, giving particular attention to the potential for factions or groups to have developed around the substantive belief or doctrinal issue at the centre of the conflict.

(E) *Master-plan the conflict*

- If the conflict is at category 3 or above, engage expert outside assistance immediately. You may then need to adjust your leadership role depending on the advice you receive from those you employ to assist.
- Ask yourselves whether there is a history of disputes over beliefs or doctrinal issues in the community. If so, what does this tell you? How were these disputes dealt with? What can you learn? Is there a cycle that needs to be broken? What do you need to do differently in master-planning this conflict? Is there a case for engaging expert outside assistance here?
- Emotions always run high in conflicts involving differences over beliefs or doctrine. Consider, therefore, the implications for the whole community. As noted in *Mapping the conflict* above, groups are likely to form around the different positions which emerge. Group dynamics, therefore, come to play a

part. So, include in your master-plan how to equip yourselves to understand these dynamics recognising that knowledge of group mentality may prove invaluable. A good summary discussion of the topic may be found in Barthel and Edling *Redeeming Church Conflicts*, p. 97ff.

- If in mapping the conflict you have determined that the differences are of sufficient importance to warrant some kind of separation, then set out a healthy process to achieve this.

11.3 *Strategies to manage the conflict in-house*

If you conclude the conflict is at either category 1 or 2, consider the following to address the issues in-house:

- Have all parties set out their issues and positions in writing, holistically and respectfully, to reduce the potential for misunderstanding.
- Use the *Sample process to facilitate active listening* provided in Part 3, Resources, 16.8(c).
- Discuss the relevance of the facts outlined in 11.1 above. The protagonists may have forgotten some of these in the heat of the moment.
- Slow down, listen intently to what each side has to say (James 1:9), taking the different beliefs or doctrinal positions and reasons for them seriously. Make notes, reflect, summarise the arguments.
- Consider what is negotiable and what is not.
- If you assess that a community meeting is necessary to address what is happening, see Part 3, Resources 16.8(d)) *Guidelines for a community meeting*, including suggested ground rules at 16.8(e).
- Ensure leaders and the chairperson remain mindful of their own presuppositions or biases concerning the beliefs or doctrinal issues at the centre of the conflict.
- Where agreement cannot be reached, develop an *interim* solution on the basis that parties agree to differ for the moment. This will buy time and allow emotions to settle so that a different *process* can be developed to resolve the conflict.

- Ultimately, if no agreement can be reached, leaders may need to make the call on the position which the organisation will hold going forward. This is a significant step. It needs to be undertaken with great care, prayer, wisdom, courage and love.

11.4 *Conclusion*

Leading theologian and pastor, the late John Stott, provides a fitting conclusion in this context:

> *Thank God there are those in the contemporary church who are determined at all costs to defend and uphold God's revealed truth. But sometimes they are conspicuously lacking in love. When they think they smell heresy, their nose begins to twitch, their muscles ripple, and the light of battle enters their eye. They seem to enjoy nothing more than a fight. Others make the opposite mistake. They are determined at all costs to maintain and exhibit brotherly love, but in order to do so are prepared even to sacrifice the central truths of revelation. Both these tendencies are unbalanced and unbiblical. Truth becomes hard if it is not softened by love; love becomes soft if it is not strengthened by truth. The apostle calls us to hold the two together, which should not be difficult for spirit-filled believers, since the Holy Spirit is himself "the spirit of truth," and his first fruit is "love." There is no other route than this to a fully mature Christian unity.*[180]

These comments not only apply in the context of the church. They can equally apply to all other Christian communities.

---

[176] Brubaker, *Promise and Peril*, p. 65, 115 reflecting on a hypothesis of Shane Hipps, *The Hidden Power of Electronic Culture: How Media Shapes Faith, the Gospel and the Church* (Grand Rapids, MI: Zondervan, 2005).

[177] Fenton, Horace L., *The Peacemakers: Resolving conflict between Christians*, Inter-Varsity Press, 1987, p. 42.

[178] Brubaker, *Promise and Peril*, p. 121. (Copyright 2009 © the Alban Institute. Reproduced with permission of the Licensor through PLSclear.)

[179] Fenton, *Peacemakers*, p. 75.

[180] John R W Stott, *God's new society: The message of Ephesians*, The Bible Speaks Today Series (Downers Grove, IL: InterVarsity, 1979), p.172.

A BETTER WAY 12

In this chapter, we reflect on:
- **what it means to practice ongoing biblical peacemaking in your community;**
- **the benefits of establishing peacemaking as a community mindset; and**
- **the role of leaders and individuals in developing and maintaining the practice of biblical peacemaking.**

This chapter offers a further step for leaders to stay steady at the helm, notwithstanding the presence of conflict. It explains how they can equip their communities for the kind of reconciliatory lifestyle which will better prepare them for the disputes which will inevitably arise. As Leroy Goertzen insightfully expresses it,

> *...conflict management, like reconciliation, is a way of life for the church and the normal state of conducting its affairs, be they substantive, interpersonal or intrapersonal... Life is conflict and conflict is to be lived in the context of reconciliation, a way of life that incarnates God's redemptive purpose in the world and embraces the reconciliatory lifestyle of Jesus.*[181]

12.1 *The context*

The practice of 'passing the peace' is embedded in the culture of many Christian communities. It echoes the expression Jesus often used when he met his disciples after his resurrection – 'Peace be with you' (Lk 24:36; Jn 20:19, 21, 26). These were words of comfort and reassurance, spoken at a time of mixed emotions for the disciples when they were both frightened about their future and joyous at his unexpected presence.

Today, the practice of 'passing the peace' often involves worshippers in a reciprocal exchange of encouragement and hope. The first person offers the statement: 'The peace of the Lord be with you', and the second responds: 'And also with you'. No doubt, many of those who participate in this mutual gesture of peace have, or have had, conflict of one kind or another in their lives.

So, we might ask: *What would it take to ensure that Jesus' words, 'Peace be with you', and today's reciprocal 'passing of the peace' genuinely mean something in the context of an actual conflict in a person's life?* Then, by extension, we must ask: *What might it take to ensure the principles of biblical peacemaking (which sit behind these words of peace) are the first things which come to mind for everyone connected to a Christian community when they face conflict in their lives?*

The thrust of this book thus far has been about responding well to conflict *after* the fact. Is it possible to get to a place where navigating conflict using biblical principles becomes so natural that the storms of conflict abate quickly at their point of origin? Is it possible that leaders can get to where they would no longer need to grapple with what to do, even as a real-life conflict erupts around them? Could they instead respond immediately from a deep communal base of shared biblical knowledge, assurance and hope?

As we know well, Jesus' desire is for all believers to live in a community characterised by 'complete unity' (Jn 17:23). Paul expressed this desire similarly, encouraging his readers to: 'Make every effort to keep the unity of the Spirit through the bond of peace...' and to persevere until '...we all reach unity in the faith...' (Eph 4:3, 13).

Paul is realistic. To live in peace takes effort and perseverance. Scripture recognises that training in biblical principles must be ongoing (Lk 6:40; 1 Tim 4:16). Paul understands that training equips people 'for works of service' (Eph 4:12). This includes addressing conflict in our lives. The writer to the Hebrews says: '...solid food is for the mature, who by constant use have trained themselves to distinguish good from evil' (5:14). John says: 'Anyone who runs ahead and does not continue in the teaching of Christ does not have God; whoever continues in the teaching has both the Father and the Son' (2 Jn 9).

God's vision, therefore, for all Christian communities is that they are characterised by constant efforts towards unity and ongoing learning to be ready to deal with inevitable conflict, positively and constructively. In such a community, a tradition of peace, the practice of biblical peacemaking, can take hold.[182]

Key advantages of proactively developing a culture of biblical peace-making include:
- people resolve their conflicts more readily and in a healthy manner;
- people find freedom rather than being bound by ingrained and destructive attitudes and behaviours;
- generally, people maintain, and indeed enhance, marriages, friendships and relationships;
- the reputation of Christ and the Christian community, its people and its ministries is protected; and
- the potential of ongoing cycles of conflict is thwarted.

12.2 *The role of leaders*

We have argued that it is a fundamental biblical responsibility of Christian church leaders to address conflict wherever and whenever it arises in their community. This includes the obligation to initiate and navigate a practice of ongoing biblical community peacemaking. As Robert Warren expressed it:

> *The church is called to be the pilot project of the new humanity established by Christ, an outpost of the kingdom of God and the 'community of the Age to Come'. Not least is the world looking for models of handling conflict... the truth remains, that there is a longing to see relationships work, so see the truth of God's call to love being practised. Conflicts in the church can seem such a distraction from getting on with the real work;* but this is the real work. *When people come near such a community they will instinctively know how real the relationships are.*[183]

Although the church is Christ's primary context to reflect his kingdom on Earth, any community where the people of God gather in the name of Christ to accomplish his purposes will also reflect his kingdom.

As we have seen, conflict provides opportunities to honour Christ, grow to be more like Jesus, and serve our fellow brothers or sisters in Christ. Conflict, therefore, offers itself as a rich source of insightful learning and personal growth. If, therefore, your community has spent time in the conflict school of hard learning, it would be tragic to forget the lessons learned. Unfortunately, there will always be further conflict to navigate and master-plan in our lives and communities. It is only a matter of time. So, now is the time to go on the front foot and develop a preventative, proactive strategy to build the practice of biblical peacemaking in our communities.

Here are some practical steps for leaders to consider:

- Form a small peacemaking team of gifted people with a brief to develop a culture of peace in the community; train them as mediators, facilitators and conflict coaches.[184]
- Develop a repository of books and resources consistent with biblical principles for yourselves, the peacemaking team and your community members to access.

- Teach biblical principles of peacemaking from time to time across multiple platforms: in large group contexts; by encouraging small group reflection;[185] by publishing relevant articles in your newsletter or magazine.
- Enter into a *leadership covenant* as a group that incorporates a commitment to addressing conflict using biblical principles (see Part 3, Resources, 16.6(a) for a sample).
- If you have not already done so, embed biblical conflict resolution principles in your foundational documentation, such as your:
  - *statement of values;*
  - *constitution* (see Part 3, Resources, 16.9(b) for a sample conflict resolution clause);
  - *grievance policy* for staff, members and others (see Part 3, Resources, 16.9(c) for a sample); and
  - *community covenant of behaviour* in times of conflict (see Part 3, Resources, 16.6(b) for a sample).
- Evaluate and learn from any *past experiences of community conflict.* Whenever leaders emerge from conflict events, there will always be lessons to be learnt. There will also be things to celebrate. These situations, therefore, provide an opportunity to review how you and your group handled them by answering questions such as:
  - What can we celebrate in what transpired?
  - What actions would we not like to repeat?
  - What strategies could we have strengthened?
  - What different initiatives could we have adopted?
  - What might still need to be done to restore health to everyone in our community fully?
- Establish a *community relations group* to proactively address minor grievances between the senior executive (rectors, pastors, principals, CEO's) and the community (see Part 3, Resources, 16.9(a) for an outline of the rationale for this group along with details on forming one).

With this understanding of the obligation and opportunity to build a culture of peace and some practical steps to guide this, leaders are equipped to take the initiative to name the issues and activate the processes to address them. Hopefully, these processes will be well understood and embedded in the culture of your community. A culture of peace normalises conflict and takes away its power. All concerned can immediately apply the life-giving skills and community processes which have been developed.

12.3 *Conclusion*

Navigating a course for a better way means proactively building a culture of peace across your community. Charting such a course is not just about 'doing things better'. Instead it calls the whole community to a total re-orientation of heart and mind, which reframes conflict as an opportunity for personal and community transformation, godly growth and organisational well-being.

---

[181] Goertzen, *Understanding*, p. 100.

[182] For an outline of this vision, and how you might develop it in your community, see Ken Sande's book, *The Peacemaker*, Appendix F, *Cultivating a Culture of Peace in Your Church*, p. 289ff.

[183] Robert Warren, *Being Human, Being Church: Spirituality and Mission in the Local Church*, London: Marshall Pickering, 1995, as quoted by Alastair McKay in *Resolving Conflict* from *How to Become a Creative Church Leader, A Modem Handbook* ed. by John Nelson, Canterbury Press, Norwich, 2008, p. 208.

[184] PeaceWise in Australia offer a wide range of courses on an ongoing basis throughout Australia as well as live video training courses accessible anywhere – see www.peacewise.org.au

[185] See further reading listed in the bibliography. Also, see Part 3, Resources, 16.9(f) for relevant courses and web-based resources.

PART 3
RESOURCES

See the book's website:
www.navigatingcommunityconflict.com

Part 3 provides the following bonus chapters:

13. **Working with Outside Professionals**
14. **Working with the Media**
15. **Working with Lawyers**

and:

16. **Resources:**
    - the resources are primarily arranged under the eight HELM principles
    - other resources are also listed
    - scriptures referenced in the book are listed on the book's website

To access the resources on
the book's website
navigatingcommunityconflict.com
enter the password:
ncc1234#

BIBLIOGRAPHY

Conflict in Churches and Christian organisations

- Barthel, Tara Klena & Edling, David V. *Redeeming Church Conflicts: Turning Crisis into Compassion and Care*, Baker Books, 2012
- Boyd-MacMillan, Eolene and Savage, Sara, *Transforming Conflict: Conflict transformation amongst senior church leaders with different theological stances,* The Foundation for Church Leadership, York, United Kingdom, 2008
- Brubaker, David R, *Promise and Peril: Understanding and Managing Change and Conflict in Congregations*, The Alban Institute, Herndon, Virginia, 2009
- Fenton, Horace L., *The Peacemakers: Resolving conflict between Christians*, Inter-Varsity Press, 1987
- Goertzen, Leroy W., *Understanding, Managing & Redeeming Church Conflict,* Corban University, 2012
- Jones, Robert D., *Pursuing Peace: A Christian Guide to Handling our Conflicts*, Crossway, 2012
- Leas, Speed B., *Moving Your Church Through Conflict*, Alban Institute Inc., 1985
- Leas, Speed B., and Kittlaus, Paul, *Church Fights: Managing Conflict in the Local Church*, Philadelphia: Westminster Press, 1973
- Lott, David B., Editor, *Conflict Management in Congregations*, The Alban Institute, 2001
- Nienaber, Susan, *Leading into the Promised Land: Lessons Learned From Resilient Congregations,* posted on July 13, 2006 by Alban Institute p. 3 https://alban.org/archive/leading-

into-the-promised-land-lessons-learned-from-resilient-congregations/
- Parsons, George D., Leas, Speed B. *Understanding Your Congregation as a System: The Manual*, The Alban Institute, 1993
- Poirier, Alfred, *The Peacemaking Pastor: A Biblical Guide to Resolving Church Conflict*, Baker Books, 2006
- Sande, Ken, *The Peacemaker: A Biblical Guide to Resolving Personal Conflict*, 3rd Edition, Baker Books, 2004
- Sande, Ken & Johnson, Kevin, *Resolving Everyday Conflict*, Baker Books, 2011
- Steinke, Peter L., *Congregational Leadership in Anxious Times: Being Calm and Courageous No Matter What*, The Alban Institute, 2006
- Steinke, Peter L., *Healthy Congregations: A Systems Approach*, Herndon, VA: Alban Institute, 2007
- Van Yperen, Jim, *Making Peace: A Guide to Overcoming Church Conflict*, Moody Publishers, Chicago, 2002

Christian leadership

- Shaw, Peter, *Deciding Well: A Christian Perspective on Making Decisions as a Leader*, Regent College Publishing, Vancouver, Canada, 2009
- Starling, David I, *UnCorinthian Leadership: Thematic Reflections on 1 Corinthians*, Eugene, Oregon: Cascade Books, 2014
- Williams, Garry, *Essential Standards of Ministry Governance For Christian Churches, Schools and Ministries*, Christian Management Australia, 2010
- Wright, Walter C., *Relational Leadership: A Biblical Model for Influence and Service*, Second Edition, InterVarsity Press, Illinois, 2009

Other books referenced and useful for further reading

- Ciampa, Roy E and Rosner, Brian S. *The First Letter to the Corinthians*, Grand Rapids, Michigan / Cambridge, UK: William B. Eerdmans Publishing Company, 2010

- Deutsch, Morton, Coleman, Peter T. and Marcus, Eric C., Editors, *The Handbook of Conflict Resolution: Theory and Practice*, Second Edition, John Wiley & Sons, 2011
- Kober, Ted, *Confession & Forgiveness: Professing Faith as Ambassadors of Reconciliation,* Concordia Publishing House, St Louis, MO, 2002
- Kober, Ted, *Built on the Rock: The Healthy Congregation*, Concordia Publishing House, St louis, MO, 2017
- Lehman, Karl, *Outsmarting Yourself: Catching Your Past Invading the Present and What to Do about It* – 2nd Edition, Libertyville, Illinois: This JOY! Books, 2014
- McKnight, Scot and Barringer, Laura, *A Church Called Tov: Forming a Goodness Culture That Resists Abuses of Power and Promotes Healing,* Tyndale Momentum, 2020
- Mitchell, Margaret M., *Paul and the Rhetoric of Reconciliation: An Exegetical Investigation of the Language and Composition of 1* Corinthians, First American Edition, Westminster/John Knox Press, Kentucky, 1992
- Ostrower, Francie & Stone, Melissa M., *Governance: Research Trends, Gaps, and Future Prospects* in W.W. Powell & Steinberg (Eds.), *The Non-profit Sector: A Research Handbook* – 2nd edition, New Haven: Yale University Press, 2006
- Stoesz, Edgar and Raber, Chester, *Doing Good Better! How to be an Effective Board Member of a Nonprofit Organization* Good Books Intercourse, PA, 1994

WITH GRATITUDE

This book would never have come together if not for the valuable input and support of many people. Foremost among these, I am immensely grateful to my uniquely gifted life partner, Carolyn. Her professional, collaborative and developmental editorial assistance, along with her understanding of my purpose, content and target audience, have all been foundational to the manuscript taking shape in the way that it has. Thank you so, so much for this and your constant encouragement and motivation. I would be bankrupt if you ever sent me an account!

A significant amount of the thinking in this work has been informed by what I have been privileged to have learnt from others. I am deeply grateful to the lecturers at Regent College, Vancouver, in the 1980s who inspired me afresh with the imperative to spend time studying scripture. They also provided me with the tools to do this and how to apply scripture to all of life. Les Scarborough and Tim Dyer of John Mark Ministries trained me in church consultancy and gave me deeper insights into the human condition. Bruce Burgess and his team at PeaceWise equipped me with the principles and methods of biblical conflict resolution through the courses I attended and the mediations I undertook. I am sincerely indebted to each of you for this input into my life.

Kristin Argall, Commissioning Editor of the Bible Society in Australia, willingly shared her vast knowledge, experience and contacts in publishing and was always an encouragement on the journey. Peter Kaldor gave me early advice on publishing. Thank you both very much.

Then there are those I reached out to for feedback at various stages in the writing process. Some read the whole manuscript and, in several cases, provided quite detailed reflections despite being fully engaged in their respective work contexts. Others read sections of the manuscript and also provided invaluable insights. So a big thank you to Bruce Burgess, Steven Cooper, Pete Davies, Tim Dyer, Barbara Friend, Les Gray, Ian Hanslow, Ted Kober, Wendy Konemann, Lloyd McKay, Paul McPhee, Bruce Meller, Steven Nicholson, Jono Shead, Greg Sorrell, Peter Stone, Rod Thompson, Lyn Thow and Phil Waugh. My sincere apology to anyone I reached out to but have omitted to mention! Much appreciation to you as well.

To those who have written endorsements, a sincere thank you. I am humbled and encouraged by your generous comments. My particular appreciation goes to Tim Costello, who immediately upon request agreed to write a foreword notwithstanding his busy life and then provided his offering in a timely manner. Thank you so much for your generosity and insights.

Throughout the writing process, I have been supported by members of several home groups from my local churches in Springwood, Canberra and then Springwood again. They took a regular interest in the project and prayed. I am truly grateful for your support. Thank you to my parents, Arthur (now deceased) and Jean, my children, Anthony, Marcella and Jeremy and my extended family, my second cousin, Ruth Ridley, my sister-in-law, Judith Carpenter and many friends along the way, including Judy Clifford, Gordon Menzies, Les and Ann Gray, Peter and Kerrie Stiles, Lloyd and Merrilyn McKay, Graham and Wendy Toulmin, Trevor Cork and my Monday morning bike rider's group. I have valued your personal interest in the project and your prayer.

At the outset of this writing journey, I had the privilege of spending six weeks researching the topic at Tyndale House, Cambridge, UK. I am grateful to that institution for its amazing research facilities and the invaluable assistance from several staff members.

Subsequently, when living in Canberra, BaptistCare NSW & ACT, and particularly their CEO, the late Ross Lowe, permitted me to occupy a desk in their Canberra offices to allow me to write. I very much appreciate that kind assistance. Thank you, as well, to those in the Canberra office who warmly accepted my presence amongst them.

Thank you, too, to the partners of my former legal practice, McPhee Kelshaw, Springwood, for the use of their board room so that Carolyn and I could edit the work together in a different environment. Peter Moss helped keep the garden together for much of the time while I wrote and re-wrote. Thank you for this and your ongoing interest. Also, I truly appreciate the excellent work on the graphics by Rosie Wheeler of Cocoon Creative.

And to the staff at Ark House Press, a big thank you for guiding me in the various steps of the publication process and setting up the book's website. I greatly appreciate your professional assistance.

At the end of the day, I alone am responsible for the work as published with all its shortcomings, of which I am sure there are many.

Finally, and above all, I am profoundly grateful to my Heavenly Father for his constant guidance throughout this project, along with the motivation to keep going during times of doubt and aloneness. Praise, honour and lasting gratitude are due to Him for his unfailing faithfulness, encouragement and protection.

For the

INDEX

and

LIST OF SCRIPTURES

see the book's website

www.navigatingcommunityconflict.com

ABOUT THE AUTHOR

Alan Kelshaw holds a law degree (LLB) from Sydney University, Sydney, Australia and a Masters of Christian Studies degree (MCS) from Regent College, Vancouver, Canada. He has undertaken extensive training in church consultancy and is accredited by his denomination as a consultant. Alan has trained in conflict resolution through several organisations in Australia and the United States.

Alan practised as a lawyer (solicitor) for nearly 30 years. He has acted as a Christian mediator, consultant and trainer in conflict resolution in churches, Christian schools, mission organisations and para-church ministries for the past 20 years.

Throughout his life, Alan has held many leadership roles, including membership of the pastoral leadership team and an elder in his church; board and committee member in his church and denomination; managing partner role in his law practice; director for a number of Christian organisations, including national, state and local board roles in Habitat for Humanity Australia. For several years, Alan chaired a governance review committee for his denomination, which resulted in the organisation adopting a refreshed model of governance for which Alan drafted a new constitution.

Alan lives in the Blue Mountains, west of Sydney, Australia, with his wife, Carolyn. They have three children and eight grandchildren. Alan loves to bike ride, bushwalk, swim, eat out, play the piano, read, and host events at home.

www.ingramcontent.com/pod-product-compliance
Lightning Source LLC
Chambersburg PA
CBHW070744270326
41927CB00010B/2088